AF612924

THE CUSTOMER SERVICE SPECIALIST

AND

PERSONAL DRIVER

TOMMY C. SEAY SR.

Copyright © 2026 by Tommy C. Seay Sr.

All rights reserved.

No part of this book may be reproduced, stored in a retrieval system, or transmitted in any form or by any means—electronic, mechanical, photocopying, recording, or otherwise—without prior written permission from the publisher, except for brief quotations in reviews.
Images labeled "Representative Image" are used for illustrative purposes only and do not depict actual individuals described in the text.

Published by Unveiling Press

Printed in the United States of America

Unveiling Press is an independent publishing imprint dedicated to works that illuminate truth, faith, and lived experience with clarity and integrity. Founded to bring forward stories and studies that reveal what is often unseen, Unveiling Press publishes memoirs, theology, and reflective works with an emphasis on substance, craft, and purpose.

Released: April 6, 2026

ISBN (Hardcover): 979-8-9950893-0-8
ISBN (Paperback): 979-8-9950893-1-5
ISBN (eBook): 979-8-9950893-2-2

Library of Congress Control Number: 2026909705

Dedicated In Honor Of

THE FITZGERALD FAMILY

(Kevin Sr., Mary, Kevin Jr., and Lauren)

THE COOK FAMILY

(Dan, Gail, and Lisa)

TABLE OF CONTENTS

PART III — THE NATIONAL FOOTBALL LEAGUE YEARS

PREFACE

Being a customer service specialist and personal driver is no walk in the park. It takes patience, awareness, and a whole lot of heart. You're dealing with people from every corner of life—some grateful, some stressed out, some just trying to get through their day. But the beauty of the job, the part that keeps you showing up with your head held high, is that moment when someone truly appreciates what you do. When a customer looks you in the eye and says, "Thank you," and you can tell they really mean it—that's the payoff. That's the quiet reward most people will never understand unless they've stood in our shoes.

People love to throw around that old line, "The customer is always right." Let me tell you, "No, they're not!" Not even close. But here's the truth: even when they're not right, they want to feel like they are. They want to be heard, respected, and understood. It is essential to make people feel validated in their opinions, not because they are right or wrong, but because when leaders listen first, cooperation and mutual respect follow. And if you've been in this business long enough, you learn that creating that feeling is part of the job. Not because it's easy, but because it builds trust—and trust keeps the wheels turning and the company growing.

But some people? They don't belong in customer service. And I don't say that to be cruel—I say it because we've all experienced it. You pull out of a drive-thru, thinking you're all set, only to find out your order is either incorrect or incomplete. Now you're sitting in your car shaking your head like, "Come on now… really?" Or you're at a restaurant and ask for water with lemon—a simple request—and every time the server comes back, that lemon is missing, like it took the night off.

Another time, you order pancakes, and when they come, you watch your server take the newcomers' orders without bringing you the syrup. When you finally finish and ask for the check, that simple request turns into a drawn-out ordeal. Strangely, it's only when you put your coat on and start heading for the door that it comes promptly. In moments like that, it's hard to tell whether the issue is a lack of heart or a lack of multitasking—but either way, the frustration is the same. You're paying for a level of service that doesn't meet your standards.

Good customer service is bigger than a job description. It's the backbone of every business, every industry, every interaction where people depend on people. When you care about the person in front of you—whether you're handing them a bag, pouring a drink, or driving them across town—something shifts. You're not just completing a task; you're creating an experience. And at the end of the day, that's what it's all about: treating people right, making them feel seen, and doing your part to make their day a little lighter than it was before. That's the kind of service that stays with people… and it's the kind of service that defines who we are.

Over the years, I've had the pleasure of meeting and serving people from all walks of life—movie stars, everyday folks, quiet souls, and big personalities. You name it, I've been there and done that. In this book, I'm sharing some of those moments—those encounters I've come to cherish. Not because they were flashy or dramatic, but because they were real. Human. Meaningful. These aren't just customer service stories; they're snapshots of life, people, and the lessons that showed up when I least expected them.

CHAPTER ONE

MOM CAST THE DEVIL OUT OF MY DADDY

A Father Under Pressure

Winter roared across Buffalo like a freight train, rattling windows and tightening belts. Inside our bustling home on Riley Street, Dad carried the weight of twelve mouths—eleven children and a wife whose prayers alone could open and close heaven. He worked like a man racing the clock, determined to keep heat in the radiators and food on the table. But long hours and constant pressure have a way of bending even strong men. And little by little, the smoke curling from his cigarette and the Gin or Wild Irish Rose glistening in his glass began following him home like shadows.

For a child, it was confusing. Here was a man—a deacon in the church—who built churches one spiritual brick at a time, taught Sunday School, and prayed as if heaven's door were just one more knock away… yet he drifted, slipping into habits that felt like strangers wearing my father's face. The house grew tense—like thunder waiting to break.

Dad's voice became sharper, his steps heavier, his late nights more frequent. And Mom, steady as a lighthouse, watched him fade like a man being swallowed by his own storm. One evening, the tension tightened so suddenly it felt like the air itself might crack. I tugged at Mom's sleeve. "Mom… what's wrong with Dad?" She didn't blink. Didn't sigh. Didn't soften her voice. She simply said:

"After tonight, there won't be anything wrong with him."

I froze. My ten-year-old heart dropped into my shoes. Under my breath, I whispered to God, "Lord, please… she's gonna kill my Daddy."

A Ride in Search of Help

With no phones, no quick calls, no lifelines, I grabbed my bicycle. The streetlights hummed overhead as I pedaled like a terrified courier racing against fate. "Y'all gotta come home!" I cried at my relatives' doorways. "Dad is going to see Jesus tonight! Mom's gonna take him out! He's done!" Doors opened. Heads shook. Shocked faces whispered. But in the end, only one person came: Aunt Dolly Jean, my mother's sister—armed with a large black leather bag that looked like it held either healing… or catastrophe.

Enter Aunt Dolly: Equal Parts Wisdom and Thunder

Aunt Dolly was not the soft-spoken type. She and Dad got along—until the Bible came up. Then it was holy wildfire every single time. "Woman, you need a real pastor to learn something about the Bible," Dad would thunder. "Silence, you vampire trout!" Dolly would snap back. (And to this day, I still don't know what a vampire trout is.) She stormed into the house and planted herself in the living room. Dropping the black bag on the floor, it felt like the house shook.

Mom looked up, calm as Sunday morning. "Dolly, what are you doing here?" "Tommy said you were going to kill Ezelle tonight. I came to help you get rid of the evidence." Mom shook her head. "Girl, I'm not killing my husband. It's a misunderstanding. Take that ungodly-looking bag out of my house and let the Lord handle Ezelle." Feeling dejected—and slightly disappointed—Dolly took the bag, gave heed to Mom's admonishment, and went home.

Midnight: The Spiritual Showdown

When Dad finally collapsed into sleep—half bear, and fully drunk—Mom waited like a general preparing for a silent battle. She sat in her recliner, listening to gospel music, calm and unshaken. At midnight, when the house finally settled, she rose with purpose. She reached for a bottle of consecrated extra-virgin olive oil—the kind she kept tucked away like spiritual ammunition.

Mom anointed herself with the oil. Then she walked through the house, whispering prayers that made the air feel different. She touched every doorway. Every window. Every wall. She even touched our dog, Trixie, when she wandered too close, leaving her blinking in holy confusion. When I saw that, I ducked under the table out of her reach, but she extended her hand and laid it upon my head. I became lightheaded while the room seemed to spin out of control.

When Mom stepped into the bedroom, moonlight fell across Dad's face. For years, the alcohol and cigarettes had Dad stinking from drinking and choking from smoking. But that night, Mom pressed her hand gently against his head, closed her eyes, and prayed—long… deep… with a faith and fervency that felt strong enough to split the Red Sea.

Dawn of a New Man

The next morning, sunlight crept through the windows like a fresh start. Dad stood up—steady, sober, present—as if yesterday had been erased from time. He showered, shaved, and stepped into the garden like a man made new. Just like that, Mom had done the impossible. She cast the devil out of my Daddy. No ceremonies. No shouting. No capes or wands. Just faith, grit, and a bottle of blessed olive oil.

From that day forward, Dad never touched another cigarette. Never reached for another drink. He lived thirty-five years clean—a number in the Scripture that symbolizes *hope*—before the Lord called him home. Word of the miracle spread like wildfire. Some praised Mom as a saint. Others—who preferred to maintain fellowship with their demons—suddenly found reasons to avoid her.

When Life Strikes Again

Years later, after retirement, Dad continued to visit the Veterans Administration Hospital, which had become like a second home to him. He loved it there—the work, the people, the sense of purpose. But it was also the place where he received the diagnosis no one wants to hear: mesothelioma. I stood beside him when the doctor explained it. Dad simply nodded, took a deep breath, and said:

"You know, doc… I've had a good life."

Even then, he carried a peace that felt like God's hand resting on his shoulder. It felt fitting—almost poetic—that the hospital he served so faithfully became the place where his earthly journey ended. On March 9, 2002, Dad entered his eternal retirement—peaceful, steady, and ready. Mom followed him years later, passing peacefully at home on May 10, 2013, leaving us with the delightful thought that she's probably teaching the angels in heaven her culinary secrets.

True North: The Legacy They Left Me

With both of my parents now resting in the Lord, the lessons they planted in us have become the compass guiding my steps. And whenever life becomes a maze—when the world tilts or grief stirs old memories—I return in my mind to that crowded home at 200 Riley Street. That was the place where chaos met love, where storms met prayer, and where a mother's midnight faith transformed a family. That place. Those people. Those lessons. They remain my true north—the inward pull that keeps me aligned with who I am… and who God always intended me to become.

CHAPTER TWO

MY TRUE NORTH & RESPECT YOUR ELDERS

A Life Shaped by Buffalo, Faith, and Family

Buffalo, New York, has always had a character all its own. You can feel it just walking down the street. Old and new houses stand side by side—some worn from decades of storms, others carefully kept by families who have lived there for generations. Even the abandoned homes seem to whisper stories of the people who once filled them with life. This is a city built on resilience, toughness, and heart. And nowhere was that spirit stronger than on the east side of Buffalo, where I grew up.

That neighborhood shaped me long before I understood how. It was a place where people knew each other, watched out for each other, corrected each other's children, went to church, and prayed together on Sundays. It was a community where you learned early that life wasn't just about you—it was about the people around you. Right in the middle of that world stood our home, filled to the brim with eleven children, two devoted parents, and lessons that would follow me for the rest of my life.

As the fifth child, I was in the perfect position to learn from every direction. I had older brothers to admire, younger siblings to look after, and a mother and father who worked every single day to make sure we had more than just food and clothes—they made sure we had values.

Lessons at the Dinner Table

Our dinner table wasn't just where we ate. It was our training ground. Mom and Dad didn't care about us being the best—they cared about us doing our best. There's a big difference. They taught us early that excellence has nothing to do with applause and everything to do with integrity.

Washing dishes, mopping floors, folding laundry—none of it was really about the task. Those chores were lessons in disguise. They taught us that even the smallest job deserves dignity. They taught us that if we were going to do something, we were going to do it right. And most importantly, they taught us about the power of quiet pride—that private moment when you step back from your work and think, I gave it my all, and that's enough.

Those lessons didn't stay in childhood. They followed me into school, into my early jobs, into my career in transportation and customer service, and into every interaction I've ever had—with VIP clients, NFL teams, or everyday passengers. Mom and Dad made excellence a habit, not a performance.

My Mother: Strength, Grace, and a Servant's Heart

The heartbeat of our family was my mother, Claudia. She was strong, gentle, disciplined, loving, faithful, and wise—a rare combination in any era. As an ordained evangelist and missionary, she lived by a simple but demanding saying:

"Holiness is right, even if no one practices it."

And she lived every word of it. Mom gave to the church with a level of generosity that still amazes me. If she had collected all she donated over the years, she probably could have bought a house in Beverly Hills—paid in full. But that was never her purpose. She gave because she loved God, loved people, and loved serving.

Before marriage, she had been an exceptional secretary—nobody could match her written or spoken English. After she started her family with my father, she poured that same excellence into raising us. And Mom didn't just raise sons—she raised capable men. She taught us how to cook, clean, sew, iron, and take care of ourselves. One day, I asked her, "Mom, why do we have to learn all these chores?" She didn't hesitate. "Because if you don't prove to be a man worthy of a woman's love, she won't stay with you long. My job is to prepare you to survive." I wasn't ready for that answer. But I never forgot it.

A Meal Fit for a United States President

On September 12, 1984, Commander-in-Chief Ronald Reagan came to Buffalo, New York, bringing with him the weight of the presidency and the energy of a nation in motion. The city responded in kind—crowds gathered, officials moved with purpose, and every detail was measured with precision as the day unfolded at D'Youville College/University. Inside, the room was set for a formal luncheon. Conversations would be held, hands would be shaken, and words about America's future would fill the air. It was a moment that would be seen, recorded, and remembered.

But beyond the public's eye… another story was taking shape. In the kitchen. There were no cameras there. No applause. Only heat rising from stovetops, the rhythm of preparation, and the quiet discipline required to get everything exactly right. Timing mattered. Execution mattered. Because this was no ordinary meal—it was being prepared for the 40th President of the United States. And at the center of it all… was my mother.

She wasn't standing at a podium or seated among dignitaries. She wasn't introduced or acknowledged before the crowd. Yet when the moment came—when the plates were completed and carried from the kitchen into that room—the meal placed before President Reagan and his colleagues had been cooked by her hands. No spotlight. No recognition. Just excellence.

While the President spoke and the room listened, history moved forward in a way most would remember. But there was another part of that moment—quiet, unseen, and just as real. A story not told from the stage, but from behind it. A story of skill, responsibility, and pride in one's work.

Years later, many may recall the visit, the speech, or the presence of a President in Buffalo. But for me, the memory carries something deeper, something personal. Because on that day—September 12, 1984—when the President of the United States sat down to eat…my mother prepared his meal. Ronald Reagan served as President of the United States from 1981 to 1989. Our whole family beamed with pride. And knowing my mother, none of us doubted that President Reagan finished his plate. She retired in 1988 to a heartfelt tribute from the staff and students.

My Father: Work Ethic, Honor, and Everyday Wisdom

My father, Ezelle, wasn't perfect—but he was steady, loyal, hardworking, and proud of who he was. A World War II veteran who served under General Douglas MacArthur in the U.S. Army Airborne, he carried himself with the quiet strength of a man who had seen the world and returned home with gratitude.

After the war, he spent his career in the Engineering and Grounds Division at the VA Medical Center on Bailey Avenue, Buffalo, New York. He was the kind of man who showed up, did his job right, and didn't complain. And while we didn't have everything we wanted, we never lacked what we needed.

Dad was a master at almost everything—landscaping, plumbing, electrical work, carpentry, and mechanics. Doctors called him. Lawyers called him. Neighbors called him. And I went with him everywhere he went. He'd give me a small task while he handled the rest. He'd watch over my shoulder, teach me patiently, correct me gently, then pay me one dollar when the job was done. At that age, one dollar felt like five hundred. I walked around feeling like a king.

Those small jobs were my first lessons in customer service—watching how he spoke to people, how he treated them, how he solved problems without ever raising his voice. To Dad, no one was a stranger. He could meet someone on the street and suddenly discover they'd met years ago. It became a family joke: Dad didn't meet strangers—he just ran into old friends he forgot he knew.

Siblings and the Neighborhood that Raised Us

Each of my siblings brought something different into our home. Terry carried quiet responsibility. Gary—the first of us to pass—and Larry were inseparable. Gerald, the singer and pianist, had that older-brother authority. Then came David, Samuel, Claude, Kelvin, Rachel, and little Lydia, the baby of the family. We argued. We laughed. We fought over the bathroom. We stole each other's clothes—well, the boys never touched the girls' clothes and vice versa. But when life got real, we stood together. Losing both our parents later in life only brought us closer.

The neighborhood itself felt like an extension of our family. People knew your name, your parents, your siblings, and your business. If you acted up five blocks away, your mother knew before you got home. Porch conversations, summer nights, neighbors sharing food, kids running everywhere—it was community in the truest sense. We didn't grow up rich. But we grew up full—with faith, love, discipline, and pride.

Becoming the Man Buffalo Raised

As I stepped into adulthood—into my early jobs, into marriage, into fatherhood, into transportation and hospitality—I began to understand just how much Buffalo had shaped me. The city taught me toughness. My parents taught me humility. My siblings taught me resilience. The neighborhood taught me community. And my faith taught me purpose. Everything I am today—from the way I treat people, to the way I carry myself, to the standard I bring to my work—comes from that childhood home on the east side of Buffalo, New York. Every compliment I receive in my career is really a reflection of my parents, my upbringing, and the values they drilled into us. Buffalo isn't just where I came from. Buffalo is where I was built.

The First Hustle: Two Jobs at Twelve

I was only twelve years old when I took my first real steps into the working world. On the weekends, I worked alongside my dad. By late afternoon during the week, I became a paperboy for the *Buffalo Evening News*. All of this had to fit around school. I'd head to class in the morning like every other kid, then race home after the final bell to swap my books for work. Back then, the city had a rhythm of its own: the *Courier-Express* commanded the mornings, and the *Evening News* wrapped up the day.

And there I was—at twelve years old, this skinny kid with a canvas bag slung over his shoulder—working two jobs in 1969. Between helping Dad, delivering papers, and finishing homework under a bedroom lamp, I was earning what felt like a small fortune. More than money, though, that paper route opened a door into a world I didn't yet realize I was being trained for: the world of service.

Learning the Heart of Service

Delivering newspapers taught me about tips—pennies, nickels, dimes, and the occasional quarter folded into a waiting hand. But it also taught me something more important: the danger hidden inside them. I learned early that if you chase the tip, you lose the meaning of the service. The moment your heart turns toward reward rather than responsibility, sincerity begins to leak out and corrupt your gift. True service only works when you're committed to doing right by people—whether a tip follows or not. Contentment, I discovered, is the quiet engine that keeps blessings flowing. As the Apostle Paul wrote: "But godliness with contentment is great gain." (1 Timothy 6:6)

Cold Days, Warm Intentions

Buffalo winters don't play fair—especially for a paperboy juggling homework, chores, and a delivery deadline before darkness settled in. Most interactions were brief: a quick exchange at the door when subscribers paid their weekly bill. To protect their papers from rain, snow, and slush, I slipped each one into the company-issued plastic sleeve. That little detail mattered. People noticed. It wasn't just a newspaper anymore—it was a message delivered with care. Service has a way of revealing your heart, even in the dead of winter.

Summer Porches and Community Roots

Then came the warm months—when Buffalo breathes a little easier. That's when the job became more than a job. I'd walk up to a house and see life happening: people tending gardens, sweeping walkways, talking with their spouse on the porch, laughing with neighbors. Those scenes reminded me of my own family, my own block, my own upbringing. Families form communities. Communities build nations. And those porch conversations were the glue that held it all together.

A Village that Raised its Children

In our neighborhood, parents corrected each other's children without hesitation. Nobody complained. Nobody argued. It was normal—because we lived by a principle as old as time:

"It takes a whole village to raise a child."

And that village had rules. When I approached a subscriber's home, I addressed them by their last name. Always. Not because it was formal—but because my parents drilled one lesson deep into us:

"Always respect your elders."

So, the exchanges went like this: "Good day, Mr. Mitchell!" "And a good day to you as well, Tommy boy!" Simple. Respectful. And without realizing it, I was learning how to carry myself long before I knew just how much I would need those lessons.

CHAPTER THREE

THE LUXURY OF GUARANTEED EMPLOYMENT

A Family Journey North

In 1948, my grandparents, Mack and Virgie Young, packed up their life in Stockton, Alabama, gathered their fourteen children—my mother was the firstborn—and headed north to Buffalo, New York. They weren't chasing fame or fortune. They were chasing stability, opportunity, and a better future for their family. They raised chickens for food, not for business. They used every part of the bird except the head. That was survival. That was culture. That was history.

Back in slavery days, enslaved people were often given the leftover cuts—wings, backs, feet, liver, gizzard, even the heart. What was rejected became tradition. What was considered undesirable became a delicacy. And without realizing it, the Young family carried the seeds of a movement that would one day change American food culture forever.

A Family that Built Each Other

Three of my mother's siblings—John, Paul, and Inez—turned cooking into commerce. They opened restaurants that didn't just sell food—they shaped neighborhoods and shaped us. In our family, we never worried about work. We had what I call **the luxury of guaranteed employment** because we were never out of a job. However, you didn't quit suddenly. You didn't walk out on family. You worked. You learned. And you gave respect. Those kitchens were our training ground. Our classrooms. The place where discipline, pride, and hospitality were instilled in us long before we realized we'd carry those lessons for the rest of our lives.

The Spark of a Visionary

Uncle John, the fourth child overall and firstborn son, had something extra—a mix of hustle, curiosity, and fearless entrepreneurship. One day, he heard about an African-American businessman in Washington, D.C., selling chicken wings dipped in a special sauce. That was all he needed to hear. His imagination caught fire. In early 1962, he and his sister Dorothy opened **John Young's House of Blair** at Carlton and Jefferson. Picture it: steam rolling out the doorway, customers lining up, and forty wings selling for four dollars.

From the beginning, John coated his wings in his special sauce. Back then, he sold **whole wings**. Today, when someone orders ten wings, they get ten pieces—barely the equivalent of five whole wings. A real wing has three parts: the drumette, the wingette, and the tip. In those days, ten whole wings cost a dollar. This wasn't Buffalo yet. This was the beginning of Buffalo.

The Height of the Wing Era

By the end of 1962, John went from selling 2,300 pounds of chicken wings a week to over 5,000. Five thousand pounds. A week. But wings were only part of it. He served ribs, oxtails, ham hocks, fish, greens, chitterlings, yams, mac and cheese, rice and red beans, lima beans, black-eyed peas, sweet potato pies, sweet potato casserole, peach cobbler—real soul food. Food that stuck to your bones and soothed your spirit. He helped his siblings build their restaurants as well. The Young family wasn't just cooking. We were building something.

"King Of The Wing" — Where a Legend was Born

In 1964, John and his wife, Christine, opened **King Of The Wing** at the corner of High Street and Jefferson Avenue. That same year—and in that very restaurant—John met Frank Bellissimo, a frequent patron. The **Anchor Bar**, located approximately one block north and three blocks west, was only a short walk away. Operating just a few blocks apart from each other, the two restaurateurs naturally crossed paths. It was the beginning of a relationship that would quietly become part of Buffalo's culinary history.

In **1965**, they moved to 1313 Jefferson at East Utica and officially registered **Wings-N-Things**. When they did, the neighborhood came alive. Cold Spring wasn't just a Black community—it was a united community. Black folks, white folks, anybody who followed the scent of frying chicken ended up at John's door. And believe me, that scent traveled. John stacked chicken in the picture window like a trophy display—wings, legs, thighs piled high like a monument.

But before you saw the chicken, you smelled it. That aroma drifted down the block, around corners, and into all areas of the community. Wings-N-Things wasn't just a restaurant. It was Buffalo culture in motion.

The Holy Baptism of the Mumbo Sauce

The secret was John's famous **Mumbo Sauce**—a blend of tomato sauce, barbecue sauce, Southern herbs, and island spices. A Jamaican elder in a sugarcane field taught him the way. Years later, when he taught me how to make it in Illinois, I could feel the weight of culture in my hands. John didn't dip wings. He baptized them. And every customer walked away converted.

A Customer Service Masterclass

John was more than a chef. He was a master of hospitality. When my mother visited, they argued every time. She insisted on paying. He insisted she wouldn't. "Sis… I love you." That was customer service in its purest form—kindness, love, humanity. John didn't treat customers like transactions. He treated them like people. That was another step forward in my education. Another lesson in what real service is supposed to look like.

The Move that Changed Everything

After Dr. Martin Luther King's assassination, riots swept across Buffalo, especially the East Side. Businesses were looted. Communities were shaken. In 1970, John moved his family to Illinois. He had reasons. Good ones. But when he left, a dangerous silence followed. And in that silence, another story grew. "The Anchor Bar invented the wing." No one can invent a chicken wing. You can only discover its use. And that's exactly what John did.

Working with a Legend

In 1978, I spent a year working with John in Decatur, Illinois. He had two restaurants and two food trucks. One truck was located inside the Wagner Casting Plant. The pace was relentless, but familiar. By then, I understood our family's rhythm: Serve with heart. Work with integrity. Never shortchange the customer. Those lessons would later define my career in hotels, at the Niagara Frontier Transportation Authority (NFTA-Metro), and at Niagara Scenic Tours.

When Myth Replaces the Record

John Young and Frank Bellissimo of the Anchor Bar were not strangers to each other. In a recorded video conversation, my Aunt Christine recalled that in **1964**, the two men often went out to breakfast together after John closed his restaurant, **King Of The Wing,** then located on High Street and Jefferson Avenue. They knew each other. They talked. They lived in the same small, overlapping world of Buffalo food and late nights. It's the nugget that didn't make it into the narrative.

Frank didn't originally claim credit for pioneering the chicken wing. The media shaped that story and it only became widely accepted after John left New York in 1970. Even the famous **1964** tale of **a mistaken shipment of wings** delivered to the Anchor Bar doesn't hold up under scrutiny. Those wings were actually intended for **King Of The Wing**.

John Young sold chicken wings for three years without a license before officially registering **Wings-N-Things** in 1965, one year after the Anchor Bar cooked its first wing piece. In the end, the difference between who gets remembered as the pioneer and who doesn't come down to paperwork, not who truly lit the match. And sometimes, history isn't written by the first—it's written by the first one who filed the forms.

The Power of Paperwork

But paperwork has a strange power. It doesn't just record history—it decides it. Once a narrative takes hold, especially one that's clean, simple, and easy to tell, it becomes stubbornly resistant to facts. Tourists repeat it. Newspapers print it. Souvenir shops build entire industries around it. And before long, the story becomes so familiar that questioning it feels almost like heresy.

The Man without a Megaphone

John Young didn't have a publicist. He didn't have a marketing machine. He had a small business, long hours, and a product that people loved. John Young was already serving chicken wings to Buffalo customers before they became a national obsession. But John wasn't chasing headlines—he was just chasing survival. When he left New York in 1970, he didn't just leave behind a restaurant. He left behind his place in the story.

How Stories Become "Facts"

Meanwhile, the simplified version of events continued to spread. It fit neatly on a placard. It fit neatly into a tourist brochure. And most importantly, it fit neatly into a headline. Over time, repetition did what repetition always does—it turned a story into "fact." But real history is messier than that. It lives in conversations like the one my Aunt Christine recorded. It lives in memories shared over late breakfasts after closing time. It lives in businesses that didn't survive long enough to hire someone to write their legend.

The Ones History Forgets

And it lives in people like John Young—men who were too busy building something real to realize someone else would one day get credit for it. Buffalo is full of stories like this. Stories where the work came before the recognition. Where the pioneer didn't get the parade. Where the foundation was poured by someone whose name never made it onto the monument.

By **1964,** John and his sister, Dorothy, went their separate ways. The chicken wing may be Buffalo's most famous culinary export, but like so much of this city's history, its true origin story is not the one that fits best on a souvenir T-shirt. It's the one that starts in a small shop, with a man who was ahead of his time—and a step behind the paperwork.

A City Tour and a Familiar Tension

At Niagara Scenic Tours, I'm the driver they call for city tours. After more than thirty years driving a 40-foot bus through Buffalo's tight streets, potholes, and surprise parades, I know this city like muscle memory. Most tours are smooth. Until we approach the Anchor Bar. That's when the historian grabs the microphone and declares:

> "This, ladies and gentlemen, is where the Buffalo chicken wing was born!"

Meanwhile, I'm gripping the wheel, talking to myself: "Lord, give me strength… here he goes again." I never say a word. I just smile and keep driving.

The Return and the Reckoning

In 1980, John came home. In 1982, the Buffalo Common Council proclaimed him the originator of the Buffalo wing. He was honored at the Buffalo Wing Festival and inducted into the National Buffalo Wing Hall of Fame. And on August 17, 2025, the *Buffalo News* finally printed the truth:

> **"Anchor Bar's wing origin story is well known; it also can't be true."**

The Legacy Lives On

John Young didn't just make food. He made culture. He made history. He made a standard. And if Buffalo wants to tell the story honestly, it begins:

...at Wings-N-Things.
...with Mumbo Sauce dripping from a whole wing.
...with the Young family.
...with John.

A Bond Forged in the Kitchen

John was very sentimental and had a way of sensing trouble before it arrived. When my brother, Larry, was in Los Angeles and weeks passed with no word, the silence grew heavy. No phones. No texts. Just worry. When John heard nobody knew where Larry was, fear crossed his face—not paranoia. Love. "Y'all need to go get him," he said, his voice breaking. "Something ain't right. Go find him." He cried openly. Not a businessman. Not a legend. Just a man who loved his nephew like a son.

A Wing Specialist

In the spring of 1998, John Mack Young made his final move. These days, I like to imagine him in heaven, sprinkling Mumbo Sauce on the wings of angels and improving the menu up there the same way he did down here. John had that gift—he didn't just serve food, he served joy. He made people feel welcome, seen, and taken care of, whether they knew him for five minutes or five decades. The world lost a good man that spring, but heaven gained a great one—a wing specialist.

CHAPTER FOUR

STOP & KOP and GET & SPLIT

A Brother's Love Turned Into a Legacy

If you really want to understand the heart of the Young family, you don't stop at John—you look at his brother, my Uncle Paul. Paul Young (May 15, 1939 – January 27, 2023) was cut from the same cloth as John: hardworking, big-hearted, and deeply committed to family. But Paul had something extra in his toolkit—a sharp, natural business instinct. John's generosity ran so deep that when Paul and his wife, Delores, wanted to open their first restaurant, John didn't hesitate. He guided them, supported them, and helped them establish **Stop & Kop** at 424 Broadway at the corner of Pratt. That spot became the starting point of a new branch of the Young family legacy.

Success Built Three Blocks from History

When John left New York in 1970, Paul stepped forward with confidence. He opened another Stop & Kop in Cold Spring—just three blocks from where Wings-N-Things had first electrified the neighborhood. Paul thrived not by trying to outshine John, but by bringing a different dynamic to the table. He watched the numbers. He monitored inventory. He studied customer patterns. Where John had heart and flavor, Paul had structure and strategy. Together, the two brothers represented the perfect combination: **Soul and system. Heart and hustle.**

A Gift Only a Brother Could Give

Despite his sharp business sense, Paul shared John's generous spirit.

At the height of its success, he did something extraordinary: he **gave** the entire Cold Spring restaurant to his sister, my mother, Claudia. That's Young family love. Across the street was Kirkland's, another respected soul-food restaurant. But Stop & Kop didn't just survive—it thrived. The aroma of fried chicken, ribs, greens, yams, and cornbread filled the block, drawing customers to the counter as if they were under a spell. The place was alive.

The Years the Streets Changed

The 1970s were not gentle on Buffalo's East Side. The neighborhood was changing fast—and not for the better. Tension lived in the air. Gang violence hovered near every storefront. And my parents felt it.

The Night that Marked our Family Forever

One evening in 1973, while working a shift alone, something happened that marked our family forever. My father had stepped out for a moment. I was behind the counter when several gang members burst through the door. They didn't come in to order food. They came to take whatever they could—**including, I believed, my life**. One gang member, the leader, jumped over the counter. I was sixteen years old. A kid. Trapped.

A Split-Second Choice and God's Mercy

My father kept a shotgun near the register for protection. With the gang leader already coming toward me, I grabbed it. I didn't want to use it—God knows I didn't. But in that moment, I believed it was either him or me. I fired. By the grace of God, the gang leader survived. He lived. But he never changed his path. Years later, that same life caught up with him. He is now serving a sentence that will keep him behind bars for the rest of his life—convicted on five counts of first-degree murder.

When Violence Came Back Again

That wasn't the only time danger reached our doors. On another occasion, my father was forced to defend himself the same way. He had to shoot two members of that same gang. Miraculously, both survived. Thank God for His mercy. But those moments shook our family to its core—not just because of the danger, but because of the emotional weight they carried.

Family First, Always

My parents realized a hard truth: no business was worth risking their son's life—or their own. They made the painful decision to return the Cold Spring restaurant to Paul. Not out of failure. But out of wisdom. Out of love. Out of survival. **Family first.** That day changed something inside me. School no longer felt safe. It no longer felt normal. Although I wasn't there, members of that gang would wait outside, hoping for a chance—hoping for retribution. Life had gotten very real. Very fast.

Protection, Fear, and a Mother's Choice

The gang leader involved, whose identity I will keep anonymous, was so notorious that the police, fearing retaliation, suggested I leave town. They even asked, "Do you have any relatives in Hawaii or Alaska?" My mother knew my stubbornness too well. Instead of sending me away or to school, she chose to bring school to me. For a while, I was homeschooled. Paul, meanwhile, kept building. He opened more restaurants across Buffalo's Black communities:

- Soul Bird
- Birdland
- Taste of Soul
- Soul Fabulous
- Meals for a Steal
- Eat Out More Often
- WINGS

Two Brothers, Two Sauces, One Legacy

Each restaurant served the same soul-food tradition—but each had its own signature sauce. John had Mumbo Sauce—rich, red, sweet, and savory, with Jamaica in its soul. Paul created Boogaloo Sauce—same roots, different rhythm. A little bolder. A little louder. Still smooth. Two brothers. Two sauces. One unforgettable legacy.

The Rise of Get & Split

Then came the third pillar. My Aunt Inez and Uncle Stanley opened **Get & Split** at 588 Genesee near the corner of Jefferson. Even the name sounded like Buffalo—direct, flavorful, full of personality. Their signature was **La-La Sauce**, named after the Delfonics' 1967 hit *'La-La Means I Love You."* And that's exactly what it was: a love letter to the neighborhood, to the food, and to the family.

Serving Buffalo, One Plate at a Time

We worked in all of them. We served everyone—working folks, families, politicians, law enforcement, strangers who became regulars, and regulars who became family. Every plate wasn't just food. It was history. Heritage. Heart.

Hearts That Fed a City

When someone in the neighborhood passed away, grief didn't stay private. It moved through churches, barber shops, beauty salons, and living rooms. And every time, my family showed up.

John.
Paul.
Inez.
My mother, Claudia.

A family would say, "We don't have much, but can you help us with food for the repass?" And the answer was always the same: **"Of course. We'll take care of everything."** No bill. No hesitation. No conditions.

Love that Didn't Wait to be Asked

John, Paul, Inez, and Mom didn't even wait to be asked. If they heard someone had passed, they started cooking. "They're gonna need this," they would say. They weren't just feeding stomachs. They were feeding souls.

Shaped by Service, Not Strategy

Looking back, those moments were bricks laid onto the foundation of who I would become. Not shaped by ambition. Not shaped by profit. But shaped by **service**. That's where my understanding of real customer service was born—not in a classroom or a manual, but at home, the family restaurants, in grief, in love, and in showing up when people needed you most

CHAPTER FIVE

NEW SKATELAND & THE HOLIDAY INN MIDTOWN

The Joy of Skating and the Need to Keep Moving Forward

As I moved through my early teenage years, I learned how to carry school on one shoulder and work on the other. And somewhere in between, roller skating became my escape—the one place where I felt light, fast, and free. So, when I landed a job at **New Skateland Arena** in 1972—the heart of our community at 33 East Ferry Street—I felt like I had struck gold.

For kids in our neighborhoods, skating wasn't just a pastime. It was a rite of passage. Once a child learned to walk, skates usually came soon after. And New Skateland was where the laughter, music, childhood crushes, and awkward falls all came together under one roof.

Working for the Goggins Family

I had the privilege of working for **Mr. Trunnis Goggins**, the father of future **Navy SEAL** and bestselling author **David Goggins**. Back then, none of us had any idea how famous the Goggins name would become—but we all knew Trunnis was a force in the community. It was one of those rare jobs where you met new people every day—kids from school, church friends, families from all over Buffalo—and somehow earned an honest paycheck while having fun.

The Many Jobs Behind the Skating Floor

My best friend's brother, Donald, worked alongside me. Donald had a gift for impersonations, especially Donald Duck—and kept us laughing through long shifts. At Skateland, we did everything:

- Serviced the skating floor
- Stripped and waxed hallways
- Stocked and cleaned restrooms
- Ran coat check
- Repaired worn-out skates
- Worked the concession stand
- Kept the building and sidewalks clean

And every now and then, I stepped into the **DJ booth**. That part was special. Each skating group had the floor for three songs. Clear the floor. Next group in. Without realizing it, I was learning how to **read a room**—something that would become a critical skill many years later as a professional driver. Mr. Goggins also hosted midnight adult skate sessions called **B.Y.O. — Bring Your Own Bottle**. Those nights had their own energy… and their own stories.

The Vermillion Room: A World Above Us

Above the rink sat one of Buffalo's slickest nightspots: **The Vermillion Room**. That was Trunnis' pride and joy. He managed a local band called *Sabata.* They didn't play original music, but they sounded so good that nobody cared. That band taught me how to **listen to music**, not just hear it. Donald and I were responsible for keeping the club clean. Even as teenagers, we knew we were stepping into a grown-up world—built on rhythm, nightlife, and adult stories.

Rick James and Buffalo Pride

Trunnis was close friends with another Buffalo legend—**Rick James**. Before Rick became a superstar, he was a local kid on wheels just like the rest of us. But when he hit it big—after *Mary Jane* and *Super Freak*—he still found his way back to The Vermillion Room, often pulling up in his yellow Excalibur with an entourage that turned heads. Through Rick, Trunnis met other industry figures who passed through the club. They may not have lived perfect lives—but in those moments, they were in their glory.

Three Years, Countless Memories

I spent about three years at New Skateland. Those memories still warm my heart. I remember little Trunnis II wobbling on skates while his sisters—Terasa, Salina, or Marina—helped lace him up. Once released, he'd take off with arms flailing and his head bouncing to the music. By the time David Goggins was born in 1975, I was already preparing for the next chapter of my life. I never met him during those Skateland years.

Seeing Trunnis Through My Own Eyes

I only knew Mr. Goggins professionally—but that was enough to know him as a warm, respectful, fatherly figure who looked out for his people. Years later, in David's book *Can't Hurt Me*, he shares painful truths about his father's darker side. My heart goes out to him and his family for what they endured, and I pray that the Lord has healed him and given him peace that passes all understanding. But the man I knew treated his staff and customers with dignity. He never demeaned us. Never stripped us of our pride. And that is the man I remember.

THE HOLIDAY INN MIDTOWN

A Life of Encounters Waiting to Be Remembered

There are moments in life when you wish you could go back and tell your younger self, "Write it all down. These memories will matter." I crossed paths with musicians, athletes, and public figures long before I understood what I was witnessing. I kept no diary. Just lived it. Decades later, I pieced together timelines through old concert listings, articles, and archives. I may not remember every date—but I remember the experience. And sometimes, that's more important.

Stepping Onto Delaware Avenue

In early 1975, my life took another turn. The **Holiday Inn Midtown** at 620 Delaware Avenue stood like a glass monument to professionalism. And I got there because of one man—my friend and brother-at-heart, **Jerome "Magoo" Croskery**. We grew up dodging gangs, drugs, and street life together. Jerome worked there and believed I'd be a good fit. He went to his boss, **Mrs. Mayzelle Russell**, the Executive Housekeeper, and spoke my name with confidence. Friday: I applied. Monday: I was in uniform. No waiting. No games. His word meant something.

Becoming an Unbreakable Duo

Jerome and I became a two-man crew that could outwork five. If one slipped, the other filled the gap. "There is a friend that sticks closer than a brother." Jerome was that friend. Still is. Being a houseman meant doing everything, and those chores are what built me:

- Glasses
- Mirrors
- Floors
- Bathrooms
- Elevators
- Linens
- Trash
- Deliveries

We didn't just clean. We maintained an atmosphere. And for the first time in my life, I wore a uniform. Olive green. Simple. Official. That uniform taught me something I've never forgotten: People see your appearance before they see your performance.

The Power of Presence

I spoke to guests because I cared. "How is your stay with us?" Some were surprised. Some were touched. But that's how I was raised. Service isn't about position. It's about presence.

Recognition in a White Uniform

Mrs. Russell began calling me into her office—not for corrections, but to hand me **letters from guests** praising my service. She was elegance, discipline, and leadership in a white uniform with gold-rimmed glasses. She didn't just run a department. She built people. And she believed in me.

A Foundation Laid in Olive Green

That hotel helped shape the man I became: A customer service specialist. A trusted professional. A man who understands that kindness, consistency, and pride matter. Every folded sheet, every polished mirror, every guest interaction became part of me. Even without a diary, those years wrote themselves into my character.

CHAPTER SIX

AN ALL-STAR CAST

LABELLE: A Trailblazing Sound and the Spirit Behind It

One of the most memorable groups I ever encountered during my Holiday Inn years was **LaBelle**—and especially their electrifying bass player, **Carmine (Carmen) Rojas**. LaBelle, the boundary-breaking female group behind the funk classic *"Lady Marmalade"* (written by Bob Crewe and Kenny Nolan), was known as much for their futuristic stage outfits as for their fearless fusion of rock, funk, and soul.

Their sound was a radical departure from their early days as a traditional 1960s girl group and stood in sharp contrast to the later solo career of Patti LaBelle. While Patti is the name most people remember, **Nona Hendryx** was another extraordinary creative force—an avant-garde songwriter who carved out her own bold path. And the group's story actually began as a **foursome**, not a trio.

The Formation of a Philadelphia Powerhouse

Before the world knew them as LaBelle, Patricia Holt and Cindy Birdsong sang in a Philadelphia group called **The Ordettes**. In 1962, they joined Wynona "Nona" Hendryx and Sarah Dash of **The Del Capris**, forming what would become **Patti LaBelle and the Blue Belles**.

Sarah Dash (August 18, 1945 – September 20, 2021) remained a foundational voice of the group. Their first major success came in 1962 with *"I Sold My Heart to the Junkman."* Though written in 1946 by Leon and Otis René and previously recorded by others, the Blue Belles' version finally broke through nationally. It charted:

- #15 on the Pop charts
- #13 on the R&B charts
- #8 on Billboard's Regional Breakouts

And just like that, they had their first hit.

The Controversial Backstory of "Junkman"

Behind that success was a fascinating and controversial story. Another group, **The Starlets** from Chicago, had recorded the song while on tour. But instead of releasing it under their name, the record was issued as a Blue Belles single. The Starlets sued and eventually settled for $5,000 per member. They won legally—but history moved on without them. If the story is true, the Blue Belles earned their first gold hit without ever stepping into the studio.

Producer Bobby Martin encouraged Patricia Holt to adopt the last name **LaBelle**, and the group was reborn as Patti LaBelle and the Blue Bells. In 1967, Cindy Birdsong left to join **The Supremes**, and the group settled into the trio that would carry them into the 1970s. Then, in 1974, everything changed.

The Rise of LaBelle

Their album **Nightbirds**, released September 13, 1974, launched them into a new stratosphere. *"Lady Marmalade"* hit #1 on both the Pop and R&B charts in early 1975, earning them their first gold album. Though later albums (*Phoenix* and *Chameleon*) were well-received, they never quite matched that moment. By 1976, the group chose to disband—not out of bitterness, but to preserve their friendship.

MEETING CARMINE ROJAS

The Bass Player Who Offered a Word of Encouragement

Between 1975 and 1976, LaBelle performed in Buffalo three times and stayed at our Holiday Inn each time. I remember one crisp Buffalo morning. I was polishing the glass doors when **Carmine** walked toward the exit. I held the door and said, "Good morning, sir." "Good morning," he replied, taking in the cool air. "Feels pretty good outside today." That simple comment opened the door—literally and figuratively—for conversation. I asked, "Are you with the band or the stage crew?" "I play bass," he said. That caught my attention immediately. When I told him I was practicing guitar, he encouraged me: "Whatever you do, don't stop practicing. You'll be surprised where your talent will take you." I was grateful for his words of encouragement, but my course in life was already determined by someone bigger than us all.

A Brother's Christmas in April

"I'm Tommy." "Carmen," he said, bumping elbows since my hands were full. During their stay, he gave me **concert passes**. I took my brother Gerald (who has since passed), and for him, that night was like Christmas. Before Carmine left, he shared a line I will never forget: "While dreams set the stage, it's persistent hard work that brings them to life."

A Bassist who Touched Every Corner of Modern Music

Carmine Rojas would go on to become one of the most respected and sought-after bassists in the world, working with:

- David Bowie (*Let's Dance, Tonight*)
- Rod Stewart
- Julian Lennon
- Paul Young
- Santana
- Todd Rundgren
- Carole King
- Michael Bolton
- Jewel
- Joe Bonamassa

He crossed genres effortlessly—rock, funk, R&B, soul, blues. But what stayed with me most was his humility. He was twenty-two. I was eighteen. And he treated me like an equal.

B.B. KING: A BLUES LEGEND AND AN ELEVATOR RIDE

The Day B.B. King Rode My Elevator

The Holiday Inn Midtown in the 1970s was a magnet for traveling stars. Thirteen floors, just over a hundred rooms, and perfectly placed between Buffalo's major venues. And when B.B. King came to town, the whole building felt different.

The Elevator Encounter

One day, I was polishing the elevator buttons and brass plate when Bob, our bellman, stepped in with a guest. In the reflection, I suddenly realized who was standing beside me. The King of the Blues. I blurted out, "Mr. King, what a privilege it is to welcome you." He smiled and said, "Thank you. I'm pleased to be here."

A Message for Lucille

When we reached his floor, the doors opened. As they stepped out, I stopped the doors from closing. "Oh, Mr. King... please extend my warmest regards to Lucille." He paused. Smiled wider. "I sure will."

The Legend Behind the Name

Most people today know the name Lucille as B.B. King's guitar. But the story behind that name is pure blues in its own right. Back in 1949, while performing at a club, two men started fighting over a woman named Lucille. In the chaos, they knocked over a kerosene barrel, and the whole building caught fire. B.B. escaped—then realized he'd left his guitar inside. Against every instinct of survival, he rushed back into the burning building and saved it. Afterward, he named the guitar "Lucille"—a reminder of the night he almost lost his life... and the woman who unintentionally sparked the flame. Every guitar he ever owned after that carried her name.

A Shared Birthday

Interestingly, B.B. King and I shared the same birthday: September 16. He was born in 1925. I came along thirty-two years later. He passed away in 2015. But that elevator ride—quiet, simple, unforgettable—has stayed with me ever since. Some moments don't need a stage. Sometimes all it takes is a reflection in brass, a smile... and a nod from the King himself.

When Ella Fitzgerald Came Through Buffalo

I remember when **Ella Fitzgerald** came through Buffalo in December of 1974. I don't remember every detail of her visit—time has softened the edges—but I remember *her*. I remember management informing me that she was coming and that I was to assist in getting her settled. I remember helping with her luggage. That part is clear.

At the time, she was 57 years old, still touring, still performing, still carrying herself with a quiet authority that never needed announcing. What stayed with me most, though, wasn't her fame—it was her spirit. She was gentle. Warm. Saturated with the kind of love that only a mother possesses. Being in her presence felt calm, reassuring, and deeply human, as if kindness had become second nature to her. There was no rush, no tension, no sense of distance. Just grace.

In our brief interaction, I felt the kind of care that doesn't demand attention, the kind that simply exists. It was subtle, but unmistakable. She was born on April 25, 1917, and passed away on June 15, 1996. Yet in that brief December moment in Buffalo, she felt timeless.

CHAPTER SEVEN

BEFORE HONOR IN HUMILITY

A Father's Lessons in the Glow of a Freshly Waxed Floor

Growing up beside my father—whether we were fixing, lifting, wiping, or waxing—came with a classroom of its own. He didn't raise his voice to teach. He spoke in simple truths that settled deep into my spirit. "Son," he would say, leaning on a mop handle or stepping back to admire a polished floor, "if you have to mop and wax floors for a living, then make 'em shine. Take pride in your work. Celebrate your victories. Learn from your mistakes. In time, people will see your character—and the rewards will follow." At the time, I didn't realize he was handing me a lifetime of wisdom. Only later did I recognize that what he taught echoed King Solomon's ancient proverb:

> "Before destruction, the heart of man is haughty, and before honor is humility."

That was one of the first seeds planted in me about what true greatness looks like. And it always began with humility.

The Quiet Power of Humility

Humility isn't shrinking back or pretending you don't have gifts. It isn't a weakness. Humility is strength dressed in discipline. It's knowing who you are—your abilities, your limits, your flaws—and remaining teachable anyway. It's the steady hand of someone who understands that life is bigger than applause and character is bigger than titles.

Humility never seeks titles like "Mopotologist, Broomologist, Janitorial Technician, *or* President of the Mop Room." It finds contentment right where

Providence has placed it, serving faithfully without needing a spotlight. In customer service—whether behind a hotel desk, inside an arena tunnel, or behind the wheel of a motorcoach—humility becomes an invisible badge. People feel it before you speak. And when they feel it, they trust you.

Humility in God's Eyes

From a biblical perspective, humility is the posture that says, *"Lord, Your will above mine."* It acknowledges that every gift we have is God-given, every opportunity God-opened, and every promotion God-allowed. Christ Himself walked in humility—never loud, never boastful—yet His impact shook the world. Humility is never advertised. But it is always seen.

Why Humility Matters Everywhere You Go

In hospitality, transportation, sports operations, or leadership, humility stabilizes a person. People follow humble leaders out of admiration, not fear. Clients remember humble service long after they forget names and titles. Humility is not a lack of power. It is **power under control**. Here's what it produces:

1. **Humility builds strong relationships**
   It helps people listen more than they speak, value other perspectives, and earn trust.
2. **Humility creates room for growth**
   A humble person never assumes they know everything—and that keeps them improving.
3. **Humility promotes unity and cooperation**
   Teams succeed when people work together instead of competing for attention.
4. **Humility strengthens leadership**
   The best leaders lead by serving. Humility makes a leader approachable and trustworthy.
5. **Humility keeps perspective**
   It helps you celebrate success without arrogance and face setbacks without collapse.

A Door Opens at the Holiday Inn

By 1977, a few years had passed since I started at the Holiday Inn. One day, Mrs. Russell, our Executive Housekeeper, called me into her office. She told me my work ethic and attitude had exceeded management's expectations. "Mrs.

Strada wants you upstairs working with Bob on the bell staff," she said. Bob was a Caucasian gentleman with a big personality and a great sense of humor.

Unless a large group or band checked in, we alternated between morning and evening shifts. While working the bell staff, I also learned the front desk—check-ins, credit cards, and room blocking. "On Monday, you'll start up there," she said. "It's been wonderful having you on my team. Congratulations."

The Woman who Opened the Elevator Door to My Future

Agnes Strada, the Innkeeper, was an elegant Italian woman with a commanding yet gracious presence. She had a gift for spotting potential—and the generosity to develop it. She moved me from behind-the-scenes work into a guest-facing role. I was issued a sharp new uniform: charcoal-gray pants, a light-blue shirt, and a dark-blue tie. I hadn't expected the tie—but I wore it proudly. For the first time, I was no longer just supporting the operation. I was representing it.

A Transition Marked by Time and Loss

The promotion came with pride—but also a quiet sadness. Jerome and I would no longer work side by side every day. Over the years, we drifted apart, as often happens in life. Now we only see each other when someone from the old neighborhood passes away. The last time was at the funeral of our childhood friend **Haywood "Boy Teeny" Paterson**, one of the ten victims of the Tops Market shooting on May 14, 2022. Later in this book, I'll return to that day—I was the lead driver of four buses that carried the Buffalo Bills to the memorial.

"Teacher" — The Nickname that Finally Made Sense

Jerome had always called me "Teacher." I never asked why—until that day. He said, "Out of everybody we grew up with, you were the only one who always made sense when you talked. Whether you were right or wrong, it always sounded right." We both laughed. But standing there, older now, I realized something: My father's lessons… the floors I waxed… the humility I carried… were shaping something in me long before I understood that one day, those very things would become lessons I would share with others.

CHAPTER EIGHT

A FRONT-ROW SEAT TO THE STARS

Buffalo's Soundtrack in the Mid-to-Late 1970s

From the mid to late 1970s, Buffalo was alive in a way that's hard to explain unless you lived it. The city didn't just host music—it *breathed* it. Soul, jazz, funk, rock, blues—every week, sometimes every night, another legend rolled into town. And right in the middle of it all stood the Holiday Inn Midtown on Delaware Avenue, where I had the privilege of working during a stretch of years that now feels almost unreal.

Buffalo had become a serious stop on the touring circuit. If Kleinhans Music Hall, Shea's Performing Arts Center, or the Memorial Auditorium had a major act booked, there was a very good chance the artist—and often their entire crew—would be staying just a few floors above my bellman's station. And they weren't just any artists. We're talking about names that still echo through music history:

> Elvis. Sinatra. Bowie. Springsteen. Ray Charles. B.B. King. James Taylor. Santana. Chicago. The Jacksons. The Rolling Stones. The Who. Fleetwood Mac. KISS. Aerosmith. Rod Stewart. Neil Diamond. Chuck Mangione.

The list goes on and on—and yes, I've preserved the full historical list separately, because it deserves to be remembered (**Appendix**). But this chapter isn't about lists. It's about what it felt like to stand in the middle of it.

Where the Artists Stayed

The Holiday Inn Midtown wasn't a luxury palace by today's standards, but back then, it was **the** place to stay. Thirteen floors high, just over a hundred rooms, and perfectly positioned between Buffalo's biggest venues, it became a crossroads for music, movement, and moment-in-time history. Over those years, many artists didn't just pass through once—they came back again and again. Some stayed for days. Some only for a night.

But all of them brought with them a certain electricity that you could feel in the lobby, in the elevators, even in the hallways. Sometimes it was quiet professionalism. Other times it was organized chaos—road cases, instruments, managers, assistants, security, and sound crews flowing in like a small traveling city. And right in the middle of all of it... was me.

Behind the Scenes of the Music

Most of the time, my role was simple: carry luggage, deliver towels, bring ice, fetch glasses, point people in the right direction, and make sure they felt welcome. And often, after helping someone to their room, they'd slip me a pair of concert tickets or backstage passes as a thank-you. But the real gift wasn't the tickets. The real gift was **watching greatness up close**—not on stage, but in the quiet, human moments in between.

I never had a single bad encounter. Not one. Every artist, every musician, every road manager I met treated me with dignity and respect. Some were quiet. Some were funny. Some were larger than life. But all of them, in those moments, were just people on the road—tired, focused, and grateful for a smooth place to land.

A Network of Hotels, A City in Motion

The Midtown wasn't alone in this. Our sister Holiday Inn properties across Western New York helped support the entire entertainment ecosystem:

- The Buffalo-Amherst location hosted many of the Melody Fair performers.
- The Dingens Street location was perfect for acts playing the Aud.
- The Airport Holiday Inn became a major hub for large productions.
- The Grand Island property housed summer performers and extended stays.

All of those hotels are gone now. Sold. Closed. Repurposed. But back then, they were **alive**—full of music, movement, and stories being written in real time.

Melody Fair: Another Giant of its Time

And then there was Melody Fair in North Tonawanda—another legendary stage that brought giants to Western New York: Nat King Cole, Harry Belafonte, Johnny Cash, Duke Ellington, Ray Charles, Little Richard, Sammy Davis Jr., Gladys Knight, The Bee Gees, and so many more. Some of them stayed at the Buffalo-Amherst Holiday Inn—under the same ownership family that employed me, but most made their home base at the Holiday Inn Midtown. Looking back now, it feels almost impossible that all of this was happening in one city, in one era, and that I was right there in the middle of it.

My Role in this Musical World

During those years, I didn't see myself as anything special. I was just doing my job. But my job put me in a position of **trust**. I was trusted with people's luggage. With their comfort. With their privacy. With their space. And I took that seriously. Whether I was delivering ice, towels, glasses, a morning newspaper, or just offering a warm smile and a "Welcome to Buffalo," I understood something even back then: **service is never small when it's done with care.**

A Season that Built Something Greater

When I look back on those years, I don't just remember the celebrities. I remember the *feeling*. The feeling of being part of something bigger than myself. The feeling of moving through a city that pulsed with live music almost every night. The feeling of being young, working hard, and standing in the current of history without even realizing it. I see it clearly now:

The Holiday Inn Midtown wasn't just a job.
It was training.
It was shaping.
It was Providence.

I wasn't chasing titles. I wasn't chasing fame. I was building upon a foundation—one bag, one towel, one respectful gesture at a time. And somewhere along the way, I learned something that has followed me my entire life: **Humility is not a stepping stone to honor. It is honor itself.**

CHAPTER NINE

THE BLIZZARD OF 1977

When Buffalo Stood Still, and Humanity Stepped Forward

There are storms you outgrow, storms you forget, and storms that become part of your identity. The Blizzard of 1977 is the kind that lives inside you forever. I'm proud—and blessed—to say I'm one of the thousands of Buffalonians who survived the deadliest winter event in our city's history.

A Storm that Came Like a Thief in the Daylight

Friday, January 28, 1977. Most storms give you warnings. This one ambushed us. By 10:45 a.m., the National Weather Service issued a severe storm warning. Within an hour, Western New York vanished behind a curtain of white so thick it felt as if the sky itself had dropped onto the streets. Winds screamed up to seventy miles per hour, stealing the breath from your lungs. Snow didn't fall—it attacked, hurled in sheets from a frozen Lake Erie.

The wind chill plunged to nearly fifty below zero. The city went still. Cars stalled and sat like tombs in the drifts. Roads closed. The airport shut down. Snowplows surrendered. People abandoned vehicles and stumbled into department stores, offices, and taverns—anywhere warm enough to wait out what felt like the end of the world.

Almost thirty lives were lost. Many froze where they stood or where they sat, trapped in cars buried deeper by the minute. Even in a city trained to handle winter, this storm brought Buffalo to its knees.

Nature's Fury, Hour by Hour

That morning had started deceptively gentle. I recall the temperature actually rising—from five degrees at midnight to twenty-six by 11 a.m. A storm luring its prey. At 11:35 a.m., the real monster arrived. Visibility collapsed to zero. Winds shifted and howled at nearly fifty miles an hour. The temperature plunged from twenty-six to zero in less than sixty minutes. By late afternoon, gusts at the airport hit 69 mph, and at Niagara Falls, an even more vicious 75 mph. With temperatures below zero and winds cutting like knives, the wind chill bottomed out near sixty below. And then the storm just… stayed.

Three more days of unpredictable whiteouts and punishing winds. February 1st finally brought sunlight, but it only revealed the damage—cars entombed, power lines dragged down, entire neighborhoods buried. The National Guard was mobilized. Even troops from Fort Bragg were flown in to help. President Jimmy Carter declared nine counties federal disaster areas. That's what it took to get Buffalo back on its feet.

A Morning that Began with Mom's Bacon

That morning started with something beautiful—my mother's bacon sizzling in the pan. The aroma alone could warm a soul. Schools were closed, so all nine of us were home. Terry and Larry were serving in the U.S. Navy at the time. Dad had already left early and made it safely to the VA Hospital. Mom gathered us around the table, prayed, and fed us like only she could. After breakfast, I looked out the window. Conditions were worsening by the minute. I wasn't scheduled to work at the Holiday Inn that day, but something told me they'd need all hands on deck. I called the hotel. They were short-staffed everywhere. "I'm on my way," I said.

Mom looked at me with that familiar mix of concern and trust. She told me to put on one of my father's snow-removal suits—an army-green, heavily insulated bodysuit with hood, gloves, and ski mask. Once you put that thing on, you step outside immediately, or you'll cook alive. I packed a small bag—toothbrush, socks, deodorant, extra uniform—hugged Mom, told her my route, wrapped my face in a scarf, and stepped into the storm. I joked, "If you don't hear from me in thirty minutes, call the United Nations." She didn't laugh. She just prayed.

The Walk through the White

We lived at 1067 Ellicott Street, less than a mile from the Holiday Inn. Under normal circumstances, a seventeen-minute walk. That day, it felt like walking through another world. The wind shoved. The snow clawed at my mask. But it wasn't yet a full whiteout, and by God's grace, I made it. When I reached the hotel, my friend Jerome was already out front, shovel in hand, battling the storm. "Give me a minute, bro," I called. "I hear you, Teacher!" he shouted back.

That was our brotherhood. I called Mom to ease her heart, grabbed a second shovel, and we went to work. But the truth was, the snow was falling faster than two young men could fight it. We ran out of places to put it and started piling it on top of buried cars.

The Hotel Becomes a Refuge

Half the housekeeping staff couldn't make it in. But for once, we were grateful the hotel was nearly empty. Every room became a lifeline—drivers, families, employees from nearby businesses who'd ventured out and gotten trapped. The front desk blocked rooms for staff still on site. Jerome and I shared a double room to make space for others. When we ran out of cots, we handed out blankets and pillows. Those who could pay did. Those who couldn't were welcomed anyway. Humanity over revenue.

Then came Mr. McKenzick, our restaurant manager—a man with a heart big enough to warm a frozen city. He turned the ballroom into a dining hall and served everyone a complimentary breakfast, lunch, and dinner. Alcohol was the only item for sale. Everything else was on the house. Housekeeping was suspended. We supplied linens and towels and let guests manage their own rooms. Jerome and I delivered supplies, vacuumed where needed, and helped wherever we could. Everyone pitched in. Everyone lifted someone else.

Strangers Became Family

Over the next few days, the hotel became something special. People shared stories, laughter, fears, and food. Parents played board games with their kids in the lobby. Workers slept beside families. Executives talked with maintenance men. The storm stripped away titles and status. When people finally left, they didn't leave as strangers. They left as family.

What the Blizzard Taught Me

Serving celebrities is exciting. But nothing in my career—before or since—has matched the fulfillment of serving ordinary people who were scared, cold, exhausted, and grateful for warmth. That's one reason I never ask celebrities for autographs. Another is professionalism—I'm there to serve, not to chase. And the truth is, I was never starstruck. I've always believed this: With or without fame, I am the most important celebrity in my own life. If I want a picture of someone important, I'll take a selfie. If I want an autograph, I'll sign my own name. The Blizzard of '77 didn't just bury Buffalo. It revealed Buffalo—resilient, compassionate, unbreakable. And it revealed something in me, too: Service is who I am… no matter the storm.

CHAPTER TEN

TWENTY DOLLARS AND A BUSINESS CARD

A Quiet Moment That Changed Everything

Working on the bell staff at the Holiday Inn Midtown meant I crossed paths with people from every walk of life—celebrities, executives, entrepreneurs, and families on vacation. Every day brought new faces, new stories, and new opportunities to sharpen my customer service instincts. I didn't take those moments lightly. I took pride in holding my head high, addressing each person with dignity, and offering the kind of service my parents raised me to give: authentic, warm, and respectful.

It was the summer of 1977—if memory serves—when I encountered a guest who carried himself with an almost royal stillness. A handsome gentleman of Asian descent, always sharply dressed, his polished shoes and black-rimmed eyeglasses made him look like a scholar—or a man descended from some noble dynasty. Although he stayed with us for several days, he moved quietly, almost invisibly. Still, whenever our paths crossed, I greeted him as I did all guests:

> "Good morning, sir. Good afternoon, sir. Good night, sir. Are your accommodations to your liking?"

He would nod, barely speaking, yet somehow letting me know he appreciated the respect. A few times, he asked for dining suggestions, and I pointed him toward the finest places in town—The Cloister, Manny's, Park Lane, and a few others that never disappointed. Even now, I couldn't tell you his line of work. He never volunteered it, and it wasn't my place to ask. My job was service, not investigation. But his presence—quiet, dignified, almost regal—was unforgettable.

A Gift, A Pause, And an Invitation

When he was ready to check out, he asked me to retrieve his luggage. I followed protocol as always—knocked, announced "Bell service," waited, and used my master key only after receiving no answer. His belongings were neatly arranged, the kind of orderliness you'd expect from a man who left nothing to chance. When I brought the luggage down, he was already outside beside an elegant black sedan, the trunk open and waiting. I loaded his bags, closed the trunk, and stepped back with the same gratitude I felt every time I served a guest. "Sir, it was an honor to have you with us. Safe travels."

He looked at me—still no smile—and said something that froze time itself, "The pleasure is all mine. Should you ever decide to join the Hilton family…" He let the words drift into the air, unfinished but powerful. For a moment, the city noise faded away. It was just the two of us, standing there in a bubble of quiet possibility. He placed a twenty-dollar bill and his business card into my hand. No long speech. No dramatic farewell. Just a brief hand gesture and the soft hum of that black sedan pulling away from the curb. Sometimes God speaks through people who never even learn your name.

A Fish Out of Water

Not long afterward, my coworker, Mike DiNardo, a clerk assigned to the Holiday Inn's front desk, approached me with unexpected news. Mike and I had always clicked—mutual respect, mutual trust—so when he said he'd been offered the General Manager position at another hotel, I was genuinely proud of him. Then he said the words that caught me off guard:

> "I want you to come with me. I need someone strong in operations—someone I can trust—as my Rooms Division Manager."

He gave me the address. 1640 Main Street, near Michigan Avenue. It didn't take long for my memory to connect the dots. The old Mohawk Motor Inn. A place my brother Gerald knew well—he'd worked there at the front desk years before. But the idea of leaving a thriving Holiday Inn for a neglected, nearly forgotten property felt… well, it felt like comparing a top-shelf apple to the seed that never made it into a seedless grape. Something that technically existed—but barely. Still, Mike spoke with conviction. Strong financial backing. A vision for renewal. A place to grow. His confidence became contagious.

A Leap that Didn't Land Where I Hoped

I went to our Innkeeper, Mrs. Strada, and shared my decision. She didn't want to lose me—she said as much—but she never stood in my way. Instead, she gave me something more valuable: "If it doesn't work out, the door is open. Don't forget that." That mattered. My parents taught me never to burn bridges, and she reinforced that truth with grace.

A Restless Spirit and a Closed Chapter

Looking back, part of me knows I was restless. Comfortable, maybe even complacent. The Holiday Inn had been good to me, but I felt that chapter closing. I wanted growth—something new. (And interestingly enough, that old Holiday Inn Midtown is now a 105-room Residence Inn.) I finished my notice and stepped into the new hotel with optimism.

This Wasn't It

But the moment I entered the building… I felt it in my spirit. This wasn't it. The owner expected rooms to fill immediately, but the property wasn't ready—not by a long shot. To put it gently, the environment was more suited for shady dealings than genuine hospitality. No amount of customer service excellence could fix what was broken. After a week—one long, eye-opening week—I pulled Mike aside, thanked him, and resigned. A Door Opens… but not the one I expected "I feel like a fish out of water," I told him. And I meant every word.

A New Chapter Down South

Later that same year, 1977, my brother Larry returned home after serving honorably in the U.S. Navy. He and his wife, Alma, and the kids, Montina and Monte, were living in Mobile, Alabama. When they visited Buffalo, he extended an invitation: "Come back south with us." No hesitation. I packed what I had and went. Over the next few years, I worked at McDonald's and Church's Fried Chicken in Mobile, Alabama, then with my uncle, John, at Wings-N-Things in Decatur, Illinois. Each job strengthened something in me—leadership, teamwork, patience, humility, and the ability to serve people from all walks of life. All of it—the twenty-dollar bill, Mike's offer, the hotel mistake, the move south—was part of a path I didn't fully understand then. But every detour was leading me home. Back to Buffalo. Back to purpose. Back to who I was becoming.

THE BUFFALO HILTON HOTEL

A Business Card, a Phone Call, and a Divine Nudge Changed My Life

In June of 1980, the brand-new Buffalo Hilton Hotel opened its doors, shining like a fresh jewel in the heart of the city. By the fall, I walked through those same doors with hope in my chest and my résumé in hand, ready to apply for any position that matched my growing experience in hospitality. My interview with the Director of Human Resources, Mrs. Wilson, went well, but had an element of uncertainty: "Right now, we're fully staffed. But if something opens up, you might be a prospect. I'd still like to schedule a second interview."

Before I could respond, her phone rang. She apologized and took the call. And as she spoke, I sat there thinking hard, searching for something—anything—that might tip the scales in my favor. Then it hit me. I reached into my back pocket, pulled out my wallet, and removed a business card I'd carried for three years. It had been handed to me by a quiet, dignified Asian gentleman who stayed with us at the Holiday Inn back in 1977.

Until that moment, I had never actually read the fine print on that card. Now I studied it carefully, over and over, while Mrs. Wilson continued her conversation. When she hung up and asked, "Any questions I can answer for you?" I slid the card across her desk and said, "No ma'am… but I believe the gentleman who gave me this expected me to give it to you." She picked it up, read it, slowly removed her glasses, leaned back in her chair, and simply asked:

"Can you start tomorrow?"

"Absolutely," I told her—calm on the outside, shouting hallelujah on the inside. Only then did she inform me: the man whose card I carried was Clement Chen Jr., the owner of the Buffalo Hilton Hotel.

The Man Behind the Card

Clement Chen Jr. (1930–1988) was born in Shanghai and moved to the United States in 1949. Trained as an architect, he became a major force behind hotel construction across the country—San Francisco, Los Angeles, Buffalo, and beyond. His firm, Clement Chen & Associates in Palo Alto, was known for its elegant, modern, and welcoming hotel designs. Ironically, the design inspiration for the Jianguo Hotel in China came from his own Holiday Inn in Palo Alto. And that's where destiny circled back to greet me again.

In late December of 1981, after receiving Employee of the Year, I was flown—expenses paid—to the 1982 Rose Bowl in Pasadena, California. My accommodations? Mr. Chen's Palo Alto Holiday Inn. The hotel was breathtaking.

The service? Impeccable. They treated me like royalty. I watched the staff the way a hungry student watches a masterclass—quiet, alert, absorbing everything. Whatever I saw done well, I added to my own toolbox.

Clement Chen's West Coast Masterpiece

The Palo Alto Holiday Inn, developed by Clement Chen Jr. in the early 1970s, was one of his signature hotel projects—so well-designed and forward-thinking that he later used it as the architectural model for the Jianguo Hotel in Beijing. The property sat just steps from Stanford University, surrounded by landscaped courtyards and a resort-like atmosphere that made it stand out among West Coast hotels of its era.

With roughly 280 rooms and Chen's attention to detail woven into every corner, it quickly became known for its elegance, comfort, and the kind of service that reflected his philosophy: hospitality done with quiet excellence. The Rose Bowl ended with the Washington Huskies defeating the Iowa Hawkeyes, 28–0. But for me, the real victory was the experience.

A Job I Didn't See Coming

When Hilton hired me, I assumed I'd be placed in a role aligned with my skill set—front-of-house, bell staff, guest services. Something familiar. Instead, they hired me… as security. Security? I had no training. No background. No experience. But I was street-smart, observant, and steady under pressure. And perhaps—just perhaps—Mrs. Wilson saw something trustworthy in me, something that mirrored the confidence Mr. Chen had when he handed me his card three years earlier. In customer service, faithfulness is the real currency. Honesty is non-negotiable. People depend on you—sometimes with things more valuable than money.

In fact, I'm reminded of a story about a Costco employee, John Sotelo. He found an envelope with $3,940 inside—money a customer had accidentally left behind. He immediately turned it in. Management reviewed the footage, located the customer, and returned the envelope. Sotelo was honored as Employee of the Month, but truth be told, he deserved Employee of the Year. That's the kind of integrity this work requires.

A Hotel Like Buffalo Had Never Seen

The Buffalo Hilton was unlike anything the city had seen in 50 years. It was a world unto itself—an entire ecosystem of comfort and recreation under one roof. Inside those walls, guests enjoyed:

- A spacious indoor swimming pool
- A full 1.6-mile running track
- Six indoor tennis courts
- Racquetball and squash courts
- Men's and women's saunas
- Three restaurants: *Justine's*, *Charlie's*, and *The Greenery Coffee Shop*
- An elegant Atrium cocktail lounge
- Two executive suites stretching across two levels, connected by a spiral staircase, with saunas and wood-burning fireplaces

In total, 500 rooms—with everything designed to make guests forget the world outside. The Buffalo Hilton wasn't just a hotel. It was an experience—one that elevated my professional life and opened doors I didn't even know to knock on. And it all began with a business card I almost forgot I had.

CHAPTER ELEVEN

YUL BRYNNER

A Night Wrapped in Drama

Some people don't walk into a building — they *arrive*. Yul Brynner was one of those men. By 1981, everyone in the world knew who he was. The King of Siam. The man with the commanding voice, the shaved head, the unforgettable presence. When "The King and I" came to Shea's Performing Arts Center in Buffalo, the city buzzed like it was hosting royalty — because in a way, it was.

I was serving as Chief of Security at the Buffalo Hilton at the time, and when Brynner's car pulled up, fans seemed to come out of thin air. Autograph seekers. Starstruck guests. Curious onlookers. He moved quickly, guarded, and purposeful, and we escorted him straight to his room with as little fuss as possible. What I didn't know then was that the real show wasn't going to be onstage that night.

A Night Wrapped in Drama

Brynner arrived with a young, striking woman — beautiful, elegant, and unmistakably poised. The tension between them was thick enough to feel before a single word was spoken. Whatever disagreement they were carrying with them into the hotel, it hadn't stayed in the car. They tried to keep things quiet in the lobby. They failed. Within minutes, the staff radar was fully activated. You know how hotels are — nothing travels faster than a whisper in a hallway. Once they reached their room, the disagreement escalated. Our acting General Manager, Mr. Daniel Rodriguez, called me and said, "Tommy, stay alert. If this gets out of hand, call the police." I remember thinking, *Lord, I hope I don't end up calling the police on the King of Siam.*

From Conflict… To Passion

Part of my responsibility was to make rounds. And yes — that included passing by their room. At first, the tension was still there. Voices. Emotion. The kind of argument that doesn't need translation. But later that night, on another pass, the tone had shifted dramatically—from sharp conflict to an intense, unmistakable passion. Peace had been negotiated. Enthusiastically.

From that point on, every time I saw Mr. Brynner during his stay, I had to fight the urge — like a curious student approaching his professor — to ask him if he might be willing to share the secret of whatever ancient royal technique he used that first night. But some lessons, I suppose, are meant to remain… royal secrets.

The Woman Behind the Curtain

Later, I learned that the young woman was Kathy Lee, a ballerina from Ipoh, Malaysia, and the woman who would become Yul Brynner's fourth wife. She was a featured dancer in "The King and I" and sometimes performed the role of Eliza in the ballet sequences. They had met during the London Palladium production of the show in 1979–1980. She was 26. He was 62. They were married in 1983. Apparently, what I witnessed that night at the Hilton was just one scene in a much longer love story.

What stood out just as much as her beauty was her kindness. Kathy Lee carried herself with a quiet grace that made everyone around her feel seen. She was warm and respectful to our entire staff at the Hilton—from the front desk and bell staff to housekeeping and food service—and that kind of character never goes unnoticed. When she entered the hotel lobby, there was a calm elegance about her presence, and when she exited, it felt as though she left a little light behind. She had the rare ability to make a room feel brighter without ever demanding attention. Her presence made the lobby glow, not simply because of who she was, but because of how she treated people.

The Report They Couldn't Put Down

As required, I wrote a full incident report. I didn't exaggerate. I didn't embellish. I just wrote what happened. The next morning, when the sales and executive teams arrived, they didn't reach for their schedules. They didn't reach for the newspaper. They reached for my report. That evening, when I came back on duty, Mr. Rodriguez approached me holding the document, grinning like a man who had just read a best-selling novel. He leaned in and said, "Tommy… the sales team is unusually cheerful today. I'm guessing they read your report. Next time, just tell me the highlights and spare the paperwork. They don't need entertainment this good." That was the first time I saw the lighter, mischievous side of him — and I couldn't help but laugh.

A Kingly Impression

Through it all, Yul Brynner and his entourage were nothing but professional and respectful to our staff. He carried himself with class, dignity, and that unmistakable presence that made him who he was. But for me? That night remains one of the funniest, most unbelievable memories of my years at the Buffalo Hilton. Only in hospitality can one evening contain:

- A legend
- A crisis
- A reconciliation
- A written report that becomes required reading

And a story better than the show. Some nights at the Hilton really were better than the performance.

CHAPTER TWELVE

SIR, I'M SECURITY

A Clock, A Purpose, And A Suit That Felt Like Armor

At the Buffalo Hilton, I had many responsibilities, but none more constant than keeping the hotel safe—inside and out. Night after night, I walked those long hallways carrying a Detex Newman Watchman Security Clock. If you saw one, you'd swear it belonged in a museum—nearly seven inches around, three inches thick, and weighing close to five and a half pounds of pure steel. Inside it, a paper disk quietly turned. All around the hotel, management had mounted small metal boxes with keys chained inside. My job was to find each one, insert the key, turn it, and stamp the exact time onto that spinning disk. It was proof that I had been there. Proof that the hotel was safe.

I wasn't licensed to carry a firearm. That clock—heavy enough to swing if things ever went sideways—was the only "weapon" I had. At the end of every shift, I wrote detailed reports about everything I'd seen. Detailed enough, in fact, that the executive staff often preferred reading them to the morning paper. Every so often, Clement Chen III—Mr. Chen's son and future successor—would visit the property. Calm, gracious, and sharp beyond his years, he would occasionally walk part of my rounds with me, cutting precious minutes out of his packed schedule. I admired him then. I still do.

The Men Who Stepped in Until One Could be Found

The Hilton needed stability—and fast. In less than three years, several general managers had cycled through the position. When I joined the staff, Mr. Chen had just terminated Laurent L. Bessou, who had replaced William J. Whittle. With no one left to hand the keys to, Mr. Chen himself stepped in as temporary general manager—the first one I served under. To help steady the ship, he summoned Daniel Rodríguez from Palo Alto. Mr. Rodríguez was the director general of Mr. Chen's California hotel and a man who looked like he lived on the cover of GQ—strong Spanish accent, sharp suits, calm authority. From day one, he treated me with respect, and I looked up to him.

Eventually, Mr. Chen found the Hilton's next general manager. But one strange thing remained true the entire time: I never received a security uniform. No name tag either. No strict dress code beyond "look professional." So, I wore what felt right. And in that era, what felt right was style. I favored clean, classic lines—Dr. King's quiet dignity, my uncles' sharp suits, Johnny Carson's timeless cool, a little Rat Pack confidence. Back then, an M. Wile suit carried more pride than a badge. My pants sat where they were supposed to. My shirt was pressed. My shoes were polished. Looking sharp wasn't vanity. It was respect for the job and for myself.

A Simple Ride that Revealed the Power of Presence

One evening, I stepped into the elevator to make my rounds. Just as the doors started to close, a voice called out:

"Can you hold the elevator?"

"Yes, sir," I said, pressing the button.

A distinguished white gentleman stepped inside, casually but neatly dressed. Something about him felt important, though I couldn't quite place it. As the elevator climbed, my customer-service instincts kicked in. "Sir, are your accommodations to your liking?" "Yes, they are," he replied. "If there's anything we can do to make them more pleasant, please don't hesitate to let us know." He looked me up and down. No uniform. No badge. Just a suit and confidence. "I'll keep that in mind," he said slowly. "But… are you an employee here?" I smiled. "Yes, sir. I'm security." The doors opened. We wished each other good night and walked off in opposite directions. I had no idea that moment would change my life.

I'LL HAVE A TANQUERAY AND TONIC WITH LIME

A Turning Point in the Lobby of Opportunity

The next day, I walked into work like any other shift. Before I could even reach the time clock, James "Jim" Lurek—our Rooms Division Manager—stopped me. "Go see Sandy in the executive office," he said. Then he added something that made my stomach drop: "And don't bother clocking in." That wasn't Jim's style. On duty, he was polished and by-the-book. Off duty? He was the life of the party—loud, hilarious, unpredictable. I admired both versions of him. But that day, his face gave away nothing. And I couldn't help thinking about the last time I'd seen him cut loose.

The Miracle-Working Toupee, Hairy

At a Hilton family bowling night, Jim had bowled gutter ball after gutter ball. Then, in a moment of pure, tipsy inspiration, he walked up to the headpin, removed his toupee, and placed it on top like a crown. He strutted back, rolled the ball… **Strike!** The place erupted. And then the pin-setting machine descended and carried away both the pins and Jim's beloved toupee—forever known as *Hairy*—like some kind of ritual offering. Now that same man had told me not to clock in. Something serious was coming.

An Unexpected Audience

Sandy Gapinski—sharp, elegant, and warm—looked up from her desk. "Come in, Tommy. Someone's eager to meet you." She pointed toward the office reserved for the incoming General Manager. I walked in… And there he was. Navy-blue designer suit. Red pocket square. White shirt. Red tie. The man from the elevator. Dennis Whitney Davis. He didn't look up right away. Just gestured for me to sit. After a few moments, he asked, "Care for something to drink?" I should've said no. But fear loosened my tongue. "Sir… if I'm terminated, I'll have a Tanqueray and tonic with lime. Otherwise, no thank you." He burst out laughing. I did too. The tension evaporated. "You certainly have spirit," he said. "Now let me tell you why you're here."

Repositioned by a Single Moment

Leaning back, he said, "After reviewing your file—and remembering our conversation in the elevator—I'm impressed. You're at the wrong end of this business." My heart pounded. "I'm moving you out of security. You'll be our **first impression**. Our gatekeeper. When transportation is needed, you are the authorized chauffeur for our VIPs.

You'll also be my driver. And Mr. Chen's." I was stunned. "Sir… in any way I can serve, I'm willing." He stood. Shook my hand. "See Mr. Lurek and get fitted for your tux. Congratulations." I walked out floating. This wasn't a promotion. It was a **calling**.

Priority One and the Facilitators

Mr. Davis wasn't just a general manager—he was a turnaround specialist.

And during his short time at the Buffalo Hilton, he transformed the culture of the entire hotel with a program called **Priority One**. On the surface, it was a guest-service training course. But in practice, it was something far deeper. It taught us to anticipate needs instead of waiting for complaints. It taught us consistency—so no matter who a guest encountered, the experience felt seamless. It taught us how to solve problems with grace, how to communicate clearly, and how to serve with purpose instead of routine.

What I didn't realize at the time was that Priority One was also working on *me*. Somewhere along the way, something woke up inside me. My confidence grew. My awareness sharpened. My sense of responsibility expanded beyond my own job description. And before I knew it, I was asked to become a facilitator. I became the **only non-management Priority One instructor in the entire hotel**. That's where my leadership was born. Not with a title. Not with an office. But with responsibility, trust, and the opportunity to help shape others.

Rehearsing for Real Life

What we *didn't* realize at the time was that those role-playing sessions were quietly preparing us for real-life experiences. At first, they felt a little awkward. You pretend to be the upset guest. Someone else plays the employee. You stumble. You say the wrong thing. You laugh. You try again. You adjust. You learn.

But something powerful was happening beneath the surface. By the time a **real guest** stood in front of us with a **real problem**, we had already been there—just not in real time yet. We had already walked through that moment in a classroom. We had already made the mistakes. Already corrected ourselves. Already found our footing. So instead of reacting with panic, we responded with confidence. Instead of freezing, we moved with purpose. Instead of guessing, we *knew what to do.*

Priority One didn't just train us, **it rehearsed us for the real world.** And looking back now, I can see it clearly: those classrooms, those scenarios, those practice moments were shaping me for everything that came next—leadership, crisis moments, VIP responsibility, and eventually an entire career built on calm under pressure and service with intention.

Make a Decision

. Mr. Davis gave me a nickname that no one else ever used. He called me **"Big T."** Before leaving on a trip with Mrs. Davis that would keep them away from the hotel for several days, he stopped at the front entrance where I was stationed. Looking me directly in the eye, he said:

"Big T., this hotel is your responsibility. Whatever you encounter, make a decision. If the decision is the correct one, celebrate it. If it's the wrong one, learn from it. Just make a decision."

He wasn't telling me to be reckless. *He was molding a leader.*

There were department heads on duty throughout the hotel, yet he chose to place that responsibility on my shoulders. For the next several days, the weight of that trust stayed with me. I was determined not to disappoint him.

THE PURGE

When Trust Was Put on Trial

One afternoon in 1982, I walked into the Buffalo Hilton and immediately felt it. Something was wrong. The building was too quiet. Not the peaceful kind of quiet—the staged kind. The kind that tells you something already happened… or something big is about to. Almost all of the management was gone. Offices that were normally alive with phones ringing and voices bouncing off the walls sat empty. No familiar footsteps. No small talk. No background noise. Only Mr. Lurek was there, and even he seemed… careful. Measured. I was given simple instructions. "Report to guest room 208 on the second floor." No explanation. No context. Just a room number.

The Room: An Unexpected Test

Inside the room sat a man I'd never seen before, surrounded by electronic equipment that looked like it belonged in a crime show. That's when it hit me. A polygraph. For a brief moment, my heart beat a little harder—not because I was guilty, but because **anyone** would feel the weight of that moment. Still, I knew exactly where I stood. I had nothing to hide. So, I sat down. Answered the questions. Let the machine do its work. When it was over, I walked back downstairs and returned to my post at the front entrance like nothing had happened—except everything had.

The Cadillac Seville: A Different Kind of Drive

Not long after, Mr. Davis pulled up to the front entrance in his two-seater Seville. I stepped forward and opened the door, expecting the usual routine: he would head inside, and I would take the car to park it. Instead, he looked at me with a faint smile and said, "Big T., we're going to 930 Maple Road." Daffodils. One of the most elegant restaurants in Amherst, New York. Mr. Davis dined there often and was well known—and well respected—by the staff. I had never been there before, and I'll admit it: I needed his help to find it. It was also the first time I had ever driven his car off property.

We made some small talk on the way, but beneath the conversation, I could feel something else in the air. His mood carried a complicated blend of emotions—**relief, satisfaction, and a quiet sadness**—as if something heavy had just ended, and something new, not yet fully named, was about to begin.

Daffodils: The Truth, and an Invitation

Over lunch, Mr. Davis finally explained. Hotel merchandise had been disappearing. Enough of it to raise alarms. Enough of it to demand action. The polygraph tests were part of a full internal investigation. Then he said something that stopped me cold. He thanked me for my loyalty. And then—without ceremony—he pulled out a list. Names. One by one, he read them. Employees who had failed the polygraph. Employees who had been terminated. Some of them weren't just staff. **Some of them were management.**

I sat there in silence, absorbing the weight of it. This wasn't theater. This wasn't politics. This was a man **cleaning house**. Then he said something I never forgot. "Tommy," he said, looking me straight in the eye, "if I ever move on to other hotel ventures, consider this lunch an invitation." I didn't fully understand what that meant at the time. But life did.

Where I Stood: No Divided Loyalties

I told him the truth—plain and simple. "Sir, I have nothing but your best interests at heart, and that includes the hotel." And I meant it. Not because I had passed a test. But because that's who I was.

Aftermath: The Cost of Integrity, The Shape of the Future

The Purge changed the feel of the Hilton. The building didn't look different, but it felt lighter in some ways, heavier in others, and everyone sensed it. It deepened my understanding of Dennis Davis. He wasn't just rebuilding a hotel; he was protecting an institution—even if it meant burning bridges and removing people who never imagined they'd be touched. Then I realized something else: trust isn't something you talk about. It's something you're willing to test. And that day, the hotel did. Years later, the Coconut Grove Hotel revealed what that lunch at Daffodils really was. It wasn't just a conversation. It was the beginning of a road I didn't yet know I would walk.

CHAPTER THIRTEEN

A NEW ROLE WITH A NEW LOOK

The First Impression of the Buffalo Hilton

Mr. Davis brought in off-duty sheriffs and Buffalo police officers to handle hotel security. Erie County Sheriff Deputy Mike Hiliker served as Chief of Security, anchoring a well-balanced team of professionals who quickly became friends of mine. Like me, they wore suits and carried themselves with that unmistakable "Hilton polish." Unlike me, they carried guns. I carried a damn clock. That didn't bother me much—not after I stepped into my new uniform.

I was dressed head-to-toe in a beige penguin-style tuxedo trimmed in chocolate brown. A matching brown top hat sat just right, and crisp white cotton gloves finished the look. Stationed at the main entrance, I wasn't just a doorman anymore. I was the **first impression** of the Buffalo Hilton. In the summer of 1982, Buffalo News reporter Karen Brady turned my daily routine into a front-page human-interest story. The headline read:

"Million Dollar Smile Puts Him Out Front at the Hilton."

The photograph—now the front cover of this book—captured that moment in time: the tuxedo, the gloves, the posture, and the pride.

The Man they Called "Mr. Charlie"

When I first arrived at the Hilton, the front entrance already belonged to a man everyone called **Mr. Charlie**. Not Charlie. Not sir. Always **Mr. Charlie**. At 6'8" and close to 350 pounds, he had the kind of presence that could quiet a room just by standing in it. He wore a black three-piece suit every day, paired with a crisp white shirt and black tie, looking like he'd stepped out of a high-end funeral parlor.

His deep, booming voice reminded everyone of Lurch from *The Addams Family*. If he asked you to stop, you stopped. But if you stayed long enough, you discovered the truth: beneath that intimidating frame was a gentle, soft-spoken man with a surprisingly tender heart. He also carried an umbrella everywhere. Rain. Snow. Sunshine. Nobody knew why. Nobody asked. That was just Mr. Charlie.

The Shift Inside Le Club

Mr. Davis had a vision not only for the front door, but for the entire personality of the hotel. After my doorman duties, he assigned me inside **Le Club**, the Hilton's elegant, high-energy nightclub. It wasn't just a bar. It was a destination—locals, travelers, entertainers, and curious visitors all mixing under one roof while more than 500 light patterns danced across the ceiling.

It was alive. But underneath the glamour, something wasn't right. There were quiet rumors that not everyone was being treated fairly at the door. Discrimination, some said. And Mr. Davis wasn't about to let that reputation live for a single second longer. At the time, Le Club was managed by Thomas Haidon—a sharp, disciplined man who ran the place like a machine. Efficient, organized… but not always warm.

Mingling with the Guests

To rebalance the atmosphere, Mr. Davis made me a floor host. My assignment was simple: Move through the room. Talk to people. Read the energy. Fix what needs fixing. Make sure **everyone** feels welcome. I became the bridge between management and the guests—the guy who floated from table to table like the owner of a neighborhood restaurant checking on friends. Eventually, Mr. Davis replaced Tom with Steven Munn, a man with softer edges and natural warmth. Where Tom leaned on control, Steven leaned on connection. And slowly, Le Club became what it was supposed to be. But storm clouds were gathering over the hotel.

The Union Storm

The Buffalo Hilton became the center of a serious labor dispute when Local Union 66 attempted to unionize the property. For privately operated hotels, unionization can bring enormous financial strain. Buffalo had already watched several properties collapse under similar pressure. Even today, the downtown Hyatt Regency continues to wrestle with it. I'll return to this issue later in the book, when I discuss the November 2, 2025, Kansas City Chiefs' visit and show how these disputes can ripple far beyond a single hotel.

MAYOR JAMES D. GRIFFIN

The Mayor Who Walked Through My Doorway

Being a doorman put me at the crossroads of Buffalo's daily heartbeat. Judges. Executives. City officials. Regular folks. Many used our parking ramp not because it was closest, but because it was free. Their daily walk through the Hilton became part of my rhythm. One of those regulars was **Mayor James D. "Jimmy" Griffin**. Every morning, newspaper tucked under his arm, moving with the purpose of a man who knew every crack in the city's sidewalks. To most, he was a headline. To me, he became something else: A familiar face who never walked past without acknowledging the man holding the door.

Where a Doorman and a Mayor met in the Middle

Our exchanges were meaningful. Never political. Never rushed. One morning, he stopped, looked me over, and reached out to straighten my tie. A small gesture. A big meaning. Weeks later, I returned the favor—pretending his tie was crooked when it wasn't. He laughed and said, "Iron sharpens iron." Those few minutes each day turned the concrete stretch between City Hall and the Hilton into something human.

The Day the Mayor Handed me my Future

During one of our special interactions, he handed me an envelope with the city seal and my name on it. "Someday, you might find a use for this." Inside was a beautifully written letter of recommendation—signed by the Mayor of Buffalo. That letter opened the door to the Niagara Frontier Transportation Authority in 1985. And it changed my life. Jimmy Griffin may have been a towering political figure. But to me, he will always be remembered as: The man who straightened a young doorman's tie… And quietly handed him his future.

CHAPTER FOURTEEN

THREE POWERFUL PILLARS

A Season When History Kept Knocking

Some seasons of life pass quietly. Others arrive like a procession—one remarkable moment after another—until you realize you're standing in the middle of something far bigger than yourself. The early 1980s at the Buffalo Hilton was like that for me. History, fame, and unforgettable human moments kept rolling through the front doors—and somehow, I kept finding myself right there in the middle of them.

THE CHINESE AMBASSADOR TO AMERICA

A Rare Moment in Buffalo's Story

In 1981, the Buffalo Hilton hosted a guest unlike any other: His Excellency **Chai Zemin**, the Chinese Ambassador to the United States. At the time, he was helping shape the early years of renewed relations between the U.S. and the People's Republic of China—a delicate, historic chapter in global diplomacy. Because **Clement Chen Jr.**, a proud son of China and owner of the Hilton, stood at the helm of the hotel, it made sense that the Ambassador chose our property. Still, none of us could have imagined how close I would come to that moment in history.

A Doorman's Once-In-A-Lifetime Assignment

Out of everyone in the building, **I was chosen to drive him**. Even now, that feels surreal. A kid from Buffalo. A former security officer turned doorman-chauffeur. Entrusted with transporting one of the world's most important diplomats. That's not luck. That's Providence.

The Limousine Fit for Diplomacy

When the Hilton opened, Mr. Chen selected a **1979 gray Cadillac limousine**—elegant, smooth, dignified. He bought it pre-owned from **Fred Silverman**, former president of NBC. On its front fenders, two magnetic flags were mounted: one American, one Chinese. They fluttered in the wind like a quiet announcement that something bigger than Buffalo business was happening.

A Ride I'll Never Forget

I stood by the rear passenger door when the Ambassador emerged from the hotel—composed, dignified, calm. He nodded politely and greeted me. Moments later, **four motorcycle police escorts** snapped into formation. Engines hummed. And suddenly, we were gliding through Buffalo like a moving piece of history. For those few miles, I wasn't just driving. I was **witnessing**. At one stoplight, he turned to me and said, in accented but clear English:

"You have a beautiful city."

I answered with the pride of a man who loves his hometown: "Thank you, sir. I'm honored you're here." He smiled. That was it. Simple. Human. Unforgettable. When we returned to the Hilton, I opened his door. He looked at me and said:

"Thank you. You did well."

Those words stayed with me. Not because of who he was—but because of what they meant: **trust, dignity, recognition**. That day taught me something I never forgot: You never know when history is riding in the back seat, watching how you drive.

MICHAEL JACKSON'S TRIUMPH TOUR

When Legends Move Through Your Lobby

By 1981, **Michael Jackson** wasn't just famous—he was mythic. That summer, the Jacksons launched the **Triumph Tour**, one of the biggest tours in the country. And on **August 23, 1981**, that whirlwind arrived in Buffalo. Their home base? Our hotel.

A Flash of Greatness

Working crowd control that night put me right at the front line. The Jacksons arrived like lightning—doors open, movement, elevators, gone. I never exchanged a word with Michael or his brothers. But I did meet their **band and crew**—warm, lively, genuinely kind people. And then something unexpected happened. They handed me a **tour jacket** and a **pass to the show**. To me, that wasn't just a gift. That was an invitation into a moment I would never forget.

The Show of a Lifetime

That night, inside Buffalo Memorial Auditorium, the building shook. Michael didn't just perform—he **commanded**. The movement. The voice. The electricity. You could feel history being made in real time. Years later, a fire destroyed the house next door and spread into ours. In the flames, I lost that tour jacket. But here's the truth: Fire can take fabric. It cannot take memory. That night is still as vivid as ever.

KRIS KRISTOFFERSON

Another Legend, Another Lesson

Not long after, **Kris Kristofferson** arrived. Songwriter. Actor. Poet. Rhodes Scholar. A man who carried wisdom in his silence. He performed at **Melody Fair in Tonawanda** on August 10, 1981, and stayed at our Hilton. He and a companion requested transportation for a quick errand. Instead of the limo, I took the hotel van. I don't remember where we went. But I'll never forget the ride back.

The Light that Changed too Fast

Returning to the hotel, traveling south on Delaware Avenue, we approached a busy intersection. Green. Yellow. Red. Warp speed. Do I slam on the brakes and put Kristofferson and his associate on the glass, or take the light? Both were unsafe. I made a split-second decision and went through the red light. My heart started racing the moment we cleared it.

Now, looking like cockeyed Jr., my right eye stayed on the road, but my left eye glanced across at Mr. Kristofferson in the rearview mirror. I expected anger. Instead, Kris leaned forward, rested a hand gently on my shoulder, and said: "Tommy, it was a rough take, but we're all okay." No judgment. No tension. Just grace.

A Lesson I've Carried Ever Since

That moment taught me something I never forgot: Never trust a stale green light. Some lessons come from classrooms. Some come from life. Some come from the back seat of a van, spoken quietly by a man who understands fear and mercy. Kris Kristofferson passed away in 2024. But that moment—and that kindness—stayed with me.

Looking Back

When I think about that season of my life—the Ambassador, Michael Jackson, Kris Kristofferson—I don't think about fame. I think about **trust**. I think about **service**. And I think about how a kid from Buffalo kept finding himself in places he never imagined—simply by doing his job with dignity. Sometimes, history doesn't announce itself. Sometimes… it just walks through the front door.

A Different Kind of Ride

I remember picking up a Hollywood mega star at **Buffalo Niagara International Airport** in the hotel limousine for the Hilton sometime in the early eighties. She was the darling of America. After dinner, entire families gathered in front of the television to watch her show—and they were never disappointed. On screen, she carried grace, beauty, and a calm confidence that made living rooms across the country feel a little more elegant for an hour. The assignment itself was routine—arrival, luggage, and a quiet ride back to the hotel.

Not long after we pulled away from the curb, she commanded me to flip the mirror above the dashboard up so I couldn't see her. I'll be honest—my first reaction stayed in my head. The thought of asking her to get out of the car and catch the bus in the rain crossed my mind, but professionalism prevailed. I didn't argue. I didn't respond. I flipped the mirror, kept my eyes on the road, and finished the ride the same way I always did—calm, professional, and on time. Over the years, I learned that professionalism meant adapting not just to schedules and luggage, but to personalities—some gracious, some guarded—and doing the job the same way every time.

CHAPTER FIFTEEN

THE HILTON IS HAVING A FEAST!

A New Kind of Midnight Rider

History remembers Paul Revere as the midnight rider. But in 1981, Buffalo met a very different figure marching down Main Street—no horse, no lantern—just a young Hilton employee dressed like he'd stepped out of a colonial painting and straight into public humiliation. And that figure… was me.

A tricorn hat wobbling on my head. A long colonial coat brushing against my legs. Boots clacking louder than my heartbeat. And slung over my shoulder, a giant blue bag stuffed with five thousand flyers tied with red ribbons. I looked like a confused extra from a school play who had wandered offstage and gotten lost in downtown Buffalo. But the Hilton needed a hero. And apparently, I was the only one willing to wear the costume.

The Embarrassing First Steps

Walking out those hotel doors felt like stepping onto a stage I never auditioned for. Cars slowed as I made my way from the hotel toward Main Street, three long blocks that felt more like three miles. People stared. A few laughed under their breath. I prayed—begged—that nobody from my neighborhood would see me, especially my ex-girlfriend who dumped me. I felt foolish. Exposed. Like a grown man playing dress-up in front of the world. I held up the first flyer with all the enthusiasm of a man holding a subpoena. Then… something happened. A woman walked over. Then a couple more. Then a small line formed on the sidewalk—hands reaching out, smiles forming, curiosity sparking. And just like that, their energy started to change mine.

Hear Ye, Hear Ye — Finding the Groove

With each flyer I handed out, my confidence grew. My shoulders straightened. My voice found its strength. And before long, I felt the transformation take hold. I stopped worrying about who was watching. I stopped worrying about how ridiculous I looked. And suddenly… I was in it. I raised my voice. I raised my arms. I raised the temperature on Main Street. "Hear ye, hear ye! The Hilton is having a feast—everyone's invited!" Now people weren't just taking flyers—they were cheering, laughing, even jogging toward me like I was announcing a parade. The pigeons scattered. Children pointed. And somewhere along the way, I crossed an invisible line—from embarrassed employee to full-fledged showman. Man… I was having fun.

Main Street to Valhalla

By the time the last flyer left my fingers, I was no longer the nervous guy hoping not to be recognized. I had become the town crier of Buffalo. And inside the Hilton, Valhalla awaited. The atrium and ballroom were ready—tables heavy with golden turkey, mountains of mashed potatoes, rivers of gravy, and pumpkin pies glowing under the lights like trophies. And the people came. Oh, did they come. Laughter filled the rooms. Plates piled high. The feast became a celebration—not just of Thanksgiving, but of community, of boldness, and of a young man who dared to look foolish and ended up feeling free.

Employee of the Year

By year's end, the story had traveled through every hallway, breakroom, and executive office. My colonial march down Main Street had become Hilton folklore. I was named Employee of the Year—not because of the costume, but because I learned something that day I never forgot: Sometimes you have to walk through embarrassment to find your voice. And once I found mine, Buffalo heard it loud and clear. "Hear ye, hear ye—the Hilton is having a feast!" And the whole city came running.

CHAPTER SIXTEEN

RICHARD HARRIS

A New Year, A New Legend at the Hilton

As 1981 slipped quietly into memory and 1982 stepped onto the stage, the Buffalo Hilton felt charged with possibility—like the curtain rising on a brand-new act. And leading that act was a man who needed no introduction, yet commanded the room the instant he entered it: **Richard Harris**. To the world, Harris was a force—an Irish titan of film, theater, and song. Born in Limerick in 1930, his voice alone could fill a hall, and his presence could still the air.

Two Academy Award nominations, a towering stage career, and a hit record with *'MacArthur Park'*—he was the kind of artist who lived boldly on every platform he touched. He had been King Arthur in *Camelot*, the rugged Captain Nolan in *The Charge of the Light Brigade*, Paddy O'Neil in *Patriot Games*, and later, the gentle, wise face of Albus Dumbledore. And just months before his passing, he delivered a powerful performance as the Apostle John in *The Apocalypse*. Richard Harris was not simply an actor. He was an experience.

Camelot Comes to Buffalo

From February 11th through February 28th, 1982, Richard Harris brought King Arthur to Shea's Performing Arts Center. And during those weeks, the Buffalo Hilton became his castle. His arrival felt cinematic. The car door opened, and out he stepped—tall, unmistakable, effortlessly commanding. His eyes carried the weight of a thousand characters, yet there was nothing pretentious about him. He was warm. Genuine. Present.

A Personal Welcome

I greeted him the moment he stepped from the vehicle, assuring him that we were fully at his service throughout his stay. He handed off his luggage without a fuss, trusting me with the quiet confidence of a seasoned traveler. After escorting him to the front desk, I passed his belongings to one of our bellmen. Before heading upstairs, he turned, smiled, and pressed a generous gratuity into my hand. A small gesture—but one that said everything. Not the movie star. Not the legend. The man.

The Star who Preferred the Sidewalk

Despite his fame, Richard Harris never hid behind doors or an entourage. He moved through the Hilton like a familiar presence—calm, elegant, approachable. And when he stepped outside, it was always with a kind of casual nobility, as if the city itself were part of his stage. I can still see him now—wearing a navy-blue cashmere coat draped loosely over his shoulders, strolling just beyond the hotel's glow, letting the February air nip at him without complaint. He never wandered far. Just enough to breathe. Just enough to feel Buffalo for himself. There was something almost poetic about it—King Arthur himself, wrapped in winter blue, walking the cold streets of our city with quiet dignity.

A Memory that Stayed

Some celebrities come and go, barely leaving a trace. But Richard Harris left an imprint—on the Hilton, on the staff, and on me. He was larger than life, yet carried that life with grace. He was a star, yes. But he was also a gentleman. And for those few winter weeks in early 1982, we had the privilege of hosting a man whose presence could warm even the coldest day in Buffalo.

CHAPTER SEVENTEEN

SUGAR RAY LEONARD

The Champ Who Brought the Spotlight to Buffalo

Ray Charles "Sugar Ray" Leonard wasn't just a boxer—he was a phenomenon. Born May 17, 1956, in Rocky Mount, North Carolina, he exploded onto the world stage like a thunderclap. Between 1977 and 1997, he reigned across multiple weight classes, collecting WBC and WBA titles with a grace and ferocity that redefined the sport. By the spring of 1982, the world was watching Buffalo, New York. The WBC welterweight championship fight—Sugar Ray Leonard vs. Roger Stafford—was coming to town.

The last time Buffalo had hosted a championship bout of that magnitude was in 1950, when Ezzard Charles knocked out Freddie Beshore in the fourteenth round. This was history swinging back around. Roger Stafford had earned his place the hard way: Marine Corps Lightweight Champion, All-Military Champion, and a disciplined warrior with 26 professional wins. Cities like Dallas, St. Louis, and Baton Rouge all wanted the fight. Buffalo won the bid. And when Sugar Ray Leonard's camp chose the Hilton as their headquarters, the excitement in the city became electric.

A Moment that felt like Home

April 19, 1982. At 10:19 a.m., USAir Flight 299 touched down. Sugar Ray Leonard, his team, and his quiet aura of greatness stepped onto Buffalo soil. When their vehicles pulled up to the Hilton's front entrance, something instantly felt familiar—almost like family. They looked like the fellas from back home: jeans, sweats, hoodies, polos, and that unspoken Black cultural signature we all recognize. The only difference was this: They were world-famous. We were famous only on our own blocks.

As Ray stepped out, he caught my eye. Without thinking, I threw a playful sparring motion his way. He grinned, snapped a single mock punch in return, and nodded—as if crowning me with that moment. "Champ, welcome to Buffalo and the Hilton," I said. "Thank you. Feels good to be here," he replied. Within two hours, the welterweight champion of the world was in a makeshift sparring ring we created by converting the hotel's indoor tennis courts into a full training arena—ropes, bleachers, and more than 300 seats filled with fans.

The Matrix Moment — Fifty Punches, Zero Touches

I watched as many sparring sessions as my shifts allowed. But there was one moment—one impossible moment—I will never forget. Victor Abraham had Ray backed into the corner. Or maybe Ray had placed himself there. Either way, Victor unleashed a storm—maybe fifty punches in a blur of fury. Not one landed. Not one touched Leonard. Not even close. It was as if the air itself moved around Sugar Ray. Years later, it reminded me of *The Matrix*—Keanu Reeves dodging bullets in slow motion. To this day, I have never seen a human being move like that. Ray slipped, pivoted, glided, then ghosted out of the corner as the crowd erupted.

Soul Food, Family Ties, and Janks Morton

During their stay, I grew closer to them all, and especially to Ray's trainer and friend, Janks Morton. One day, Janks asked me, "Where can we get something good to eat?" I ran through the usual categories—steak, Mexican, seafood—then said the magic words: "Soul food." His face lit up. I took them straight to my Uncle Paul's restaurant—Soul Bird on Delavan Avenue, across from the Chevrolet plant. The kind of place where the aroma alone could raise both your blood pressure and your spirit. Greens. Yams. Mac and cheese. Catfish. Haddock. Ribs. Oxtails. Apple pie. Sweet potato pie. Food that hugged you.

They loved it so much that even though I only drove them there once, I'm convinced they went back on their own. The "Soul Bird" takeout bags I kept seeing around the hotel were all the proof I needed. Janks himself had a story: former fullback, kick returner, sparring partner to Ken Norton, brief stint with the Cleveland Browns, and eventually a wildly successful insurance entrepreneur. But with Ray, he found his true calling. He trained champions—and remained one of the kindest, most grounded men I ever met.

A Secret Basketball Game at Canisius

One day, the team wanted to play basketball. When a guest wants something, my job is simple: make it happen. So, I called the athletic director at

Canisius College. At first, he thought I was joking. "This is not a hoax," I told him. "But if you can't accommodate us, we'll go to Alumni Arena at the University at Buffalo. Just know… you might see your name in the news tonight." The tone changed immediately. He cleared the gym. We entered through the discreet lower entrance on Main Street. The court was empty except for a few quiet spectators tucked into the bleachers. Then Sugar Ray Leonard picked up a basketball.

Swish.
Swish.
Swish.

Three-pointers all day. His movements were so smooth they almost made you dizzy. The athletic director just shook his head. "This man is great at everything." Honestly, if boxing hadn't claimed him, Ray might have made the NBA—and the Hall of Fame after that. Word spread. Students and staff trickled in. Ray signed autographs, talked with people, and carried himself like a true gentleman the entire time.

The Cloister — A Night I will never Forget

The only other restaurant I recommended was The Cloister—a Buffalo landmark built on the former site of Mark Twain's residence. When the team wanted a fine dinner, I drove them there in the limousine. Chauffeur duty. I stayed with the car. Then the door opened. "Tommy, come on in and join us." I hesitated. They insisted. Surf and turf arrived—steak and lobster dressed in elegance. I tried to order the cheapest thing on the menu. Janks stopped me. "Order what you want." So, I did. And I ate with champions. When I finished, I excused myself and let them enjoy their evening. But that night lives in me forever. They treated me like family. And truth be told… we were family—culturally and spiritually—long before we ever met.

The Blow He Never Saw Coming

Then came the twist no one expected. A detached retina during training. The fight was canceled. Leonard retired. Buffalo's dream night vanished. It wasn't just a sporting loss—it was an economic gut punch. Muhammad Ali had booked the presidential suite and a block of rooms. ABC personnel—including Howard Cosell—had reservations. Limousine companies had cleared entire fleets. The Chamber of Commerce had invested thousands. All gone with one announcement. But none of that mattered compared to a man's eyesight. A man's future. Sugar Ray eventually returned in 1984 to fight Kevin Howard and later faced legends—Hearns, Duran, Hagler. But Buffalo would always remember the fight that never happened.

A Final Word to the Champ

Buffalo may have lost two million dollars. But what I gained was priceless. I met Sugar Ray Leonard. I met Janks Morton. I served them. I broke bread with them. I laughed with them. I shared moments that stitched our lives together. Ray and Janks, it was an honor. You gave this city memories it will never forget. And you gave me memories that still shape who I am today. Thank you, Champs. I send you my very best. **Respect. Gratitude. Brotherhood**.

CHAPTER EIGHTEEN

A LITTLE GLORY ON THIS SIDE OF HEAVEN

Favor Ain't Fair

It's often been said, *"Favor ain't fair."* Well, I am living proof of that. If God had lined up the great biblical couples—Abraham and Sarah, Isaac and Rebekah, Jacob and Rachel, Joseph and Mary—and asked me to choose my parents before birth, I still would have walked right past every one of them. My heart would have led me straight to **Ezelle and Claudia Seay**.

Those other couples were extraordinary in their own right. But the simple, humble, God-fearing life my parents lived made them even more remarkable to me. They were my first celebrities. My first heroes. My first examples of dignity wrapped in simplicity. On June 10, 1950, they said "I do," beginning a journey that would shape my entire world.

A Son's Gift for their 32nd Anniversary

Fast-forward to Thursday, June 10, 1982—their thirty-second anniversary. I wanted to give them something unforgettable. A quiet dinner at **Justine's**, the Hilton's elegant in-house restaurant, felt like the perfect celebration. There was just one hurdle: as a Hilton employee—and the general manager's personal driver—I couldn't simply walk into the restaurant on personal business. Every employee needed permission from management. So, I skipped the chain of command and went straight to the top, Mr. Dennis Davis, our general manager. His response hit me like a tidal wave of kindness. Not only did he approve the dinner, but he also told me to pick up my parents in the Hilton's limousine. Then he added the part that almost took my breath away:

"Tell them to pack a bag for the weekend. Everything is on the Buffalo Hilton."

This wasn't just generosity. This was leadership with a heart. And Dennis Davis was, without question, the most compassionate supervisor I ever served under.

The Limousine Arrival

When I called my parents, they didn't believe a word of it. Not until I rolled up to their house in the Hilton's gleaming limousine. I laid on the horn—not once, but several times—just to summon the neighbors to their doors and windows. As expected, curtains moved, eyeglasses were adjusted, and heads craned like royalty had arrived. And honestly… they had. Even though I was off duty, I wore my full uniform.

I stepped out, placed my top hat firmly on my head, opened the rear door, and waited for my royal passengers. My brothers loaded the suitcases—along with a garment bag holding two outfits: one for dinner, one for church. As we drove away, I watched their reflections in the rearview mirror—those wide-eyed, childlike looks of wonder you never forget. Their heads turned back and forth like spectators at Wimbledon.

A Royal Welcome at the Hilton

When we arrived, my colleague Joe Shaw met the limousine. He opened the door for my father while I assisted my mother. The joy in her eyes alone was worth the entire moment. I handed Joe their bags, slipped him a ten-dollar tip, gave him the key to their suite, and introduced him properly: "Mom, Dad—this is Joe. He'll escort you to your room. Explore the hotel all you want. Meet me at the front entrance at six." And just like that, they stepped into the Hilton—not as my parents, but as **honored guests of the hotel**.

Dinner at Justine's

After changing out of my uniform, I met them and escorted them into Justine's. Our server was my colleague, Kenny Kessler—professionalism carved into human form. Before the entrées arrived, the Food & Beverage Director, Mr. Jim Mitchell, came over. I stood up to greet him, but he gently placed a hand on my shoulder and signaled me to sit. He introduced himself to my parents, spoke kindly about the value I brought to the Hilton, and then told me to sign the check. "Justine's will take care of the rest," he said with a smile. To me, Mr. and Mrs. Mitchell and their son Jamie were celebrities in their own right.

The General Manager Joins Us

Mom enjoyed the six-ounce filet mignon. Dad savored the glazed salmon. Then came the moment that turned a beautiful evening into an unforgettable one. Out of the corner of my eye, I saw Dennis Davis walk into Justine's. I stood immediately. He shook my hand, greeted my parents—and then, instead of leaving, he pulled out the fourth chair at our table. And sat down. That simply didn't happen. "Happy Anniversary," he said. What followed was a conversation filled with warmth, humor, sincerity, and quiet admiration. When it was time for him to go, he placed a hand on my shoulder, looked my parents in the eyes, and said:

> "I know you want to keep this one. But if you ever have
> another just like him, I'll gladly take him off your hands."

That sentence lived in my parents' hearts forever. My father replied, "Sir, we are deeply thankful that you've taken our son under your wing. Our family is forever indebted to you." Mr. Davis stood, shook their hands, and said: "Anything you need—charge it to the room." And then he walked away like a man who understood the power of kindness.

The Weekend, The Church, And The Celebration

My parents loved every moment of their stay at the Buffalo Hilton. On Sunday morning, after breakfast at the coffee shop, they checked out. I put my uniform back on and chauffeured them one last time—this time to **St. Mark Church of God in Christ**, the church they had helped found decades earlier. When we arrived, the congregation was already deep in praise and worship. But when I escorted my parents inside… It was like the Holy Spirit hit the sanctuary with a second wind.

Hands went up. Voices rose. Feet stomped. Shouts filled the air: "Glory to God!" "Praise the Lord!" If the church had chandeliers, somebody would've tried to swing from one. The congregation knew what God—and the Hilton—had poured into Ezelle and Claudia. And that Sunday, the celebration wasn't just for them. It was for what God had done **through them, for them, and because of them**.

CHAPTER NINETEEN

DIANA ROSS

The Queen of Motown Arrives in Buffalo

Diana Ross wasn't just a superstar—she was a cultural force. By the time she arrived at the Buffalo Hilton in October of 1982, her name carried a kind of shine that turned ordinary people into wide-eyed admirers. Born March 26, 1944, in Detroit, Michigan, she rose from humble beginnings to become the unmistakable voice of The Supremes—the group that defined Motown's magic in the 1960s. Her voice didn't just lead the group—it lifted them. Classics like *"Baby Love," "Stop! In the Name of Love,"* and *"You Can't Hurry Love"* didn't merely top the charts; they became chapters in America's soundtrack.

By 1970, Diana left The Supremes and launched a solo career that only deepened her legend. *"Ain't No Mountain High Enough," "Touch Me in the Morning," "Upside Down," "Endless Love"*—her catalog felt endless, her influence undeniable. And as if conquering music wasn't enough, she graced the silver screen with the same elegance, portraying Billie Holiday in *Lady Sings the Blues*—a performance that earned her an Academy Award nomination. She was an artist who excelled everywhere she stood—on stage, in the studio, and on film.

A Superstar in our Lobby

On October 23, 1982, the Buffalo Memorial Auditorium pulsed with anticipation—Diana Ross was in town. And while the city buzzed with excitement, I had the rare honor of seeing her in one of her quietest moments: stepping into our hotel lobby. Even from a distance, she radiated like royalty. Grace. Calm. A beauty that didn't demand attention—it simply commanded it. She wasn't accessible to the public, not this time.

But as we handled her luggage, I caught a glimpse of the woman behind the legend. No entourage could overshadow her presence. She was elegance, personified. While Diana herself remained mostly behind the velvet rope of stardom, her band and road crew were warm, approachable, and genuinely good people. They blessed me with concert tickets—close enough to the stage that when the lights came up, it felt like I had stepped *inside* the music.

The Concert: A Curtain, A Breath, A Revelation

That night's performance was a master class in artistry. Diana Ross delivered every lyric with the kind of confidence that only comes from a lifetime of mastery. Her small band played so tight and so full that you'd swear you were hearing a full orchestra. And then came *the moment*—the one none of us would ever forget. Midway through the show, she paused, addressed the crowd with a few heartfelt words, then playfully fanned her face and said:

"My, it's stuffy in here. Can someone please open a window?"

Instantly, the massive stage curtains rolled back. What we thought was a modest group of musicians suddenly exploded into a full orchestra—more than a hundred strong. A collective gasp rippled through the auditorium. It felt like we had been transported into another world—one that Diana Ross commanded with a flick of her hand. She closed with her 1970 anthem, *"Reach Out and Touch (Somebody's Hand),"* and we did. In that moment, strangers became a choir. It was a night Buffalo would never forget.

When Friendship Becomes Family

Diana's story touched my life in a more personal way than most people know. To this day, I remain close friends with her cousins, Reginald and Joyce Ross. Joyce, the sister of my friend and former NFTA-Metro coworker Raymond Powell, became part of our extended family in a deeply meaningful way. When our son, Tommy Jr., earned a full scholarship to The Ohio State University—for swimming and academics—Reggie and Joyce were living in Columbus. With no family nearby, they became our safety net. Our *"in case of emergency"* people. The ones we trusted with our child. Their kindness wasn't just appreciated—it was treasured.

From ACT 1 To Special Delivery

Reginald Ross isn't just Diana's cousin—he's a gifted musician in his own right. In 1972, he joined George Parker and Roger Terry to form the group **ACT 1**. By 1974, Terry Huff had come aboard, collaborating with producer Rafael Gerald, and the group recorded its debut under Spring Records. Later rebranded as **Special Delivery**, the group—Huff, Ross, Parker, and Chester Fortune—released a deeply emotional ballad titled *"I Destroyed Your Love."* Written by Huff, the song found a home on Quiet Storm stations across the country, climbing the R&B charts.

It was one of those late-night songs. The kind that drifted through speakers like a confession. But as happens too often in the music business, success met friction. Business disputes and personal differences pulled the group apart before a second album could be released. Still, their contribution remains stamped into the era forever. And to Reggie and Joyce, and to your family—Sarah and Christina: May the Lord's face continue to shine upon you always, in Jesus' name.

A Quiet Lesson from a very loud World

Years later, when I look back on that night—on the lights, the orchestra, the applause, and the magic—I realize something deeper was happening in my own life at the same time. I was a young man then, standing at the front doors of the Buffalo Hilton, learning what it really meant to serve people with excellence, dignity, and humility. I was rubbing shoulders with legends, yet being shaped by something far more important than celebrity: character.

Diana Ross reminded me that greatness doesn't have to shout. True class doesn't demand attention. It simply *shows up*, does its work beautifully, and leaves people better than it found them. But just as powerful as the concert itself were the friendships that came with it—the kind that don't fade when the curtain closes. Reggie and Joyce weren't just relatives of a star. They became family to us when we needed family the most.

In a season when our son was far from home, God placed the right people in the right city at exactly the right time. That's been the quiet pattern of my life. From my parents, Ezelle and Claudia Seay, to the hotel lobbies, to the stadium tunnels, to the front seats of motorcoaches carrying the world's most famous names—I've learned that the real story is never just about who you meet. It's about **who you become while serving them**. And somehow, in God's gentle way, He has allowed my ordinary hands to touch extraordinary moments—while teaching me to keep my feet planted firmly on the ground. Long after the applause fades, that is the part I'm most grateful for.

CHAPTER TWENTY

BURT REYNOLDS

A Legend Before He Ever Reached Buffalo

Before he ever set foot in the Buffalo Hilton, **Burt Reynolds** was already a force of nature—a name spoken with the kind of affection and curiosity usually reserved for kings, quarterbacks, and rock stars. Born Burton Leon Reynolds Jr. on February 11, 1936, in Lansing, Michigan, he grew up under the Florida sun, chasing dreams on the football field at Florida State University. A devastating knee injury ended that chapter—but sometimes destiny speaks clearest through disappointment. Acting became his unexpected path, and Hollywood quickly learned what football had lost.

Rise of a Hollywood Icon

Reynolds cut his teeth in the late 1950s on shows like *Gunsmoke* and *Perry Mason*, gradually finding his footing. By the 1960s and '70s, he had become a familiar face thanks to *Riverboat*, *Dan August*, and a magnetic edge that made people lean in whenever he appeared onscreen. Then came *Deliverance* (1972)—the film that didn't just give him a breakthrough, it blasted him into superstardom. The rest of the decade was his playground: *The Longest Yard. Smokey and the Bandit. Semi-Tough. Cannonball Run.*

Burt wasn't just famous—he was bankable. He was the man who made you buy a movie ticket before you even knew what the movie was about. And beneath the flash and the stunts was a sharp, thoughtful mind. He directed films like *Gator* and *The End*, adding artistry to swagger. Decades later, his role in *Boogie Nights* earned him an Academy Award nomination, reminding the world that the charisma was real—but so was the talent. When Burt Reynolds passed away on September 6, 2018, at age 82, Hollywood didn't just lose an actor. It lost an era.

Buffalo on the Hollywood Map

In 1982, **Burt Reynolds and Goldie Hawn arrived** in Buffalo to film *Best Friends*, a romantic comedy directed by Norman Jewison. While the story followed a couple navigating love and marriage, the decision to film in Buffalo gave the movie a charm and freshness that big coastal cities couldn't offer. The cast and crew stayed at the Hilton. And that meant Buffalo's front door ran straight through me.

First Encounter with Royalty

As the gatekeeper of the Hilton, I was the first face Burt Reynolds and Goldie Hawn saw when they stepped out of their vehicles. And let me tell you—the moment felt cinematic all by itself. Goldie Hawn floated through the entrance with the grace of a queen—soft, radiant, warm. Burt followed with that unmistakable swagger, a smile bright enough to light the lobby, and a presence so commanding yet so relaxed that it instantly put people at ease. But it wasn't the fame that impressed me. It was his manners.

To this day, Burt Reynolds remains the most well-mannered celebrity I have ever met. He had a rare gift for lifting people—meeting you where you were, or gently pulling you upward with him. No hierarchy. No ego. Just a man who understood humanity. Though fame limited his freedom to roam Buffalo, he still found ways to be gracious. He even brought his personal chef into our hotel kitchen. And whenever he did step out, he made those brief encounters feel warm, real, and unhurried.

Jim Reynolds: The Free Spirit

While Burt—and especially Goldie—kept a low profile, there was one Reynolds who embraced Buffalo like a long-lost cousin: Jim Reynolds. James "Jimmy" Hooks Reynolds was Burt's childhood friend, later adopted into the family in his forties. He was a stuntman with credits in *Bad Boys* (1995) and *Nine Months* (1995), and he worked transportation on *L.A. Confidential.* Jim had a personality that filled the room—gregarious, witty, instantly likable.

He and Dennis Davis hit it off so well that Dennis often invited him along on errands. Sometimes Dennis drove his flashy 1979 yellow convertible Cadillac Seville. Other times, I chauffeured them in the hotel limousine. Jim enjoyed every bit of it. Buffalo became his playground. He even invited me to be an extra in *Best Friends*, but I declined as humbly as I could. The first time I ever saw the movie was when I decided to write this book—and I truly enjoyed it. Jim passed away in March 2019, just six months after Burt. Two brothers in spirit—gone too soon.

The Parting Moment I will never Forget

When filming wrapped and the cast prepared to check out, Burt Reynolds approached me with the same warmth he had shown from day one. He pressed a crisp $100 bill into my hand—a generous gesture, yes. But what he gave me next is what stayed with me forever. A bronze-looking belt buckle. Not just any buckle—one engraved on the back with the address to his ranch in Jupiter, Florida, and a message that read:

"With respect and admiration. Burt!"

To this day, it remains the only piece of celebrity memorabilia I own. As far as I know, only three other people in Buffalo ever received one: Dennis Davis, Mayor James D. Griffin, and William "Bill" Hanbury, Vice President of the Buffalo Chamber of Commerce. I keep mine not because it's rare… …but because of the man who handed it to me. A star who didn't just shine—he made others shine with him.

A Quiet Measure of Greatness

Over the years, I've stood face-to-face with many famous people. Some were kind. Some were forgettable. A few were unforgettable. Burt Reynolds was unforgettable—not because of who he was to the world, but because of who he was to the people standing right in front of him. He taught me that real greatness doesn't announce itself. It notices people. It honors them. It leaves them better than it found them. That belt buckle isn't a trophy to me. It's a reminder. That character outlives applause. That humility outshines fame. And that the finest thing a man can ever be—no matter how high he rises—is **kind.**

CHAPTER TWENTY-ONE

ANDREA TRUE

The Song Everybody Knew… But the Woman Few Really Did

More, more, more, how do you like it… how do you like your love?"

If you lived through the 1970s or early '80s—if you ever walked into a club, a bar, a wedding, or even a supermarket—you heard that anthem. People danced to it, laughed to it, lived to it. That song had a way of slipping into your bloodstream before you ever knew the name of the woman singing it. But behind that iconic hook was a real person: Andrea Marie Truden—known to the world as **Andrea True**—a Nashville-born singer and actress whose name might not ring bells for everyone, but whose voice could still pull a crowd to the dance floor decades later. She was born July 26, 1943. She passed on November 7, 2011. And somewhere in between, she left a permanent fingerprint on pop culture.

A Star with an Unexpected Path

Before Andrea True became a disco sensation, she had already lived a complicated, unconventional life. She first built a career as an actress, including work in adult films under the name **Inger Kissin**—a chapter that was controversial, bold, and undeniably part of her story. Then came 1976. She and her band, **The Andrea True Connection**, recorded *"More, More, More,"* and the world instantly took notice. The song rocketed up the Billboard charts, traveled the globe, and stamped her name forever into the disco era. Even when she returned to acting in the 1980s, nothing could ever eclipse that one shimmering anthem that made people feel alive under spinning lights.

A Quiet Visit to Buffalo

I can't tell you the exact date she walked through the Hilton's doors—sometime in those first three years of the 1980s—but I remember the moment. No setlist showed her performing in Buffalo. No concert calendar placed her here. That told me she wasn't in town for the spotlight. She was here for business. Or rest. Or simply life. And somehow, in the steady swirl of celebrities and dignitaries who passed through that lobby, Andrea True became one of the most surprising and charming encounters I ever had.

A Presence that Drew you In

Andrea had a kind of energy that didn't need a stage. She walked in with a blend of charm, intelligence, and quiet confidence—the kind that made you feel like you could talk to her about anything. She was funny, sharp, and down-to-earth, the type of woman who made the room feel lighter just by being in it. She was close to forty then, but she carried herself like someone who knew exactly who she was—and liked who she was, too. Still glamorous. Still magnetic.

I didn't recognize her. But my bell staff brothers—God bless those perverts—were more than happy to educate me. Next thing I knew, they were humming, singing, and even dancing their best disco moves to *"More, More, More"* right there in the service area. And yes—I'm listening to that same song right now as I write this. Life has a funny way of looping back.

A Star who Never hid behind her Stardom

What struck me most was how approachable she was. Some celebrities needed a buffer. Andrea didn't. She signed autographs without hesitation—black-and-white copies of the *White Witch* album cover. One for me. One for every bellman on duty. She didn't rush. She didn't seem bothered. She just smiled, talked, and treated us like people—not props. It wasn't a long meeting. But it was meaningful. One of those brief moments that stays with you long after the ink dries.

A Hilton Memory I'll Always Carry

My years at the Hilton were filled with unforgettable encounters, but Andrea True sits near the top—partly because of who she was, and partly because of how she made you feel. Seen. Respected. Human. And I never forget why I had access to these moments in the first place. The Chen family opened that door. It was an honor to serve them, to serve their guests, and to stand at that doorway representing their vision and their hotel. And as I remember and cherish those years, I also honor **Mr. Clement Chen Jr. (July 27, 1929 – February 19, 1996)**—a leader whose legacy gave me opportunities I could never have scripted. May he rest in peace.

A Song, A Smile, And A Small Lesson

It's strange how life works. Some people give the world one unforgettable song. Some people give you one unforgettable moment. Andrea True gave me both. Not because she was famous—but because she was kind, open, and unguarded. She reminded me that behind every voice on the radio is a human being… and that sometimes the greatest thing a star can do is **not act like one**. And standing there in that lobby—between legends, luggage, and everyday life—I was learning a lesson that would follow me for decades: That real impact isn't measured in applause. It's measured in **how people treat you when they don't have to**.

CHAPTER TWENTY-TWO

THE CROSSROADS

When Dennis Davis Changed Everything

In 1983, Dennis Davis—who had served as general manager and vice president of the Buffalo Hilton Hotel for two years—made a decision that sent shockwaves through the building. He resigned his position and accepted the role of general manager at the Coconut Grove Hotel in Coconut Grove, Florida. To the staff, it felt sudden. To many of us, it felt impossible. I took it especially hard. By then, I had grown to feel like part of the Davis family. The Hilton wasn't just where I worked—it was where I belonged.

The Davis Family and Benson

Dennis's wife, Liz, a striking blonde, was one of the most refined and generous women I had ever met. She treated me with dignity and respect from day one. She was also a gifted businesswoman, applying her talents at the Marriott Hotel on Millersport Highway in Amherst, New York. I was especially close to their son, Scott—and to Benson, their giant schnauzer. Benson and I took nightly walks around the hotel grounds. He was so well-behaved that when the Davises were out of town, he sometimes came home with me at night. During the day, I made sure he stayed in his familiar environment—their suite.

An Unexpected Invitation

When Dennis told me he was leaving, I shared both my sadness and my fear that the hotel might suffer in his absence. Then came the surprise. He invited me—along with seven other key Hilton employees—to join him in Florida and help run the Coconut Grove Hotel. Just like that, my life split into a before and an after.

Choosing Between Loyalty and Opportunity

I wrestled with the decision. Not just because Buffalo was home. Not just because a new general manager might treat me differently. But because **Mr. Chen had given me a chance**. I felt loyal to him. He was the kind of leader who allowed people to grow and thrive. Leaving felt almost like betrayal. Still, I was young. And when I weighed stability against uncertainty, I chose the risk—believing I had time to recover if things didn't work out.

And Then… There Was Suzi

Around that same time, another complication walked into my life. Her name was **Susan—Suzi—Brant**. She was witty, intelligent, beautiful, and a redhead—already a dangerous combination. She worked as an executive assistant to Russell Baker, owner of Baker, Frazier, and Tucker Advertising, the agency behind the Buffalo News story about me. A radio station operated on the third floor of the Hilton, and Suzi regularly came in to swap advertising tapes.

A Rocky Start

Although we eventually married and have three amazing sons, Tommy, Michael, and James, three beautiful daughters-in-law, Breanne, Christine, and Cassidy, and three precious grandchildren, Jayden, Melania, and Beckham, it was **not** love at first sight. It was war! She insisted on parking at the front entrance instead of in the ramp. Hazard lights on. Dash inside. Ignore me completely. I repeatedly explained that the area was a no-parking zone. Her response? "I'll just be a moment." She would breeze right past me while I stood there turning beet red beneath my uniform, even though I'm black. Despite her beauty and wit, her refusal to follow the rules drove me crazy. She was clearly a source of irritation.

The Day She Crossed the Line

One day, she really went for it. She parked, dashed past me, and whispered: "I saw your name and number on the ladies' restroom wall at Crawdaddy's." I was stunned. Crawdaddy's was a famous waterfront spot in downtown Buffalo—dining, dancing, memories. Years later, Suzi and I would celebrate many anniversaries there before it eventually declined and was replaced by Templeton Landing. That place taught me a lesson too: Excellence has to be maintained every day—because once it fades, it rarely announces its departure.

An Olive Branch and a Misunderstanding

I decided to try diplomacy. I sent roses to her office with a simple card: "Can we all just get along?" But Maria Tucker—one of the owners—thought the flowers were for her and opened the card. She realized the mistake, apologized, and handed them to Suzi. Suzi kept the flowers. And kept parking in front.

The Showdown

One day, I stepped directly into her parking spot and planted myself there. Arms crossed. Face serious. She drove around me, parked anyway, and said:

"I'll just be a moment." I thought, "What a crazy lady."

From Adversary to Soulmate

What I didn't know was that this "crazy lady" would become my wife. Somewhere along the way, irritation became curiosity. Curiosity became admiration. Admiration became something I couldn't ignore. I started looking for her car. Listening for her footsteps. And then—we started dating.

The Florida Question

But looming over all of it was Florida. Dennis Davis had opened a door most young men would run through. But my heart wasn't made of paper. Every time I thought about leaving, I thought about Suzi. And slowly, the opportunity started to feel like heartbreak waiting to happen.

A Decision that Changed Everything

It became the hardest crossroads of my life: Chase a rising career… Or stay with the woman who had unexpectedly captured my heart. And as I would soon learn…That decision would shape everything that followed.

CHAPTER TWENTY-THREE

THE COCONUT GROVE HOTEL

A New Beginning in a New World

With promises made and a future still uncertain, I left Buffalo and joined the management team Dennis Davis had assembled to take over operations at the Coconut Grove Hotel in Coconut Grove, Florida. I was given the role of **swimming pool manager**. My responsibilities were practical and precise: maintaining proper water chemistry, hiring and scheduling staff, and making sure every guest who stepped onto the pool deck felt safe, comfortable, and well cared for. It wasn't exactly the position I imagined for myself at that stage of life—especially as someone newly devoted to living a Christian life—but it was honest work. And I intended to do it with excellence.

Temptation by the Pool

The challenge revealed itself immediately. Day after day, I worked in an environment filled with temptation—like a kid turned loose in a candy store. Or, to put it in my own language, like someone with a sweet tooth staring down a hot apple pie. And if there's one thing I've always loved, it's pie. Out by that pool, some of the most beautiful women in the world lounged in the latest, most revealing swimsuits. Every day became an exercise in discipline, focus, and prayer. I had made commitments—to God, to myself, and to Suzi. And with effort, intention, and more than a little tribulation, I kept them.

A Hotel with a Long Memory

The Coconut Grove Hotel stood at **2649 South Bayshore Drive**, just steps from Biscayne Bay. It was originally built in **1882** as the Bay View Inn, making it one of the oldest hotels in Miami. Over the decades, it had been expanded, renovated, and renamed, eventually becoming the Coconut Grove Hotel. It was known for its tropical gardens, its proximity to the water, and its long history of hosting celebrities, politicians, and winter visitors during Miami's early tourism boom. It was a beautiful place. But beautiful places, like people, can carry hidden fatigue.

A Hotel of Memories—And Challenges

Like many historic properties, the Coconut Grove Hotel had lived through changes in ownership, economic downturns, and shifting times. It was still known for its social events and lively gatherings, but underneath the surface, something wasn't right. The atmosphere among the staff was heavy.

A Troubled Workforce

The greatest obstacle to the hotel's success wasn't the building. It was the **spirit** of the workforce. Across departments, there was resistance. Frustration. A sense of bitterness that hung in the air. Whether it stemmed from rivalries between the Miami Dolphins and Buffalo Bills, resentment over promotions, or simply years of accumulated disappointment, I never fully figured it out. I only knew this: You can't build excellence on top of discouragement. And discouragement had taken root.

Monty's Coconut Grove: A Place to Breathe

When the days got heavy, I found refuge just a few steps away at **Monty's Coconut Grove**. The food was wonderful, and the service was exceptional. The atmosphere was warm. And the live reggae music—often provided by **Dink Ramsey (July 10, 1943 – January 7, 2022)**—washed some of the hotel's shadows right off my shoulders. For a little while, sitting there, listening to music and watching the marina, I could breathe again.

When Reality Doesn't Match the Dream

I had come to Florida full of hope. Full of ambition. Full of belief in the opportunity Dennis had offered me. But slowly, quietly, I began to understand something: Not every open door leads where you think it will. Some lead to growth. Some lead to testing. Some simply teach you what you're not meant to stay in.

A Season, Not A Forever

I did my job. I did it well. I kept my standards. But in my heart, something was shifting. I was learning that this chapter of my life wasn't a destination. It was a season. And seasons, by their nature, eventually change.

Looking Ahead

What I didn't know yet was that one ordinary decision—getting a haircut—would lead me into one of the most meaningful and unexpected encounters of my entire time in Miami. It would take me far from the pool. Far from the hotel. And straight into a place that felt strangely… like home.

CHAPTER TWENTY-FOUR

LIBERTY CITY

A Haircut That Became A Journey

My most unusual experience in Miami began with something simple. I needed a haircut. Not knowing the city very well but feeling adventurous, I boarded a city bus and rode until I saw a neighborhood that looked familiar—one that reminded me of the places where I had grown up. Only later did I learn I had wandered into an area most people would've warned me to avoid. It was called **Liberty City**. In many ways, it felt like parts of Buffalo I knew by heart—Madison and Sycamore, Riley and Masten, Cold Springs. And I've learned something in my life: As long as you don't walk into a community with fear, arrogance, or disrespect, people usually meet you with humanity.

A Place with A Deep Story

Liberty City traces its roots to **Liberty Square**, a housing project built in 1937 under Franklin D. Roosevelt's New Deal. It was the first public housing development in the American South designated for African Americans. It was built as a response to the overcrowded, unsanitary conditions in Overtown, Miami's main Black community at the time, where discriminatory housing practices left families with few options. In its early years, Liberty Square was seen as a model—so much so that the surrounding area earned the nickname **"Model City."**

But history has a way of changing neighborhoods. In the 1960s, urban renewal projects and highway construction—especially Interstate 95—cut straight through Overtown, displacing thousands of Black families. Many of them were relocated to Liberty City. Over time, disinvestment, unemployment, and segregation took their toll. What began as a promise became a struggle.

The Barbershop

I stepped off the bus and wandered until I found a small Black-owned barbershop. I don't remember the street. But I remember what happened when I opened the door. The place was alive—laughter, conversation, clippers humming. Then I walked in. Everything went silent. All eyes on me. One of the barbers—who clearly ran the place—asked: "Can I help you?" Trying to sound cool, I said: "Yeah, I was hoping to get a haircut and my dashboard trimmed." The silence exploded into laughter. He grinned and said, "Man, we never heard anybody call a mustache a dashboard. Take this chair, brother." He sat me right in the middle seat—letting me skip someone he said was his cousin. And just like that, I wasn't a stranger anymore.

Finding Familiar Ground

What amazed me was what they were talking about. The conversation drifted right back to **the Bible**. As a former Sunday school teacher, I felt like I'd walked into a room of old friends. Faith has a way of doing that—turning strangers into family in a matter of minutes.

"Hollywood in the Ghetto"

The barber looked at me and said, "You're obviously not from here. Where you from?" I told him I was from New York and working as the swimming pool manager at the Coconut Grove Hotel. He laughed and said, "Oh, you Hollywood in the ghetto." The whole shop erupted again—and this time, I laughed with them. I told them my name was Tommy. He told me his. I wish I could remember it. But I will never forget his kindness. He was professional, respectful, and served his customers with care.

An Invitation, Church, Fellowship, And A Miracle

Before I left, he invited me to his church. I accepted. The service lifted my spirit. Afterward, he invited me to his mother's house. She served me the **best fried chicken and pigeon peas with rice** I have ever eaten. I had never even heard of pigeon peas before. It tasted like love. Then she shared her testimony. She had once been paralyzed from the neck down, bedridden, and hopeless. She prayed:

"Lord, either heal me or take me home."

On Mother's Day, God answered. He healed her. She never returned to that bed in that condition nor for that reason. I sat there in awe.

A Brother I Never Forgot

There were several young men in that barbershop that day—all around my age. Perhaps one of them was you. Maybe you're even the barber. If you ever read this and recognize this story, I would love to reconnect. To confirm it's you, tell me the **denomination of the church** you invited me to. That detail will prove it.

What that day Taught Me

I went looking for a haircut. I found **brotherhood**. I found **faith**. I found **home** in a place I was told to avoid. And I learned something I've carried with me ever since: God is already present in the places people are afraid to go.

A Quiet Truth

That day in Liberty City reminded me of who I was. Not a hotel manager. Not a visitor. Not an outsider. Just a man… among other men… in the presence of grace.

Looking Ahead

I didn't know then that my time in Miami was already nearing its end. That this season, like all seasons, was about to close. And that home—real home—was waiting for me in Buffalo.

CHAPTER TWENTY-FIVE

THE WAY HOME

When Seasons End

Nothing dramatic announced the end. No trumpet. No argument. No explosion. Just a quiet realization that the season was changing. Not long after we arrived, Dennis Davis—born in St. Louis, Missouri, on June 2, 1940—made the difficult decision to resign and return to New Orleans, where he had grown up, to help his brother Jim run the family restaurant. That was the last time I ever saw or spoke to him. When I later learned of his passing in 2018, my heart was heavy. He had been more than a boss to me. He had been a mentor, a door-opener, and for a time, the man who changed the direction of my life.

The Team Disbands

With Dennis gone, the vision that had brought us all to Coconut Grove slowly unraveled. One by one, the Buffalo team resigned and moved on. The experiment was over. The hotel would continue, of course—but our chapter in it had ended.

The Decision that was Already Made

I could have stayed in Florida. With my restaurant background, I could've joined Dennis and Jim in New Orleans. On paper, that probably made sense. But my heart had already decided.

Her

Somewhere between designated parking area arguments and quiet conversations…Between laughter and stubborn standoffs…Between Buffalo winters and Miami sunsets…**Suzi had become home.**

Choosing Love Led Me Back to Buffalo

So, I returned to Buffalo. Not as a man who had failed. But as a man who had **learned**. Learned what ambition feels like. Learned what temptation looks like. Learned what faith requires. Learned what really matters. We got married. And somehow, without fanfare or fireworks, I stepped into the most important role of my life, **Husband.** Today, more than forty years have passed. We're still together. Still married. Still in love. Still grateful. We've built a life—not from perfect plans, but from faithful choices.

What Miami Gave Me

Miami gave me:

- Perspective
- Humility
- A test of my faith
- A deeper understanding of myself

And it gave me a story I'll carry with me forever.

What Buffalo Gave Me

Buffalo gave me:

- Roots
- Purpose
- Community

And the woman who would walk beside me for the rest of my life

A Quiet Truth

Looking back now, I see it clearly: I didn't go to Florida to find my future. I went there to confirm where my future already was.

The Real Arrival

Some people think the big moments in life are when you leave. Sometimes… The real moment is when you **come home**.

The Best Decision I Ever Made

I've stood in front of famous people. I've opened doors for legends. I've lived in extraordinary moments. But the greatest decision of my life wasn't a career move. It was a **commitment**. To a woman. To a life. To a journey built on love, faith, and choosing what matters most. And every road I traveled… Every door I opened… Every city I left… Led me right back to where I was always meant to be.

CHAPTER TWENTY-SIX

THE HYATT REGENCY BUFFALO

A New Beginning at Fountain Plaza

February 12, 1984, rose crisp and bright over Buffalo as the brand-new Hyatt Regency at **2 Fountain Plaza** prepared to open its doors for the very first time. Inside that excitement—amid the swirl of movement, hope, and polished brass—there I stood, part of the original staff. And to this day, I still marvel at how I got there. Just weeks earlier, I had returned from Florida with no particular plan. I didn't apply to the Hyatt. I didn't drop off a résumé. I didn't stand in line hoping to be chosen. They found me. Out of nowhere, the phone rang. Someone heard about my work—about my service, my standards, the way I treated people. My reputation arrived before I did. Sometimes, favor steps into the room before you.

Joining the Bell Staff

I had hoped to work the front desk, but those positions were already filled. So, I joined the **bell staff**—the first impression of the hotel—with the promise that a front-desk opportunity might come later. From day one, that lobby was alive: luggage wheels whispering across marble, elevator chimes rising and falling, conversations blending into a warm, welcoming hum. It felt like stepping into a brand-new story.

Ron Mann, the Hyatt's first General Manager, guided us through those early days. He reminded me of Dennis Davis—not because they were the same, but because they shared something rare: positivity, fairness, patience, and leadership rooted in wisdom.

More than carrying Bags

Working the bell stand was never about luggage. It was about **people**. A tired traveler. A nervous executive. A family juggling kids and suitcases. Every guest was a story walking through the door. And I tried to treat each one like it mattered—because it did. With every thank-you, every surprised smile, every small moment of connection, I was reminded: Hospitality isn't just a job. It's a calling.

Charlie Murphy: Eddie's brother, but a Star in his own Right

It was in 1984 at the Hyatt when I first met **Charlie Murphy**—Eddie Murphy's older brother, but a man who carried his own gravity. He had a quiet swagger, a sharp wit, and a smile that told you he saw life from an angle most people missed. The resemblance to Eddie was obvious—but the spirit was all Charlie: comedian, actor, storyteller, protector.

The year before, Eddie had performed at Shea's, likely staying with his close friend Rick James, who had known both brothers since 1981. Around that time, Rick wrote and produced *"Party All the Time,"* with Eddie on vocals. The song climbed to #2 on the Billboard Hot 100 in 1985. My conversations with Charlie were brief—but memorable. Born July 12, 1959, in Brooklyn, New York, he passed away April 12, 2017. But if you ever met him—even once—you remember the spark.

RAY "Boom Boom" MANCINI & GENE "Mad Dog" HATCHER

Two Fights, One Ring, One Unforgettable Night

Also, in 1984, the Hyatt Regency Buffalo became a crossroads for two more unforgettable boxing figures. **Raymond M. Mancini**, born March 4, 1961, in Youngstown, Ohio, was the reigning WBA Lightweight Champion. The son of a boxer whose career had been cut short by World War II, Ray carried his father's dream all the way to the top.

Ronald Hatcher Jr., BKA "Gene Hatcher." born June 28, 1959, in Fort Worth, Texas, was on the rise. An intense competitor in the ring, but outside of it—warm, respectful, and generous with his time. They were like brothers in spirit. They signed autographs, talked with staff, and treated everyone with dignity. After meeting their parents, it was easy to see where that character came from.

Tickets to History

Both men gave me tickets to their **June 1, 1984,** fights at the Buffalo Memorial Auditorium. I invited my best friend Jerome to join me. What happened that night became boxing history. Gene Hatcher stunned the world, stopping Johnny "Bump City" Bumphus in the 11th round—an upset later named **Upset of the Year**. Ray Mancini, heavily favored, fought bravely but was stopped by Livingstone "Pit Bull" Bramble in the 14th round. Two champions. Two very different outcomes. One unforgettable night.

Men of Character

What stayed with me wasn't the belts or headlines. It was **who they were**. Champions in the ring. Gentlemen everywhere else.

A Doorway to the Future

The Hyatt gave me a front-row seat to the world: entertainers, athletes, executives, families, and quiet stories passing through polished marble halls. But the hotel industry also had a truth you couldn't ignore: The hours are long. The schedule is unpredictable. And the demands are relentless. Hospitality is exciting in your twenties. But it isn't always friendly to family life—unless you climb into the executive ranks. And in **September 1984**, Suzi and I got married. Suddenly, my priorities had a new center.

A Season of Preparation

The Hyatt gave me experience. Confidence. Perspective. And unforgettable encounters. But even then, something in me knew: This was a season. Not a destination. And once again… The phone was going to ring.

CHAPTER TWENTY-SEVEN

THE CALL THAT CHANGED EVERYTHING

When Experience Begins to Outweigh Excitement

There comes a moment in every life when experience starts to outweigh excitement. By late 1984, I had collected many such moments—inside hotel lobbies, along polished corridors, opening doors for people beginning their journeys. The Hyatt had sought me out. Trusted me. Given me a place on its opening team. For that, I was grateful.

When Responsibility Enters the Room

But marriage changes the way you hear the clock. It introduces a quiet realization: Showing up every day can no longer be driven only by passion. It also has to be guided by permanence. The hotel industry offered excitement and opportunity—but not guarantees. And for a man building a future, **guarantees start to matter**.

Waiting on something I couldn't see yet

In October 1984, I submitted my application to **NFTA-Metro (Niagara Frontier Transportation Authority)**. But let me be honest—I didn't just mail it in and sit around folding my hands, waiting on fate to do the rest. That's never been my style. I **called**. And then I called again. And then I called again. Every time, I tried to be respectful. I'd say something like:

> "I don't mean to be a nuisance… but I do intend to be a great asset to your team."

I wasn't begging. I was **presenting myself**. I wanted them to know that if they hired me, they wouldn't just be getting a body in a seat—they'd be getting someone who showed up early, stayed late, and took pride in doing things right. Week after week, I checked in. Politely. Persistently. At some point, I'm pretty sure they didn't hire me because I was quiet and patient. They probably hired me so I would **stop calling**.

But here's the truth: I wasn't being annoying. I was being **determined**. I could feel that something was coming—I just couldn't see it yet. And I wasn't about to let that opportunity pass me by without making sure somebody on the other end of that phone remembered my name.

The Call

Then the phone rang. Not a bell captain. Not a general manager. Not hospitality at all. It was the **Niagara Frontier Transportation Authority**. A class was starting **in one hour**. A last-minute cancellation had opened one seat. If I could get there in time… The opportunity was mine.

From Opening Doors to Taking the Wheel

That day, I stopped opening doors for other people's journeys. And stepped into my own. I moved from the front of the hotel… To the front of a bus. And without fully realizing it in that moment, I had just stepped onto the road that would define the rest of my professional life.

The Turn in the Road

Looking back now, I can see it clearly: The Hyatt was a classroom. Hospitality was a training ground. And that phone call was a **calling**. Some doors you open, and some doors open you.

CHAPTER TWENTY-EIGHT

NIAGARA FRONTIER TRANSPORTATION AUTHORITY

Earning a Seat Behind the Wheel

In November of 1984, I was granted what few people received without influence: a seat behind the wheel at NFTA-Metro—the Niagara Frontier Transportation Authority—here in Buffalo, New York. I call it elite, not out of ego, but out of accuracy. At that time, Metro was highly political. Getting hired usually meant knowing someone. The Authority took its workforce seriously, prioritizing safety, responsibility, and customer service—not just anyone made the cut.

Competitive wages and full benefits attracted the best candidates, but those conditions didn't come as a matter of goodwill from management. They were hard-won through collective bargaining between the Authority and Amalgamated Transit Union Local 1342. It was my first union job. And unlike the hotels I had worked for—private enterprises vulnerable to ownership changes and economic shifts—public transportation was funded through government resources. It offered something entirely new to me: **stability**.

The Three Lessons that Defined the Job

Metro sharpened three skills that would become foundational in my professional life: **safety, time, and patience**. During orientation, instructors Carl Smith and Roland Reese drilled that lesson relentlessly. Safety always came first—but time came right after. Public transportation runs on precise schedules. If the driver is late, the passengers are late. And when the passengers are late, frustration climbs right up the bus steps with them.

Serving the Public, Not the Assembly Line

For more than three decades, I served the public in a role that demanded constant adaptability. This wasn't factory work or steel labor, where routines repeat and human interaction is minimal. Working face-to-face with the public meant every day was different—and **patience became the cornerstone** of everything else: empathy, listening, judgment, and problem-solving.

Metro was also personal. While the system carried suburban professionals to offices and medical facilities, roughly ninety percent of its riders came from Buffalo's inner-city neighborhoods—the same streets where I grew up, played, and went to school. I knew these communities. I understood them. Metro alone could fill a thousand-page book with stories—some difficult, some heartwarming, all unforgettable.

Safety Above All

Safety was sacred at Metro. Every year without a chargeable accident earned an operator a safety pin. Ten consecutive years earned a gold watch, engraved with the Authority's emblem. And if you did have a chargeable accident, it stayed on your record for one year before being cleared—a system that balanced accountability with grace.

The Day James Brown cost me a Perfect Record

I earned my watch in my eleventh year—but not without a lesson. Near the end of my tenth year, I made a small mistake with lasting consequences. As I pulled out of the garage to start my route, my attention drifted where it shouldn't have. I had one earphone in, listening to James Brown's *"I Got the Feelin'."* Relaxed just enough to forget where I was, my bus clipped the control box operating Door Eleven.

When I sat with my supervisor, Mr. Carr, he shook his head. "Tommy, you were doing so well. What happened?" I told him the truth. "Boss, I was listening to James Brown, 'I Got the Feelin,' and relaxed a little too much." He looked at me and said, "Well, you also got that accident on your record, too. Get back out there—and focus on what you're supposed to be doing." Lesson learned. **Permanently.**

What Every Transit Operator Learns the Hard Way

A transit operator faces challenges most people never think about—false complaints, verbal abuse, even assaults. Every time the doors open, a new personality steps aboard. One rider can shift the mood of an entire bus with a single breath. To survive—and serve—I kept a few truths close:

- **Handling Frustrated Passengers:** Many board with problems already weighing on them. Patience keeps situations from escalating and makes people feel heard.
- **Ensuring Clear Communication:** Not everyone can explain their issue clearly. Patience allows space to clarify without rushing or dismissing.
- **Building Trust and Rapport:** When passengers don't feel hurried or brushed aside, trust grows.
- **Problem Solving:** Complex issues take time. Patience prevents shortcuts that create bigger problems.
- **Personalizing the Experience:** Everyone is different. Patience lets you meet people where they are.
- **Reducing Stress for the Specialist:** Staying calm protects not just the passengers—but the operator too.

When One Passenger holds up the whole Bus

Eventually, every operator encounters a passenger whose sole purpose seems to be disruption. When protocol alone wasn't enough, relationships—and judgment—mattered. After safely securing the bus, I would address everyone onboard:

> "Ladies and gentlemen, I understand how important it is for you to get where you're going on time. Unfortunately, today we'll be delayed—because this individual is holding everyone up."

Something powerful happens when responsibility is shared. The instigator, who expected a one-on-one confrontation, suddenly faced a busload of angry commuters instead. Most situations resolved themselves quickly. Still, judgment is everything. When tension escalated or safety felt compromised, I didn't hesitate to call the Dispatcher and request law enforcement assistance. **Pride never outranks safety.**

A Seat on the Safety Board

Because of my driving record and reputation for customer service, I was later selected to serve on NFTA-Metro's Safety Board—the Accident Review Committee—where we evaluated incidents to determine preventability. That seat gave me a deeper appreciation for fairness, accountability, and the weight of every decision an operator makes.

Thirty-Two Years, Done the Right Way

After thirty-two years, I retired in June 2017. It wasn't an easy decision. A new collective bargaining agreement required employees—including long-tenured veterans like me—to begin contributing to medical insurance premiums. Rather than surrender benefits I had earned over decades, I chose to step away with them intact. I wasn't yet eligible for Social Security, but my age and years of service qualified me for my pension. It was a quiet, steady reward for a lifetime of showing up, staying patient, and keeping people safe. And I walked away knowing something that mattered even more: **I had done the job the right way.**

From a Route Map to a Compass

When I walked away from NFTA-Metro in June of 2017, I wasn't walking away from work. I was walking away from a chapter. Thirty-two years behind the wheel had given me more than a pension and a gold watch. It had given me instincts. Judgment. A deep respect for safety. And above all, patience—the kind that can't be taught in a classroom, only earned one passenger, one problem, one day at a time. Metro taught me how to carry people. Niagara Scenic Tours would teach me how to **carry missions**.

At Metro, I moved the public. At Niagara Scenic, I would move **teams, organizations, expectations, and reputations**. The equipment would be bigger. The schedules tighter. The stakes higher. The margin for error thinner. But the principles would be exactly the same. Safety first. Time always matters. And patience makes everything else possible.

I didn't know it yet, but every snowy route, every delayed passenger, every hard-earned lesson—even the day James Brown cost me a perfect record—had been preparing me for what was coming next. I wasn't just changing jobs. I was changing **arenas**. And in the next chapter, I would discover that the most demanding, most precise, and most meaningful driving of my life was still ahead of me.

CHAPTER TWENTY-NINE

NIAGARA SCENIC TOURS

From Humble Beginnings to a Western New York Institution

What began nearly a century ago as a small hauling and moving operation has become one of Western New York's most trusted names in transportation. Niagara Scenic Tours, a Fisher Group, proudly marks a historic milestone—**more than 90 years in the transportation industry** and nearly a century since its humble beginnings on February 21, 1927.

In 1947, the Fisher family launched Fisher's Bus Service, planting the seeds for what would become a full-service transportation network. Over the decades, the company expanded its services to include everything from student transportation and luxury motorcoach travel to moving and storage solutions.

Still family-owned and operated by the third and fourth generations of the Fisher family, Niagara Scenic Tours continues to uphold the values that built its foundation: **reliability, community commitment, and personalized service**. In celebration of its 90-year milestone, the company unveiled a commemorative decal on each vehicle—a symbol of pride and a visible reminder of its enduring presence throughout the region.

Finding Home on a New Road

In June of 2017, I retired from NFTA-Metro and joined Niagara Scenic Tours the following month. From day one, I felt honored—not only to be part of one of the premier motorcoach companies in the country, but to feel genuinely welcomed into what I proudly call **the Fisher family**.

Since my days under Dennis Davis at the Buffalo Hilton, no manager I had ever served under came close to filling his shoes—**until** I met Niagara Scenic

Tours' CEO, **Mr. Keith Fisher**, and his son, **President Hadley Bos Fisher**. They certainly did.

Leadership with Heart—And Humor

Both men possess remarkable personalities—warm enough to melt the ice at the North Pole—yet always anchored by professionalism. And when they choose to show their humorous side, it's unforgettable. At one of our Annual Employee Meetings and Luncheons, we lined up for a company photo. Mr. Keith Fisher positioned himself alone in the front row, with the staff standing behind him. After the photo was taken, we burst into laughter. There he was—nowhere near the size of a sumo wrestler—yet posing like one ready to enter the ring, while the rest of us looked perfectly normal. When you're successful, grounded, and blessed with a great sense of humor, you can enjoy life however you please.

Like Father, Like Son—Leadership on the Front Lines

That same spark runs through Hadley. As the saying goes, *like father, like son*. During one of my assignments in Jamestown, New York, I was tasked with shuttling convention attendees between the Chautauqua Hotel and the National Comedy Center. Two buses were scheduled, and I was the lead driver. Just before the shift began, my coworker on Bus 2 fell ill, leaving us scrambling for a replacement. The only available operator was none other than the heir to the empire himself—**Mr. Hadley Bos Fisher**. Not just a great president, but also a professional operator. He's the kind of leader who rolls up his sleeves, grabs a set of keys, and climbs into the driver's seat without hesitation.

"Just order from the Left Side of the Menu"

Things finally slowed down and gave us a chance to grab a bite to eat. I asked Hadley what he was in the mood for. After giving him a few options, he suggested dining at the Chautauqua Hotel restaurant. As we sat and looked over the menu, I said, "Boss, order whatever you want, and I'll pick up the check." "Absolutely not," he said, firm and unwavering. "I'll take care of it. Just order from the **left side** of the menu." Our drinks arrived—water for Hadley and lemonade for me. As I scanned the left side of the menu, I saw appetizers, chicken fingers, salads, soup, cheeseburgers, and fries. Meanwhile, the **right side** held the real treasures.

Truth be told, Hadley is not a cheap man by any means. In fact, he is one of the most generous people I have ever met and had the pleasure of serving under. During this situation, however, I just wanted to have some fun.

"I'll have exactly what he's having"

The waitress returned, ready for our order. Hadley went first: a garden salad and honey-glazed salmon with garlic mashed potatoes and mixed grilled vegetables. All of it from the **right side** of the menu. Silently, I thought, *This man has some nerve.* I was the one who offered to pay. He refused. Then he told me what side of the menu I could order from. I thought he might need a check-up from the neck up. So, when the waitress turned to me, I smiled and said, "I'll have exactly what he's having." And handed her the menu. Hadley didn't protest—but he did give me a look like I had completely lost my mind. It was the kind of look that could easily earn its own spot in the **National Comedy Center**.

No, not that kind of Surprise

That Jamestown charter unpacked more than passengers that evening—it delivered a surprise I never saw coming. Hadley radioed me and said, "Tommy, there's a lady here asking about you. She says she'll be waiting at the hotel." Now, after more than four decades of *marriage*, the very last thing a man needs is a surprise visit from someone claiming you've got children you never knew existed. My mind went there immediately—and I actually debated whether I should leave the passengers at the National Comedy Center and go home.

But I did return to the hotel. After the passengers finished unloading, I walked over to the woman standing nearby. She looked at me and asked, "Are you Tommy Seay?" "That depends," I said cautiously. She smiled. "My name is Joanne Conley. Your son, Michael, is dating my daughter, Christine." "OMG!" I blurted out, and before either of us knew what was happening, I was giving her the biggest hug she'd probably received all year. Instantly, she became the nicest lady you could ever meet. Christine's family is from the Adirondack Mountains region, a five-hour drive from us.

Joanne was in town for the convention. We took a photo together right there outside the hotel. At the time, Michael and Christine, who met and were living in Los Angeles, happened to be out to dinner. I sent them the picture, and they couldn't believe it. Out of all the people on earth, the odds of me randomly meeting Christine's mother had to be about one in a billion. Even better? Michael and Christine have their wedding planned for October 3, 2026. Sometimes life doesn't just write stories—it drops them right at your feet.

One Vote. One Winner. One Knockout Blow.

The year 2023 ended with another unforgettable moment: the company's first-ever **Operator of the Year Award**. It meant even more knowing it was voted on by my peers—and that I was the first to receive it. One afternoon, curiosity finally got the better of me. I was preparing the bus for a day trip when I ran into Hadley in the parking lot. "Boss," I asked, "how many votes did I win by?" "One vote," he replied. That alone amazed me—my own vote had been the deciding factor. Then I asked, "How many votes were cast?" He smiled and said, "Just one." And that was the knockout blow.

Gratitude for Leadership that sets the Tone

I want to take a moment to express my deepest gratitude to **Mr. Keith Fisher** and **Mr. Hadley Bos Fisher** for your outstanding leadership and for giving me the opportunity to be part of this incredible team. Working under your direction has been both an honor and a privilege. Your vision, integrity, and commitment to excellence set the tone for the entire organization. You lead not only with wisdom and strength, but with genuine care for the people who serve alongside you. Your example inspires me daily and reminds me why being part of this team means so much to me.

A Salute to the Team behind the Scenes

In alphabetical order by first name, I want to sincerely thank the executive team, office staff, talented and dependable mechanics, and everyone who works behind the scenes to keep this operation moving forward every single day:

> Andrew Satterly, Anne Davis, BrieAnna Koehler, Brittany Norris, Chad and Mary Schumacher, Dave Ehrke, Emmariah Dankosh, Geoff Nowak, Gina Marie Kimmick, Georgia Trekyak, Joanna Miller, Joe Rallo, Josh Seiler, Keith Petti, Kerry Wasinger, Maria Burridge, Michael Harrington, Mike Eberl, Riley Moran, Shawn Evingham, Steve Bohn, Sue Sivula, Tammy Kurszka, Tim Rockwood, Veronica Knittel, and Yon'Taya Hicks.

Your hard work, organization, and steady support make a real difference. So much of what you do happens quietly in the background, but it's felt every time we show up prepared and ready to do our jobs. And to our incredible Scenic Excursions hosts and hostesses—thank you for being the heartbeat of the daily operation. Please know this: **your efforts do not go unnoticed. Your work matters. And you are appreciated more than you may ever hear.**

CHAPTER THIRTY

2021 MAJOR LEAGUE BASEBALL

Turning a Minor League Park into a Major League Stage

Sahlen Field was never meant to host Major League Baseball. It was a beautiful, well-kept minor league park—but the difference between Triple-A and the big leagues is measured in more than just talent. It's measured in infrastructure, technology, security, broadcast capability, and standards that leave no room for improvisation.

In a matter of weeks, the city of Buffalo and the Blue Jays organization pulled off something that felt impossible. Clubhouses were expanded. Lighting was upgraded. Video and replay systems were installed. Broadcast facilities were overhauled. Security zones were redesigned. Even the visiting facilities had to be reimagined to meet Major League specifications.

What had once been a proud minor league home was suddenly transformed into a fully functional Major League ballpark. And it wasn't just concrete and steel that changed. The **identity of the city changed** with it. Overnight, Buffalo became a big-league town. You could feel it in the air. In the way downtown buzzed. In the way people walked a little taller. In the way kids pressed against the railings, dreaming bigger dreams.

Driving through a season the world will never forget

The 2021 MLB season was unlike anything professional sports had ever experienced. Everywhere we turned, there were new procedures, new expectations, and new responsibilities. The bus wasn't just a mode of transportation anymore—it was a **mobile health zone**, a protected environment that had to meet strict protocols to keep players and staff safe. Before every pickup, my team and I were required to:

- Sanitize every handrail, seat, window frame, and storage compartment
- Maintain masked interactions at all times
- Keep front rows empty for distancing
- Manage staggered boarding to limit close contact
- Coordinate with medical personnel for clearance before arrivals
- Follow MLB's color-coded access system to determine who was allowed where

Some days, it felt less like operating a motorcoach and more like commanding a **rolling quarantine unit**. But we approached every trip with discipline and pride. We understood the importance of preserving the integrity of the season. These athletes relied on us not only for transportation, but for **protection**. The world was still reeling from the pandemic. Vaccines were rolling out unevenly. Travel regulations changed daily. One positive test could sideline an entire series. Through it all, Major League Baseball pressed forward, adopting what they called the **Tier System**.

- **Tier 1** covered players, coaches, and trainers.
- **Tier 2** included operational support.
- **Tier 3**… that was us—the transportation professionals who kept the whole system moving.

That meant our job wasn't just to drive. It was to remain vigilant, disciplined, and reliable. We weren't only carrying teams—we were carrying **seasons, standings, broadcast contracts, and entire cities' hopes** on our buses. And we were carrying them safely.

A Minor League City Hosting Major League Legends

By the time the Blue Jays settled into Buffalo full-time, the city had transformed. Downtown buzzed with national media attention. Local businesses revived after months of shutdowns. Kids leaned over the railings at Sahlen Field to watch batting practice, hoping for a glimpse of:

- **Vladimir Guerrero Jr.**, launching baseballs into orbit
- **Bo Bichette**, with his flowing hair and lightning-fast swing
- **George Springer**, bringing championship pedigree from Houston
- **Teoscar Hernández**, whose bat could turn a game around instantly
- **Lourdes Gurriel Jr.**, as charismatic as he was talented

Night after night, Buffalo lit up like a true big-league town. And on the road, I transported some of the biggest names in the game.

The **New York Yankees**, with Aaron Judge towering like a redwood tree.
The **Houston Astros**, with Dusty Baker's calm leadership guiding every move.
The **Boston Red Sox**, a well-oiled machine of discipline and swagger.
The **Miami Marlins**, young and hungry.
The **Baltimore Orioles**, building for the future.
The **Tampa Bay Rays**, head high with confidence.

Each team brought its own rhythm, its own routines, its own level of star power. And I watched Buffalo welcome all of them with open arms.

A Gesture That Meant More Than Money

The pressures of the pandemic amplified everything—fatigue, stress, travel complications, and last-minute changes. Yet through all of that chaos, one individual shone like a lighthouse in the storm: **Max Thomas of the Miami Marlins**. I transported championship coaches, MVPs, All-Stars, and Hall of Fame legends—but Max Thomas stands among the most memorable for his **character alone**. In those two games, the Marlins came up short, losing 2–1 on Tuesday, June 22, 2021, and 3–1 on Wednesday, June 23, 2021.

After days of structured movement under tight pandemic protocols, we reached the airport drop-off point to send the Marlins home. Max and the team exited the bus and retrieved their luggage. After saying our goodbyes, Max handed me an envelope—quietly, sincerely. As the Marlins went through security and boarded their flight, we waited for the plane to take off before leaving the airport. That's when I opened the envelope. What Max Thomas gave me was generous—far beyond anything customary—but it wasn't the amount that stayed with me. It was what he said when I called him. With appreciation in his voice, he said:

> **"Tommy, you managed your team very well. You met all our needs without us having to ask. You earned and deserve it. Thank you."**

In an industry where gratuities are inconsistent—and often nonexistent—his acknowledgment struck deeply. At a time when the world was divided and exhausted, Max Thomas extended something rare: **appreciation, humility, and respect**. Those qualities matter far more than any superstar statistic.

A Son Driving His Father's Game

Every time I drove an MLB roster—from rookies to household names—I imagined my father sitting behind me, hat ready, waiting to talk baseball with the first person who made eye contact. He would've loved it all. The players. The staff. The routines. The behind-the-scenes world few ever get to witness. Sometimes, when the bus was quiet and the night was long, I felt his presence beside me. Baseball was his passion. Service and hospitality became mine. And in 2021—during a global crisis—I somehow found myself standing at the intersection of both. Driving through the pandemic wasn't easy. But driving **Major League Baseball**—after growing up with a father who worshipped the game—felt like something beyond duty. It felt like **honoring him**. Mile after mile.

CHAPTER THIRTY-ONE

THE NATIONAL FOOTBALL LEAGUE

THE BUFFALO BILLS

A Season of Change

In 2018, Buffalo stood on the edge of something new. The energy around One Bills Drive felt different, as if the cold Western New York winds were carrying a promise. That season, I was assigned to several Buffalo Bills charters while Grand Tours Motorcoach still held the NFL transportation contract. At the time, I had no idea I was about to meet the man who would transform the franchise—and eventually the entire spirit of Buffalo football. His name was Josh Allen.

Before the Bills: The Firebaugh Foundation

Josh Allen's journey didn't begin under bright stadium lights. It began in Firebaugh, California—a small agricultural town where work ethic isn't preached, it's lived. That toughness carried him to the University of Wyoming, a place defined by relentless winds and unforgiving weather. While others struggled just to complete passes in that climate, Josh learned to master it. He learned to throw through the wind. In his junior season in 2017, he threw for 1,812 yards and added 767 rushing yards, proving he wasn't just a gunslinger—he was a true dual-threat quarterback built for hard conditions and harder expectations.

The Draft that Changed Everything

The 2018 NFL Draft became a turning point for Buffalo. With the seventh overall pick, the Bills selected Josh Allen—a bold decision that divided analysts but ignited the city. And he wasn't alone. That same draft brought in a group that would help shape the team's culture for years to come:

- Tremaine Edmunds, LB – 1st Round, 16th overall
- Harrison Phillips, DT – 3rd Round, 96th
- Taron Johnson, CB – 4th Round, 121st
- Siran Neal, S – 5th Round, 154th
- Wyatt Teller, OG – 5th Round, 166th
- Austin Proehl, WR – 7th Round, 255th

In time, I would drive and interact with every one of them—each talented, humble, and determined to prove they belonged.

The Beginning of Something Bigger

By the time I transitioned to Niagara Scenic Tours, the Bills were already regular partners with the company. I had a strong feeling I'd be assigned to their charter operations—and I was right. The 2018 draft class was temporarily housed at the Staybridge Suites in West Seneca, New York. My assignment was simple: pick them up, take them to practice at One Bills Drive, and bring them back. But nothing about meeting Josh Allen would be ordinary.

Where my path crossed with a Rising Star

I still remember that morning, even though the exact date escapes me. The hotel doors opened, and out walked Buffalo's highly anticipated first-round pick. This wasn't just another rookie. He was the embodiment of hope for a city starving for a championship. As he approached the bus, I called out, "Josh, you're the man!" He stopped, looked at my name tag, smiled, and fired back without missing a beat:

"No, Tommy—you're the man!"

We both laughed, exchanged a high-five, and just like that, the ice was broken. It was a small moment—but it told me everything. He was humble. Grounded. Respectful. Real.

The Seat of a Leader

From that day forward, Josh always sat in the front seat—directly across from me. It wasn't about comfort. It was instinct. Leaders sit where leaders belong. I never overwhelmed him with conversation. Young quarterbacks already carry enough weight on their shoulders. But one day, I did tell him what the fans were feeling. "Buffalo is excited, Josh. They believe in you." He didn't hesitate. "I'm going to give it my all to achieve that," he said. "Whatever it takes." There was no script in his voice. No performance. Just conviction. He meant it.

Becoming the Face of a Franchise

Over the years, his promise became reality. The raw tools were always there—the cannon arm, the mobility, the toughness. But now they were joined by refined accuracy, sharper decision-making, and a relentless competitive edge. By 2020, he delivered a breakout season that changed the league's perception of him and the Bills. By 2021, he had firmly established himself as one of the NFL's elite quarterbacks and the undisputed heartbeat of the team. I had the privilege of seeing the beginning—before the headlines, before the commercials, before the national spotlight fully arrived.

Character Above All

What impressed me most about Josh was never just the talent. It was the character. Quiet confidence. Genuine politeness. A respectfulness that spoke of strong values and a solid upbringing. Transporting him and that 2018 class wasn't just another assignment. It felt like watching the roots of something special take hold. It was the beginning of a cultural shift that would reshape the Buffalo Bills.

The Honor of the Assignment

Driving the future face of the franchise felt less like a job and more like having a front-row seat to history. Every mile carried anticipation. Every trip felt like the opening pages of a story still being written. Those early rides taught me something no statistic ever could:

- Josh Allen was built for Buffalo.
- And Buffalo was built for Josh Allen.

Transition: The Journey Continues

But my story with the Buffalo Bills didn't end with Josh Allen. His arrival was only the first chapter in a much larger narrative. Behind him stood:

- Visionary leadership

- Coaches who shaped the culture
- Front-office architects who built the roster
- Security teams, coordinators, and staff who kept the machine running

And in my world—behind the wheel—there were more relationships to build, more players to transport, and more unforgettable encounters with the people who make this franchise what it is. This was only the beginning. The next Bills chapter picks up right where this one leaves off—because the story of Josh Allen was just the doorway into my deeper journey inside Buffalo Bills football.

The Day My Body Said Stop

During that summer of 2018, I had the assignment of shuttling the Buffalo Bills rookies to practice at One Bills Drive. Josh Allen wasn't on board that day, but I do remember Tremaine Edmunds and Taron Johnson were. The rookies were staying at the Staybridge Suites in West Seneca, New York—about a five-mile drive to Highmark Stadium. A simple, routine run. Or so I thought.

As we approached the intersection of Slade Avenue and Ridge Road, something suddenly went wrong. My body began to overheat—fast. Then came the stomach cramps. Severe. Crippling. For the first time in my life, I was dehydrated, though I didn't know it yet. All I knew in that moment was this:

> **I would not risk driving any vehicle that could turn a medical emergency into a tragedy.**

I couldn't imagine the national—and even international—headlines if something had happened. But this one thing was certain: I wasn't about to risk becoming a headline. I secured the bus immediately. Instead of calling 911—which, in hindsight, probably should have been my first call—I called my boss, Dan Youhess, who could get to me faster than the fire department. My only thought was getting the team where they needed to go and getting them there safely. There was a female Buffalo Bills staff member on board that day. Her name was McKenzie. I'll never forget her. She stayed with me, calm and steady, helping me until the medical team arrived. I am forever grateful to her. Truly. Thank you, M… wherever you are.

By the time the ambulance arrived, Dan was already in the driver's seat, ready to take over. What happened next still moves me to this day. The rookies didn't leave. They stayed right there on the scene—and they prayed for me. Before the ambulance pulled away to take me to Mercy Hospital, I saw their faces. Concern. Respect. Sincerity. Once inside, the EMT started an IV, and almost immediately, I began to feel better.

I've thought about that day many times since. Not because it scared me—though it did. Not because it stopped me—because it didn't. But because it reminded me of something easy to forget when you've spent a lifetime being the one people depend on: Even the driver needs a driver sometimes. That summer of 2018 was the beginning of a new era for the Buffalo Bills. A new quarterback. A new core. New hope. I was there to help move it all from point A to point B, like always—quietly, reliably, in the background. But for one unexpected moment, I wasn't the one carrying the load. And the world didn't fall apart. A calm staffer stepped in. A bus full of rookies prayed. My boss took the wheel. The system worked—not because of one person, but because of all of us.

A few days later, I was back on the job—right back in the seat—transporting those same rookies again. When they saw me, they were genuinely happy. They told me they had been worried. They told me they were glad I was ok. And I could feel it. It wasn't polite concern. It was real. In this line of work, you spend your life taking care of other people—getting them where they need to go, making sure everything runs smoothly behind the scenes. That day, a team of young men—and a calm, professional staffer named McKenzie—took care of me. I will always remember it.

Braking only for Coffee

In 2017, I signed on with Niagara Scenic Tours. The interview was conducted by Dan Youhess, and to this day, it remains the fastest interview I've ever had that still ended with a job offer. Dan glanced over my résumé and nodded. It checked every box. Experience, credentials, professionalism—it was all there. But then he leaned back slightly, as if weighing one final thought. "I do have one concern," he said. "Our drivers seem to burn through brakes like it's part of the job description." I understood exactly what he meant. Anyone who's ever handled a motorcoach understands how the way you drive determines everything. Equipment doesn't wear out by accident; it wears out by habit.

So, I looked him square in the eye and said, "Sir, I don't brake for anything but coffee." For a moment, there was silence. Then came the laughter. Not just a chuckle—but the kind that tells you the message landed exactly where it needed to. Because behind the humor was discipline… experience… and a driver who understood the machine. Still smiling, he closed the interview with just a few words:

"See you on Monday."

And just like that—I was in. And from that day forward, I didn't just drive their buses—I preserved them. Dan Youhess was the embodiment of professionalism—sharp in appearance, precise in conduct, and deeply rooted in customer service excellence. Always well-groomed and dressed to impress, he never operated a bus without his signature blue blazer, name tag, and his tie, a symbol of the standard he lived by.

Dan believed that presentation spoke before words ever could, often reminding his drivers, *"Your blazer, name tag, and tie are just as important as your license."* To him, the role of a driver extended far beyond transportation—it was about representing the company with dignity, instilling confidence in every passenger, and upholding a culture of safety and pride. He took great care in developing operators who reflected those same values: disciplined, professional, and always well put together.

.

CHAPTER THIRTY-TWO

COACH SEAN MCDERMOTT

Early Life and Foundations

Sean Michael McDermott was born on March 21, 1974, in Omaha, Nebraska, before his family relocated to the suburbs of Philadelphia. They lived first in West Chester and Paoli, eventually settling in Lansdale while he was still in elementary school. He began high school at North Penn High School before transferring to La Salle College High School, where his athletic identity truly took shape.

As a defensive back, he earned All–Southeastern Pennsylvania honors in 1992 and graduated the following year. But football wasn't his only arena. McDermott was also a national prep champion wrestler in both 1992 and 1993—early evidence of the discipline, toughness, and competitive fire that would define his life.

Discipline on the field and in the classroom

McDermott carried that same standard to the College of William & Mary, where he majored in finance and became an all-conference safety in 1997. One of his teammates was a young defensive back named Mike Tomlin—two future NFL head coaches sharing the same secondary long before either knew where life would take them. Sean wasn't just committed to football. He earned Academic All-Conference honors in 1996 and 1997 and received NSCA Strength and Conditioning All-America recognition, proving that preparation, structure, and accountability weren't just coaching philosophies for him—they were personal standards.

A Coach in the Making

His NFL coaching journey began in 1999 with the Philadelphia Eagles as a scouting coordinator. Over the next decade, he climbed the ladder—defensive assistant, defensive backs coach, and eventually coordinator—helping to build consistently tough, disciplined defenses. In 2011, he took that identity to the Carolina Panthers as defensive coordinator. For six seasons, his units became some of the most feared in football, culminating in the Panthers' run to Super Bowl 50 during the 2015 season. By then, Sean McDermott's reputation was firmly established: detail-oriented, demanding, and deeply respected.

A New Era in Buffalo

In January 2017, the Buffalo Bills hired Sean McDermott as their head coach, marking a turning point for a franchise searching for stability, identity, and belief. What he brought was more than schemes. He brought a culture. Accountability. Toughness. Precision. Team-first discipline. Under his leadership, the Bills returned to consistent playoff relevance and, in 2020, captured the AFC East title for the first time in twenty-five years. By 2023, McDermott had taken on dual responsibilities as both head coach and defensive coordinator—another sign of how deeply he is wired to the craft.

The Day Buffalo Was Wounded

May 14, 2022, is a day this city will never forget. A white supremacist gunman entered the Tops Supermarket at 1275 Jefferson Avenue and opened fire on innocent shoppers. When it was over, ten precious lives were lost, and three others were critically wounded—most of the victims were African American. Among them was my childhood friend, Hayward "Boy Tenny" Patterson.

We grew up together on Riley Street, just one block from where the tragedy occurred. As kids, Hayward, my brother Gerald, and I formed a singing group called *Queen City Express*. Hayward's first-tenor voice carried shades of The Temptations' Eddie Kendricks and Earth, Wind & Fire's Philip Bailey—pure, soaring, special. Later in life, he became an ordained deacon and ran a jitney service, helping neighbors get to and from the very Tops Market where his life was taken. His priorities were simple and unshakable:

God.
Family.
Country.
Community.

The Bills Show Up

Four days later, on May 18, 2022, the Buffalo Bills organization came to Jefferson Avenue. Four buses were assigned to transport the team and staff from Highmark Stadium to the Frank E. Merriweather Library. I served as the lead operator. On my bus were Coach McDermott, several members of the coaching staff, and General Manager Brandon Beane. Coach sat in the front seat across from me, by the window. Next to him, in the aisle seat, was Chief of Security Chris Clark—someone I'd worked with many times by then. Even in that heavy moment, his greeting was warm and familiar.

Tight streets and a Human moment

The route took us along East Ferry, down Verplanck, across East Utica, and finally onto Welker Street. Maneuvering a 45-foot Prevost through those narrow residential streets caught Coach McDermott's attention. With a smile, he said, "Tommy, can you teach my kids how to drive?" Those were the first personal words he ever spoke to me. Without missing a beat, I replied, "Coach, I'd be happy to assist however possible." He smiled. And in that small exchange, I saw exactly who he is: observant, grounded, respectful, and appreciative of skill—no matter where it comes from. The man behind the headset.

A Ride, A Compliment, and a Perfect Punchline

Coach McDermott has a way about him. He genuinely enjoys conversation, and he carries a quiet, effortless sense of humor that makes time pass quickly and moments feel lighter. As we were riding back to One Bills Drive, he turned toward me and said, "Tommy, you're obviously not new to providing good service."

"Coach, I really appreciate that," I replied. "But I've driven for some of the most high-profile and influential people in the world, and I enjoy what I do. I've got one piece of memorabilia—a belt buckle Burt Reynolds gave me. Other than that, all I really have are good memories. And now I get to add one more. I can tell my grandchildren that I drove for the greatest coach in Buffalo Bills history."

Without missing a beat, he shot back, "You drove for Marv Levy?" The bus erupted. I laughed. He laughed. Everyone within earshot laughed. It was one of those perfect, unscripted moments—part compliment, part humility, part Buffalo—and exactly the kind of memory you don't need a souvenir to keep forever.

More than a Coach

That day wasn't about football. It was about presence. It was about leadership. It was about standing with a wounded city. And in that moment, I understood something clearly: Sean McDermott isn't just coaching a team. He's helping lead a community. Which is why what happened in 2026 felt so deeply wrong.

After the Denver Broncos eliminated the Buffalo Bills in the second round of the 2025 season playoffs, the organization made a decision that devastated Bills fans. They didn't just move on from a coach—they let go of a leader.

As Bills Mafia watched Coach McDermott leave Buffalo, I couldn't help but appreciate the privilege of having known him—not merely as a successful coach, but as a man whose leadership reached far beyond the football field. Coach McDermott, thank you for the wonderful memories. God bless you and your family.

CHAPTER THIRTY-THREE

2022 NFL SEASON

Another Rising Star in Buffalo

James Cook was born on September 25, 1999, in Miami, Florida, and grew up in one of the most competitive football environments in the country. As the younger brother of NFL star Dalvin Cook, he could have lived in someone else's shadow—but James chose to build his own name. At Miami Central High School, his speed and versatility made him one of the most sought-after recruits in the nation. He took that talent to the University of Georgia, where he developed into a dynamic, multi-dimensional weapon—part runner, part receiver, part matchup nightmare.

Across four seasons with the Bulldogs, he proved he could hurt defenses in more ways than one. And in 2021, he helped power Georgia to a College Football Playoff National Championship, cementing his place on the NFL radar. In 2022, the Buffalo Bills selected James Cook with the 63rd overall pick in the second round of the NFL Draft. Buffalo wasn't just getting a running back. They were getting speed. Versatility. And a champion's mindset.

From Rookie deal to Major Extension

James entered the league on a four-year rookie contract worth $5,832,057, including a $1,421,496 signing bonus. But his trajectory didn't take long to announce itself. By 2025, his production and growing importance to the offense positioned him for a major payday. That summer, he and the Bills agreed to a four-year, $48 million extension with $30 million guaranteed. The deal ended a brief "hold-in" and sent him right back to full participation. In today's NFL, there's a difference:

- **Holdout:** A player skips camp and risks fines to force a new deal.
- **Hold-in:** A player reports but limits participation as leverage.

James chose the professional route—present, respectful, and patient—while still standing up for his value.

Quiet Nature, Violent Running Style

Off the field, James Cook is calm. Soft-spoken. Almost reserved. He carries himself with a quiet, inward energy. On the field, that switch flips. Restraint becomes explosion. Stillness becomes acceleration. And defenders quickly learn that his running style is anything but gentle. He doesn't just run. He **detonates through space**.

First encounter with James Cook

During his rookie season, I had the privilege of transporting James and a group of rookies and hopefuls between their hotel and the Bills' training facility. It was warm outside, so I kept the bus set to a comfortable 70 degrees. The players loved it. James did not. Coming from Miami, he prefers heat. Real heat. The first time he boarded the bus, his arms weren't even in his sleeves—they were tucked inside his shirt, trying to stay warm. He walked up politely and said: "Sir, can you turn the AC down or off?" He wanted it off. But he said *down*—out of consideration for his teammates. That told me everything I needed to know. Respectful. Thoughtful. Quietly assertive. Even in something as small as adjusting the air conditioning, his character showed up.

A Beloved Member of Bills Mafia

It didn't take long for Buffalo to embrace him. Bills Mafia saw the speed. They felt the energy. They recognized the spark. Today, many fans hope James Cook remains in Buffalo for the long haul—and maybe, one day, even retires in red, white, and blue. From Miami heat to Buffalo snow, he fits here. And like so many before him, he's becoming part of the story of this city.

CHAPTER THIRTY-FOUR

THE INDIANAPOLIS COLTS

Welcome Home, Frank Reich

Frank Michael Reich Jr. was born on December 4, 1961, in Freeport, New York, but his story truly began in the football soil of Lebanon, Pennsylvania. Raised in a close-knit family grounded in faith, discipline, and humility, Frank learned early that leadership isn't about volume—it's about presence. His father, Frank Sr., a former center at Penn State, taught him the language of teamwork and quiet toughness. His mother, Pat, taught him steadiness and compassion—traits that would define him both on and off the field.

At Cedar Crest High School, Frank starred in both football and baseball. But it was at the University of Maryland where his name entered the history books. Playing behind future NFL quarterback Boomer Esiason taught him patience—how to wait, prepare, study, and stay ready for moments most people never see coming. That preparation produced one of the most legendary moments in college football history. In 1984, Frank led Maryland back from a 31-point deficit to defeat Miami 42–40—the greatest comeback in NCAA history at the time. It wouldn't be his last.

The Backup who became a Legend

In the 1985 NFL Draft, the Buffalo Bills selected Frank Reich in the third round. Though he spent most of his career as Jim Kelly's backup, Frank carried himself like a starter every day. He understood the assignment:

Stay ready.
Stay humble.
Stay supportive.

And when his moment came, he delivered something eternal. On January 3, 1993, with Jim Kelly injured and the Bills trailing the Houston Oilers 35–3, Frank stepped onto the field at Rich Stadium with calm, unshakable resolve. What followed became known simply as **"The Comeback."** The greatest comeback in NFL history. Frank didn't yell. He didn't panic. He led. The Bills won 41–38 in overtime, and a soft-spoken backup quarterback became part of Buffalo forever. That was Frank Reich:

Quiet.
Humble.
Unbreakable.

New Season, A Familiar Face

In 2022, I was assigned as a lead driver on several NFL charters. The first team I had the pleasure of driving that preseason was the Indianapolis Colts. The Bills had just opened the preseason with a road loss to Carolina and were returning home to face the Colts—now coached by a very familiar face, Frank Reich. It was also the first chance for Buffalo fans to see Ken Dorsey at work as offensive coordinator after Brian Daboll left to become head coach of the New York Giants. On the Colts' side, it marked the debut of former Falcons quarterback Matt Ryan in an Indianapolis uniform.

The details behind the Scenes

The silver lining for Buffalo was that Jonathan Taylor was sidelined, so at least no one had to relive his five-touchdown performance from the year before—though, of course, this was only preseason. On August 11, 2022, I spoke by phone with Paul Spall from Colts security—a true servant-hearted professional who goes out of his way to take care of people. We finalized the itinerary and coordinated pickup times. During preseason, teams often travel with nine or ten buses. Everything was set.

Welcome Home

On August 12, 2022, the Colts arrived at Buffalo Niagara International Airport. When Frank Reich stepped off the plane, I greeted him with three words that came naturally:

"Welcome home, Coach."

And I meant it. His place in Buffalo history was sealed long ago. We loaded up and headed to the hotel without a hitch.

A Quiet Moment of Gratitude

Coach Reich sat across from me on the bus. I took a moment to tell him how much those years—and those memories—meant to Buffalo. He smiled, warm and soft-spoken, and said: "Thank you. That means a lot. And it was certainly a lot of fun." That was Frank Reich.

The Closing of a Chapter

On August 13, 2022, the Bills defeated the Colts 27–24 in a well-played preseason game. Sadly, that season would not end the way Indianapolis hoped. After a 3–5–1 start, the Colts released Frank Reich. He had served as head coach from 2018 to 2022, and the team turned to former All-Pro lineman Jeff Saturday as interim head coach. After we dropped the Colts at the airport, we wished them well and watched them head home. And I couldn't help thinking about how life—and football—always has a way of bringing things full circle.

CHAPTER THIRTY-FIVE

THE DENVER BRONCOS

A Quarterback, A Bus, and a Lesson in Character

August 20, 2022, marked the second consecutive week the Buffalo Bills faced a familiar quarterback in a new uniform—and this one was a Super Bowl champion. Russell Wilson, longtime face of the Seattle Seahawks, arrived in Buffalo wearing Denver Broncos colors after a blockbuster offseason trade. Historically, the Bills' second home preseason game is "Family Day" at the stadium. With only three preseason games now on the schedule, it also served as the annual "dress rehearsal," when starters usually see meaningful first-half action. Buffalo made a statement that day, winning 42–15. But for me, the real story began before kickoff.

Working with Josh Bruning

My point of contact for the Broncos was Josh Bruning, the team's Director of Operations. Friendly, professional, and easy to work with, he made coordination smooth from the start. The Broncos touched down at Buffalo Niagara International Airport, and the players began boarding the buses. Some quarterbacks ride on Bus 2 or Bus 3. Not this one.

First encounter with Russell Wilson

I saw Russell Wilson coming down the plane's stairs and assumed he'd head to one of the other buses. Instead, he walked straight toward the lead bus. I met him halfway, took his bag, and said, "Mr. Wilson, welcome to Buffalo. Sir, it's an honor to drive for you and the Broncos." He smiled—warm, genuine—and replied, "Thank you. Glad to be here."

A Quarterback with Presence

Russell Wilson stands about 5'11"—not the biggest man in the room—but he carries himself like someone who has been there and done that. And he has. He owns a Super Bowl XLVIII ring, earned when the Seahawks defeated the Broncos 43–8. While linebacker Malcolm Smith won the MVP that night, Russell was the engine that drove that championship team. I placed his bag in the luggage bay as he boarded.

A Rare Seat Choice

Usually, the front seat across from the lead driver is reserved for the head coach—in this case, Nathaniel Hackett. But Russell Wilson took that seat. Since I began driving for the NFL, he remains the first and only quarterback to ever sit there. The ride to the hotel was smooth and uneventful. But what happened when we arrived—that's what stayed with me.

Meeting The Fans

As we pulled up to the hotel on Millersport Highway in Amherst, a small group of Broncos fans—many with their children—waited near the entrance, dressed in orange and blue, hoping for autographs. Russell was the first to step off my bus. Instead of heading straight inside, he walked over to the fans. He gave high-fives. He signed everything they handed him. He took his time. Meanwhile, his bag was still in the luggage bay. He could wait.

A Study in Contrast

I've seen plenty of stars step off buses and walk straight past fans—no wave, no nod, no acknowledgment. Fans call out their names, not even asking for autographs, and some players act as if they're invisible. Something as small as a wave would mean the world to those people. Russell Wilson showed what real gratitude looks like.

Russell Wilson's Quiet Class

He stayed with those fans until everyone had their moment. Only then did he come back to the bus, retrieve his bag, and say to me, "Thank you for the ride." I replied, "Russell, it's a pleasure to serve you. Sleep well. See you in the morning." If I handed out awards, he'd get this one:

“Most Grateful to the Twelfth Man.”

Game Day and Beyond

On game day, Russell was inactive as he continued learning the Broncos' system. Josh Johnson played the first half, and Brett Rypien took over the second. The following year, on November 13, 2023, Russell returned to Buffalo as the starter and led Denver to a 24–22 regular-season victory over the Bills. It was a pleasure serving the Denver Broncos. But more than that, it was a privilege seeing—up close—what true class looks like when nobody is forcing you to show it.

CHAPTER THIRTY-SIX

THE TENNESSEE TITANS

A Wave, a Night, and the Weight of the League

The 2022 NFL season opened with a statement. On September 8, the Buffalo Bills walked into Los Angeles and dismantled the defending champion Rams on Thursday Night Football. With the football world watching, Josh Allen delivered a masterclass in command and confidence, guiding Buffalo to a convincing 31–10 victory.

It was the kind of opening night that didn't just set expectations—it raised them. Less than two weeks later, Western New York buzzed again. On Monday Night Football, the Bills returned home for their 2022 opener, hosting the Tennessee Titans before a sold-out crowd at Highmark Stadium. I wasn't the lead driver that evening, but I was assigned to Bus 3—close enough to witness the rhythms, the personalities, and the quiet moments that unfold behind the scenes on game day.

A Wave that Caught me off Guard

Game days usually follow a familiar script—precise timing, controlled movement, professionalism at every turn. But that afternoon gave me a moment I didn't see coming. As the Titans exited their hotel, head coach Mike Vrabel stepped outside and paused before boarding the lead bus. Then he raised his hand and waved—directly at me. Standing beside my bus, I turned around instinctively, certain there had to be someone else behind me. There wasn't.

For a brief second, I even wondered—half-smiling to myself—whether he had received some word of knowledge from Providence that one day I might be his lead driver. I can't say. I called out, "Coach," and returned the wave. Vrabel nodded and boarded the bus as if it were the most natural exchange in the world.

In that small, unexpected moment, I saw him not just as an NFL head coach, but as someone approachable and genuine—grounded in presence, comfortable in his own skin. He struck me as the kind of leader who could serve as a role model for anyone striving to live with purpose, discipline, and clarity of direction.

A Long Night in Buffalo

Once the lights came on, the game turned brutally one-sided. The Bills overwhelmed the Titans 41–7. For Tennessee, it was a humbling night—one that echoed far beyond the final whistle. The loss proved to be part of a larger unraveling. The Titans closed the 2022 season at 7–10, followed by another difficult year in 2023, finishing 6–11. Eventually, the weight of expectations caught up with Mike Vrabel. Coaching at that level demands a resilience few can fully understand. The pressure is relentless. The margin for error is razor-thin. And yet, somehow, most of them find a way to land on their feet—carrying forward lessons learned the hard way.

The Quiet after the Storm

After the game, we made our final run to the airport. Goodbyes were exchanged—professional, respectful, understated. The Titans boarded their flight and headed home, leaving Buffalo behind along with the echoes of a long night. For me, it was another reminder that every NFL trip carries more than just players and equipment. It carries pride. Expectation. Disappointment. And the humanity of those who live through the highs and lows of the game. And sometimes, it carries something even smaller. A simple wave. The kind that stays with you long after the buses pull away.

CHAPTER THIRTY-SEVEN

THE PITTSBURGH STEELERS

MIKE TOMLIN

Built for Leadership

Mike Tomlin is one of the most respected figures in the National Football League—a coach known as much for his presence as for his results. He was born on March 15, 1972, in Hampton, Virginia, and attended Denbigh High School in nearby Newport News. He went on to play wide receiver at the College of William & Mary, where he earned a degree in sociology—an education that would later show up in the way he leads, communicates, and commands a room.

His coaching journey began in college football, with stops at VMI, Memphis, Arkansas State, Cincinnati, and the University of Minnesota. From there, he moved to the NFL, serving as defensive backs coach for the Tampa Bay Buccaneers and the Minnesota Vikings—quietly building a reputation as a teacher, a motivator, and a leader of men.

The standard in Pittsburgh

In 2007, Mike Tomlin became the head coach of the Pittsburgh Steelers. A year later, he became the youngest head coach in NFL history to win a Super Bowl, leading the Steelers to victory in Super Bowl XLIII. Since then, he has become the embodiment of the Steelers' standard: tough, disciplined, consistent, and accountable. Year after year, his teams compete. Year after year, his locker rooms hold together. Playoff appearances, division titles, and league-wide respect have followed. But more than any statistic, Tomlin is known for something harder to measure:

Presence.
Command.
Credibility.

A Difficult Afternoon in Buffalo

On October 9, 2022—Week 5 of the NFL season—the Pittsburgh Steelers came to Highmark Stadium to face the Buffalo Bills. It was a long, hard day for Pittsburgh. The Bills won decisively, 38–3. After the game, I was the lead bus operator assigned to take the team to the airport. Coach Tomlin sat quietly across from me. He wasn't angry. He wasn't animated. He wasn't making a show of anything. He just sat there—still, thoughtful, carrying the weight of the afternoon. You could almost see the film already running in his mind. The corrections. The adjustments. The responsibility.

The Man behind the Headset

In that quiet ride, what struck me wasn't frustration. It was composure. Even in defeat, Mike Tomlin carried himself with dignity and restraint. His presence was calm. His spirit, remarkably humble and reserved. That's leadership. Not just in winning. But in losing. And in everything that comes after.

A Final Thought

Driving NFL teams, you get used to seeing every side of the game. The joy. The celebration. The disappointment. The long, quiet rides that follow hard days. And sometimes, you get a front-row seat to what real leadership looks like when no one is giving a speech. Mike Tomlin didn't need to say a word. Everything was already being said.

CHAPTER THIRTY-EIGHT

THE MINNESOTA VIKINGS

The Wait, the Catch, and a Name You Don't Forget

Before their Sunday, November 13, 2022, meeting, the last time the Vikings and Bills faced each other in Buffalo was back in Week 3 of the 2018 season, when the Bills won 27–6. My point of contact for the Vikings was Chuck Petersen, Senior Manager of Team Operations and Liaison to Player Personnel. And let me tell you—personality-wise, there was no comparison. Chuck is a high-spirited, natural-born conversationalist. His connection to the Buffalo area immediately gave us something in common, and from the very first text messages days before the trip, I knew this assignment was going to run smoothly. In my book, Chuck Petersen was the biggest star on that team.

Saturday Pickup and Airport Coordination

On Saturday, November 12, 2022, I picked Chuck up at the team hotel. From there, we headed to the airport to meet the rest of my drivers and receive the team. Everything about the operation was routine—smooth, professional, exactly how you want these things to go. Head Coach Kevin O'Connell was seated across from me. We were loaded, ready to roll. Then Chuck said, "Hold on, Tommy. There's one more player still on the plane."

The Pause Everyone Felt

And just like that, everything stopped. We waited. The Vikings, of course, knew who it was. My team and I didn't. We started guessing. Was it Kirk Cousins? Dalvin Cook? Eric Kendricks? Whoever it was, he was taking his time.

The Arrival of Justin Jefferson

A moment later, a figure appeared in the doorway of the plane. For a second, he just stood there—almost like he was posing for a photo shoot. Casually dressed. Designer sunglasses. A thick rope chain—white gold, maybe even platinum—resting on his chest. Then he started down the steps. It was Justin Jefferson. He walked over and boarded Bus 2. Inside my own head, I said what any honest person would have said:

That dude is too cool.

Draft-Day Roots and Game-Day Greatness

Back in the 2020 NFL Draft, the Buffalo Bills traded their 22nd overall pick to the Minnesota Vikings for Stefon Diggs. With that pick, the Vikings selected LSU wide receiver Justin Jefferson. Looking back, Bills fans can admit that trade still stings a little. The biggest difference between Justin Jefferson and Stefon Diggs is attitude and demeanor—on the field, they're both absolute monsters. And on Sunday, November 13, 2022, Justin Jefferson made a catch that sealed a 33–30 overtime victory over the Bills. The sports world called it, **"The catch of the year."** Some called it, **"The game of the year."**

A Celebratory Send-Off

After the game, the ride to the airport was—understandably—a celebration for the Vikings. Later on, Chuck Petersen began giving other teams a heads-up before they came to Buffalo. The word going around was:

"Tommy is going to take good care of you guys."

Chuck, thank you for making it easy for us to serve you and the Minnesota Vikings. God bless you, and your wonderful family. And God bless the Minnesota Vikings.

CHAPTER THIRTY-NINE

THE CINCINNATI BENGALS

When Football Stopped Being the Point

On Sunday, January 8, 2023, the Buffalo Bills closed their regular season at Highmark Stadium with a 13–3 record and turned their attention toward the playoffs. But that season will always feel unfinished in one profound way. Six days earlier, on Monday night, January 2, 2023, the football world stood still. What was supposed to be a nationally televised showdown between the Buffalo Bills and the Cincinnati Bengals at Paycor Stadium suddenly became something far bigger than a game.

Early in the first quarter, Bills safety Damar Hamlin made a routine tackle on Bengals wide receiver Tee Higgins, stood up—and then collapsed. As medical personnel rushed onto the field and CPR was administered, shock rippled through the stadium and across living rooms around the world. It was horrifying. It was sobering. And for some of us, it was deeply personal.

I had the honor of meeting and driving for Damar during his rookie season after the Bills selected him in the sixth round of the 2021 NFL Draft. He struck me as intelligent, respectful, and thoughtful—one of those young men you root for without even realizing it. Watching him fight for his life on that field drove home a hard truth:

> Football, no matter how much it means, will always come second to life.

The NFL made the only decision it could. The game was canceled. And in that moment, the league showed the world that humanity still comes first.

All Business in Buffalo

Fast forward to January 22, 2023. The AFC Divisional Playoff. Bills vs. Bengals. This one would be played to the end. On January 19, I connected with Jeffery Brickner, the Bengals' Director of Team Operations. Our exchange was efficient, respectful, and straight to the point. His tone matched their mindset:

No chatter.
No drama.
Strictly business.

The Bengals required six buses. The airport transfer to the hotel was smooth, professional, and seamless. And just like their arrival, the game itself unfolded with unsettling efficiency—at least for Cincinnati. Buffalo weather is usually the great equalizer. Cold. Wind. Snow. It has humbled plenty of Southern teams over the years. Not this one. The Bengals played as if it were July. Calm. Composed. Surgical. The final score said everything: **Cincinnati 27. Buffalo 10.** Another brutal ending for Bills Mafia.

All Access and a Rare Moment

On this visit, the Bengals became the first team to grant us full **All Access** credentials—including access to the field itself. Opportunities like that are rare, and we knew it. I usually pride myself on restraint. No selfies. No fan moments. But even the most disciplined professionals slip once in a while. After snapping a photo of the legendary Peyton Manning and exchanging a quick high-five with him moments later, I allowed myself to get caught up in the moment. I found myself taking photos of Joe Burrow and several Bengals and Bills players as they exited the locker room, walked through the tunnel, and stepped onto the field. For a brief moment, I wasn't the seasoned professional. I was just a man standing inside a moment he knew he would never forget. Photographs from this visit are available for viewing on the Unveiling Press website at unveilingpress.com.

Quiet Confidence

What stood out most about the Cincinnati Bengals was their sameness—in the best possible way. No egos. No grandstanding. No one bigger than the team. Every player, coach, and staff member carried themselves with the same calm, respectful professionalism. As usual, the Bengals' dignitaries, coaches, and several offensive stars rode on my bus.

Driving for Head Coach Zac Taylor and his team was an absolute privilege. Their focus, discipline, and mutual respect were evident from start to finish. It was a loss for Buffalo. But it was also a masterclass in how professionals carry themselves—especially in heavy moments. As that caravan pulled away, one thought stayed with me: I hope I get the chance to serve this team again. Because moments like these—quiet, heavy, deeply human—are why this work matters.

CHAPTER FORTY

2023 NFL SEASON

THE BUFFALO BILLS' ROOKIES AND TRYOUTS

A Ride to the Edge of the Falls

Few experiences humble you as quickly as Niagara Falls. The roar. The mist. The reminder that nature is very much in charge. The Maid of the Mist captures that feeling perfectly. Operating on both sides of the border, the boats drift between the U.S. and Canada, momentarily blurring boundaries as passengers pull on blue ponchos on the American side and red ones on the Canadian side. On June 9, 2023, I had the privilege of transporting the Buffalo Bills' rookie class to Niagara Falls for that unforgettable ride. On board were Dalton Kincaid (TE, Round 1), O'Cyrus Torrence (OL, Round 2), Dorian Williams (LB, Round 3), Justin Shorter (WR, Round 5), Nick Broeker (OL, Round 7), Alex Austin (CB, Round 7), along with several others fighting for a chance to make the team. It was a rare day to exhale—a pause between expectations and reality.

Dalton Kincaid, Front and Center

Sitting directly across from me was Dalton Kincaid. I greeted him, welcomed him aboard, and as we pulled away from One Bills Drive—eyes forward, hands steady on the wheel—I couldn't resist having a little fun. "Now hear this, Mr. Kincaid," I said. "I'm a member of Bills Mafia, and on behalf of my constituents, we expect you to show Travis Kelce how to play football. Are you up for the task?" Without missing a beat—voice low, crisp, almost military—he replied:

"Yes, sir. I'll do my best."

That told me everything I needed to know. Dalton has a priceless personality—respectful, grounded, confident without being loud. Add in that bright smile and composed presence, and you quickly understand why a room notices him without him ever asking for the attention.

Behind the Wheel of the NFL

In 2022, Hadley Bos Fisher, President of Niagara Scenic Tours, secured the 2023 NFL transportation contract. As a result, I was appointed the official **lead driver for the NFL**. Most of the season ran smoothly—though no season at this level ever goes perfectly. There was one situation involving a star player and a staff member on one of our buses. I won't name names—that's not how professionals operate—but I reported the matter directly to the Director of Team Operations and trusted it would be handled internally. Moments like that remind you: no matter the level—professional, amateur, or youth—leaders must constantly reinforce standards, especially when teams are traveling in public spaces.

Visiting Teams, Neutral Ground

Although we regularly drive for the Buffalo Bills and their families, on home game days my drivers and I are assigned to the **visiting team**. On average, an NFL team requires six buses. That balance requires discipline. Loyalty stays in the heart. Professionalism stays on full display.

When Words Travel Further than Intended

One game day, while tailgating near the buses, one of my drivers—Niles Hardy, assigned to Bus 3—told me about something that bothered him. A star player from the visiting team had openly criticized not only the Bills, but the **city of Buffalo itself**. A woman on board—likely a staff member—went right along with it. Niles found it unnecessary and disrespectful. So did I. Trash talk comes with the territory. Criticizing the team? Fair game. But disrespecting the city? That crosses a line.

Wearing the Hat that Burns

There's a long-standing custom: when we drive for visiting teams, they provide us with their team hats—and out of respect, we wear them. Now, let me be honest. I'm a die-hard Bills fan. So are many of my drivers. Wearing the opposing team's hat feels almost sacrilegious. Like a vampire getting splashed with holy water mingled with garlic—it burns. But professionalism doesn't care about comfort. I wear the hat. And if a driver wants to be on my team, I expect the same. This job is about service. Period.

"Yo, what's that on your head?"

Almost every African American has a friend named Willie and a cousin named June Bug. During one Bills game, I heard someone yell, "Tommy!" I turned and saw Willie—an old friend—decked out head to toe in Bills gear. His eyes went straight to the hat. "Yo, bro," he said, "what's that crap on your head?" I laughed. "I'm the lead driver for the NFL today. I'm assigned to the visiting team. When I'm on duty, I wear their hat—out of respect." We caught up, shared a laugh, and went our separate ways.

Silence on the Ride Home

That day, the Bills handled business. The beating was decisive. The bus ride to the airport afterward? Quiet as a cemetery. Credit where it's due—Niles maintained his professionalism the entire time. A seasoned customer service agent knows when not to engage. The better course is to report the matter and let leadership handle it. That kind of restraint is professionalism at its finest. And in this line of work—whether you're behind the wheel or on the field—professionalism isn't optional. It's the standard.

CHAPTER FORTY-ONE

THE LAS VEGAS RAIDERS

The Class of the Silver and Black

The Buffalo Bills opened their 2023 regular season at home, hosting the Las Vegas Raiders—a franchise defined by tradition, pride, and an unmistakable sense of identity. For privacy reasons, I prefer not to disclose the last names of security personnel unless permission has been granted. With that in mind, on Thursday, September 14, 2023, I reached out by text to Derek Haithcock, Director of Football Operations for the Raiders. The goal was simple but essential: to establish contact and let him know we were ready—and honored—to serve the Raiders organization. Among seasoned customer service specialists and professional drivers, early communication is standard practice. A call or a text breaks the ice, sets expectations, and eases any pre-arrival tension. Our exchange was smooth and easy. Derek came across as genuine, grounded, and refreshingly humble.

Arrival In Buffalo

On Saturday, September 16, the Raiders arrived at Buffalo Niagara International Airport. Ordinarily, I would pick up the coordinator at the hotel or rental car location and head to the airport. On this occasion, Derek met us there. The Raiders required seven buses for their escorted motorcade to the team hotel.

I also had the pleasure of meeting Bob Stiriti, Vice President of Team Security, who rode on my bus along with members of the organization's leadership. Bob greeted us with an easy warmth, making everyone feel seen and respected the moment he spoke. His manners were impeccable, and his presence carried a natural professionalism that would immediately put anyone at ease. Even while we were moving through the organized chaos of arrivals, Bob stayed alert and attentive—always aware of what was happening around him and ready to step in when needed.

After the game, as the team prepared to board their flight home, we shared a lighthearted moment. I noticed the communications earpiece he was wearing and joked that he looked like a Secret Service agent. In response, he let out a low, playful lion's roar. It fit the Raiders perfectly—professional, confident, and fun. From top to bottom, this was an organization that carried itself with warmth and class.

Game Day Class

On Sunday, September 17, at 8:30 a.m., the Raiders did something we will never forget. Each driver was personally handed a hot breakfast—eggs, sausage, bacon, and home fries—delivered directly to the buses. When the catering team approached, we assumed the food was for the players. Instead, they gently placed the breakfasts on each driver's seat. Other teams have provided meals in the past. However, the Raiders were the only team that season to do it in such a personal and thoughtful way. That small gesture said everything. They didn't treat us like outside contractors. They treated us like family.

Inside the Raider Family

The Raiders integrated us seamlessly into their operation. We truly felt like part of the Raider family that weekend. Head Coach Josh McDaniels rode on my bus. He has a warm, approachable demeanor and an easy, genuine smile—someone comfortable leading with both authority and humility. On the field, the Bills earned a decisive 38–10 victory.

But football always has a way of circling back. In Week 5 of the 2025 season, McDaniels—then serving as Offensive Coordinator for the New England Patriots—returned to Highmark Stadium and delivered a narrow 23–20 victory over the Bills. And in the rematch in Week 14, the Bills returned the favor, defeating the Patriots 35–31 at Gillette Stadium. Call it poetic symmetry.

A Moment with Jimmy G

As the Raiders boarded the buses to head to the airport, I had a brief interaction with James "Jimmy G" Garoppolo, who boarded Bus Three. If he weren't an NFL quarterback, he could pass for a supermodel. He was wearing a sleek gray slim-fit suit, an open-collared white shirt, and polished black shoes—effortlessly sharp.

Typically, we offer to assist with luggage, though sometimes players prefer to handle it themselves. With only a two-day stay, they usually travel light.

I opened the cargo bay for him. "It's been a pleasure driving for the Raiders," I said. "I'm proud of you. Good luck the rest of the season. Go Raiders!" He smiled and replied, "Thank you. I appreciate that. And you guys did a great job." He placed his bag in the bay and boarded the bus. Class, both ways.

Mutual Respect

The Raiders roster reflected that same professionalism across the board—Josh Jacobs, Davante Adams, Jakobi Meyers, Hunter Renfrow, Maxx Crosby, and many others. When greeted, they greeted us right back. Respect was mutual. Consistent. And sincere.

Final Word

As always, we remained at the airport until the aircraft was airborne—wheels up—before departing ourselves. That's our standard. A few days later, on Thursday, September 21, 2023, the Raiders submitted their evaluation to Niagara Scenic Tours:

> "You guys were fantastic, and we could not have asked for a better group of drivers. Tommy was invaluable, and all drivers were polite and friendly to our team. We appreciate you all. We look forward to working with you in the future."
>
> Derek

It was a fitting close to a weekend defined by professionalism, appreciation, and genuine human connection. That was the Raider way.

CHAPTER FORTY-TWO

THE MIAMI DOLPHINS

A Rivalry, A Return, and the Quiet Work That Makes It Happen

Matchups between the Buffalo Bills and the Miami Dolphins have always carried extra weight. Since their first meeting in 1966, these AFC East rivals have faced each other twice every season—except when fate brings them together in the playoffs. The games are rarely simple, and they're rarely forgettable. The clash on Sunday, October 1, 2023, promised to be no different.

A Familiar Foe and a Fresh Resolve

The memory of Miami's heartbreaking 34–31 loss to Buffalo in the January 15, 2023, Wild Card game was still fresh. The Dolphins arrived in Buffalo determined to flip the script. During that playoff matchup, I had the privilege of serving as the lead driver for the Dolphins. That's when I first crossed paths with Nate Hammett, Miami's Senior Manager of Team Operations. Nate is precise and thorough in his expectations, yet his approachable, professional manner makes it easy to meet—and exceed—his requests.

Setting the Stage

On Monday, September 25, 2023, I reached out to Nate regarding the team's upcoming trip to Buffalo. The timing was perfect. Just one day earlier, Miami had delivered a historic 70–20 victory over the Denver Broncos, a performance that sent a jolt of energy through the entire league. I had no doubt he was riding high—and rightfully so.

Arrival Day Logistics

On Saturday, September 30, six buses were assigned to transport the Dolphins from the airport to the hotel. Despite several last-minute adjustments from Nate, our flexibility and adaptability ensured everything ran smoothly, as it always does. Unless instructed otherwise, the lead bus is staged at the aircraft's front door, while the remaining buses are positioned methodically at both the forward and rear exits. It's choreography more than chaos.

Brief Encounters, Lasting Impressions

As the Dolphins deplaned and made their way toward the buses, I was close enough to greet several players who were assigned to other motorcoaches: Tua Tagovailoa, Tyreek Hill, Jaylen Waddle, Raheem Mostert, Christian Wilkins, Zach Sieler, and others. Each acknowledged the greeting. Simple exchanges. Still meaningful.

Game Day in Buffalo

Once again, both on arrival and departure, Head Coach Mike McDaniel took the front seat directly across from me. On Sunday, October 1, 2023, the Miami Dolphins and the Buffalo Bills met at Highmark Stadium, with Buffalo earning a decisive 48–20 victory. Make no mistake—Miami is an outstanding football team. And it was a true pleasure serving them.

Professional Courtesy

Given their follow-up meeting on January 7, 2024, the possibility of a third encounter in the playoffs was very real. For the October 1 game, driver passes were not available. Even so, I want to extend my sincere appreciation to the Miami Dolphins organization for their professionalism, respect, and courtesy throughout the entire visit.

Leadership Behind the Scenes

I also want to recognize Bob Karmazyn, the Embassy hotel's General Manager, who hosted the Dolphins during their stay. In all my years in the hospitality industry, I've never seen a general manager personally assist bus drivers with parking logistics. That responsibility is almost always delegated to bell or valet staff—not the hotel's top executive. Bob's hands-on approach spoke volumes about his humility and leadership. It set a tone. And it set an example.

When The Work Gets Quiet

The buses, already lined up for departure, and the final logistics were checked off, the routine returned. Headcounts complete. Doors secured. Engines humming in unison. These moments are never loud or dramatic—but they matter just as much as kickoff. This is where preparation meets trust.

Another Chapter Closed

The Dolphins calmly boarded the buses—focused, professional, and already turning the page. Coach McDaniel took his seat once again, eyes forward. There were no speeches. No lingering gestures. Just a team moving on to what's next—as professionals always do. One by one, we rolled out of Highmark Stadium under the Buffalo sky and disappeared into the traffic.

At the airport, we exchanged final handshakes and quiet goodbyes. I wished Coach McDaniel, Nate, and the Dolphins staff safe travels and success the rest of the way. There were no speeches—just mutual respect, professional courtesy, and the unspoken understanding that our paths would likely cross again. Another assignment completed. Another chapter quietly closed. No headlines. No spotlight. Just the quiet satisfaction of a job done right. Because in this line of work, **consistency is the legacy**.

CHAPTER FORTY-THREE

THE NEW YORK GIANTS

Sunday Night Lights at Highmark Stadium

Sunday night, October 15, 2023, brought the Buffalo Bills back home beneath the bright lights of Highmark Stadium. Still shaking off a 25–20 loss to the Jacksonville Jaguars in London a week earlier, the Bills were eager to reset against the 1–4 New York Giants. But this game carried extra weight. On the opposite sideline stood Brian Daboll—former Bills offensive coordinator, now head coach of the Giants—returning to Buffalo for the first time since his departure. Familiar faces. New colors. And a little unfinished emotion in the air.

First Contact: Operations Before Kickoff

Three days earlier, on Thursday, October 12, I connected with Jeff Conroy, the Giants' Director of Operations. Our conversation was smooth and professional, setting the tone for the weekend ahead. On Saturday morning, October 14, I picked Jeff up at the team hotel and drove him to the airport to meet the arriving Giants. Once there, we joined the other buses already staged in position. As is standard when servicing an NFL team, all drivers assembled on Bus 1 for a pre-arrival briefing led by the Director of Team Operations. Precision. Clarity. Coordination. Everything in its place.

Organized Chaos on the Tarmac

When an NFL team steps off a plane, the scene is controlled chaos. Security fans out. Luggage crews spring into motion. Players move with purpose toward their assigned buses. In those moments, identifying who's who can feel nearly impossible. The Giants were staying at a hotel that held personal meaning for me—I had been part of its original staff when it first opened decades earlier. Some places never stop feeling like home. Most of the buses were done for the evening after drop-off. Mine wasn't. That night, I had the privilege of chauffeuring Coach Brian Daboll and several members of the Giants' staff to a steakhouse in Williamsville, New York. Quiet conversations. Relaxed smiles. A brief pause from the grind of game week.

Game Day Conversations and an Unexpected Cameo

Game day arrived crisp and cool—classic Buffalo football weather. While waiting for the Giants to board their buses for the trip to the stadium, I found myself talking with Erie County Sheriff Sergeant Warren Luick, our lead escort. We were discussing this very book when one of the Giants' security team members overheard us. "That sounds like quite an intriguing book," he said with a grin. I turned and replied, "Jim, it's going to be riveting—and I'd like to mention you in it. But for security reasons, I'll leave out your last name." Without hesitation, he laughed. "No, please include my full name!" Sergeant Luick and I shared a good laugh at his enthusiasm.

Kojak in a Giants Jacket

So here it is—a special shout-out to **Jim Ryan**, the Giants' Team Security Coordinator. With his resemblance to Telly Savalas and his easygoing humor, I couldn't resist calling him **Kojak**. Jim wore the nickname proudly, and it fit him perfectly. The Giants are fortunate to have someone of his character, humor, and professionalism watching over their team.

A Strange Game and a Familiar Face

The game itself felt strange. Much like the week before, the Bills struggled—but this time, they escaped with a 14–9 victory. Former Bills quarterback Tyrod Taylor started for the Giants, filling in for the injured Daniel Jones. After the game, Bus 3—operated by my colleague David Cercone—was parked parallel to mine near the tunnel. Tyrod, assigned to that bus, was about to board when I called out:

"T-Mobile!"

He stopped, smiled, walked over, and extended his hand. "Thanks for taking care of us," he said sincerely.

Respect, Style, and Gratitude

Tyrod carried the same quiet confidence he had during his time in Buffalo. He was dressed sharply—a beige sweater, brown pants and shoes, and neatly braided hair with an intricate, clean design. We thanked him for the excitement and memories he gave Bills fans during his years in Buffalo. He smiled warmly and said, "Thank you. It means a lot to hear you say that." As our conversation wrapped up, two chefs from Mission BBQ—the restaurant providing the Giants' postgame meal—approached Tyrod and asked for a photo. He happily agreed. Without a word, David noticed the moment. With a quick nod from me, he stepped in and took the photo on one of their phones. Unscripted. Genuine. Perfectly human.

One Last Ride into the Night

As is customary, the coaching staff and front office rode on the lead bus. Coach Daboll sat directly behind me. Once everyone was accounted for, our police escorts guided the convoy back to the airport. There was a mutual exchange of gratitude—not just for the gratuity, but for the professionalism, humor, and respect shared throughout the weekend. Before boarding their flight, Coach Daboll and several staff members thanked us once more. I wished them a safe trip home.

Moments later, the team passed through security, boarded the plane, and disappeared into the cool, calm October sky. Another chapter closed. And another reminder that even in the high-stakes world of professional football, it's the moments of kindness, respect, and simple human connection that linger the longest.

CHAPTER FORTY-FOUR

THE TAMPA BAY BUCCANEERS

A Short Week and a Long Road

Fresh off a tough 29–25 loss to the New England Patriots, the Buffalo Bills returned home looking to steady themselves. Waiting for them were the 3–3 Tampa Bay Buccaneers, arriving in Buffalo for a highly anticipated Thursday Night Football matchup. Short weeks in the NFL carry a special kind of tension. Everything moves faster, and the margin for error is thin.

On Monday, October 23, 2023, I reached out to Zach Orth, the Buccaneers' Senior Team Operations Coordinator. His response came almost instantly—energetic, sharp, and full of personality. From that very first exchange, I knew this assignment would be different. Zach has that rare mix of charisma and quick wit that turns routine logistics into memorable moments. His one-liners are legendary, and his presence alone can lift the energy in any room.

An Unusual Setup in Niagara Falls

This visit came with a twist. Downtown Buffalo had no hotel availability, forcing the Buccaneers to stay in Niagara Falls, New York—a major departure from the norm. For NFL teams, staying close to the stadium is standard practice. This time, the commute would be more than twice as long. When the Buccaneers landed on Wednesday, October 25, they touched down not at Buffalo Niagara International Airport, but at Niagara Falls International Airport—a rarity. Earlier in the season, only the Indianapolis Colts had used it, and that was for a preseason game. From the moment the plane arrived, you could feel this trip would carry its own rhythm—and its own challenges.

First Impressions Matter

I expected to pick Zach up at the hotel before heading to the airport. Instead, he met me there—nearly sprinting from a white SUV, smiling from ear to ear. I've met a lot of energetic personalities in this profession, but Zach's energy was different. It wasn't performative. It was genuine—the kind of authenticity that reminds you why human connection still matters more than schedules and spreadsheets.

As the team boarded the buses, I was introduced to **Andres Trescastro**, the Buccaneers' Director of Team Security Operations. If personality could be mirrored, Andres and Zach would be twins. Both brought an effortless blend of professionalism, warmth, and humor that made working with them feel natural from the start.

The Ride In—and a Rare Misstep

The owners and coaching staff rode on my bus, with Head Coach **Todd Bowles** seated across from me. Quarterback **Baker Mayfield** rode on the second bus. The ride itself was smooth—until we reached the hotel. A minor misstep had us entering the drop-off area backward. No damage. No injuries. But in our world, precision matters. I immediately apologized to Zach and later spoke with our lead escort, **Erie County Sheriff Sergeant Warren Luick**. This was the only time all season our timing slipped. Warren, as always, handled the situation with professionalism and cooperation. After sharing the blame, we moved forward.

Thursday Night Traffic Chaos

Game day—Thursday, October 26, 2023—arrived with gridlock across Western New York. Fans. Commuters. And a series of unexpected incidents turned the roads into a maze. The I-190 South, usually the fastest route, had been briefly closed due to a shooting and later slowed by two separate accidents. With only five buses, the margin for error was razor-thin.

Ben, driving Bus 6, made two trips from Niagara Falls to Highmark Stadium, with the second trip moving up unexpectedly. A request for an escort couldn't be fulfilled—approval rested solely with the team. What should have been a forty-minute drive stretched into a nerve-wracking **hour and forty minutes**. Every turn the wheels made felt heavier than the last. Still—through patience, communication, and coordination—we got it done.

A Close Game and Quiet Respect

On the field, the Bills prevailed 24–18. After the game, I crossed paths again with Andres Trescastro. Born in Cuba and now working on a book of his own, his story added another layer of depth to an already memorable visit. As the Buccaneers boarded the buses, I exchanged a brief word with Baker Mayfield. After a loss, words are often unnecessary—and sometimes best left unsaid. In moments like that, **respect speaks louder than conversation**.

The Final Ride Home

The return trip to the Niagara Falls International Airport carried its own tension. One Buccaneers owner, seated behind me, leaned forward, clearly frustrated. "Can we please stick to the speed limit?" he asked. Calmly, I explained the constraints placed on us by the escort vehicles, whose role is to guide us safely through traffic and intersections. Minutes later, we arrived. Before they departed, I wished Coach Todd Bowles—whom I regard as something of an NFL diplomat—and his team a safe journey home. Every member of the Buccaneers responded warmly. Zach, Andres, and I shared final goodbyes before they disappeared through security and into the night.

Final Thoughts

The drivers didn't receive game passes, but a generous gratuity and heartfelt thanks were more than enough. Logistics matter. Money matters. But memories matter more. Seeing a team operate behind the scenes—the laughter, the pressure, the professionalism—offers a rare glimpse into the human side of the NFL. To the Tampa Bay Buccaneers: Thank you for your respect, warmth, and for letting us share a small part of your journey. Best of luck as you continue your pursuit of another Super Bowl. You've earned every opportunity that comes your way.

CHAPTER FORTY-FIVE

THE DENVER BRONCOS

A Different Script Under the Lights

The last time the Buffalo Bills and the Denver Broncos met in Buffalo was Saturday, August 20, 2022—a preseason game that felt more like an introduction than a rivalry. Russell Wilson was on the Broncos' roster, but he didn't play. Instead, he stood on the sideline, learning a new playbook, wearing a new uniform, and quietly stepping into a new chapter of his career—his first season away from the Seattle Seahawks. That night at Highmark Stadium, the Bills dominated, cruising to a 42–15 victory. Fast-forward to Monday Night Football, November 13, 2023, and the story had completely flipped. This time, Russell Wilson wasn't watching—he was leading. And the Broncos would leave Buffalo with a narrow but decisive 24–22 win. Different night. Different script.

First Impressions and Familiar Energy

On Thursday, November 9, 2023, I met Josh Bruning, the Broncos' Director of Operations. From the very start, Josh carried himself with the same professionalism and approachability I've come to appreciate in the best operations people in the league—easy to talk to, thorough, respectful, and calm under pressure. Two days later, on Saturday evening at 6:45 p.m., I picked Josh up at the hotel and headed to the airport to meet our team of drivers. The ride was relaxed and upbeat—the kind of conversation that quietly sets the tone for everything that follows.

Arrival Night in Buffalo

At exactly 9:08 p.m., Atlas Air Flight 8248 touched down at Buffalo

Niagara International Airport. As the aircraft doors opened, players and staff descended the steps and began flowing toward the buses. In the middle of that controlled chaos stood Coach Sean Payton. I greeted him as he approached. "Welcome to Buffalo, Coach." He smiled and replied warmly, "Thank you. I'm glad to be here."

Moments later, Russell Wilson appeared—headphones on, music playing, calm and composed. He acknowledged me with a nod as he stowed his bag and boarded the bus. The year before, he had sat across from me. This time, he chose the seat directly behind me, with Coach Payton sitting across the aisle. That night, six buses carried the Broncos from the airport to the hotel. On game day, we'd add a seventh.

A Quiet Moment, A Lasting Impression

Sunday morning, five buses took the team to Highmark Stadium for a light practice. Afterward, as players filtered back to the buses, Russell Wilson lingered outside his bus, waiting for teammates. I took the opportunity to say something I'd been holding onto since the year before. "Russell," I said, "last year I saw something you did that really stood out to me." He looked at me, curious. "Which game?" I reminded him of that preseason night in Buffalo—how, while most players went straight inside the hotel, he stayed behind to sign autographs for a group of Broncos fans who had waited patiently. Without hesitation, he smiled and said, "I love my fans." Simple. Genuine. No performance. Just who he is.

Game Day Recognition

Monday, November 13, 2023, game day arrived. Russell Wilson stepped out of the hotel looking like he belonged on every front cover issue of GQ Magazine—black dress pants, black sport coat, polished black shoes, and a collarless white soft silk shirt. As drivers do, I was stationed at the door as players boarded. He stowed his bag, extended his hand, and said quietly:

"Hey, Tommy."

For a brief moment, I thought to myself, "Did that future Hall of Fame quarterback just say my name?" It was small. Personal. And unforgettable.

An Unusual Stay and A Respectful Farewell

Unlike most visiting teams, the Broncos didn't head straight to the airport after the game. They stayed in Buffalo until Tuesday afternoon, departing at 3:00 p.m. Their visit—from Saturday through Tuesday—was the longest stay by any NFL team in Buffalo that entire season. As the Broncos disembarked for the final time, we congratulated them on their victory, thanked them for allowing us to serve them, and expressed our appreciation for their generosity throughout the visit. Josh Bruning and his supervisor, Chip, returned the gratitude, thanking us for the hospitality.

And then, one by one, the Denver Broncos boarded their plane—lifted into the sky—and disappeared into the clouds…leaving behind another chapter in a season full of unforgettable moments. As their plane vanished into the gray Buffalo sky, I paused for a moment longer than usual. Not because the work wasn't done—but because moments like these remind me why I've stayed in this profession for so many years. Different teams. Different personalities. Different stories. Same responsibility. Same standard. And there was no time to linger. Another opponent was already on the schedule. Another chapter already waiting to be written. And in Buffalo, that next name always carries a little extra weight. The New York Jets were coming to town.

CHAPTER FORTY-SIX

THE NEW YORK JETS

A Rare Exception in a Season of Consistency

Sunday, November 19, 2023, marked the only time during the entire 2023 NFL season when Niagara Scenic Tours did not serve as the primary transportation provider for a visiting team in Buffalo. That weekend, the New York Jets arrived aboard Atlas Air Flight 5Y 8334, requiring seven motorcoaches for their operation. Because of a driver shortage, the carrier contracted by the Jets requested assistance. Niagara Scenic Tours stepped in to supply three of the seven buses.

I operated Bus 2 of 7. Ben Petryszak drove Bus 4. Mary Schumacher—our dispatcher and a member of our management team—operated Bus 5. The contracted carrier supplied the remaining four buses. Our role was simple but important: assist with the airport-to-hotel transfer. After that, our part of the operation was complete.

An Unprepared Leader

Over four decades in this business, I've worked with many skilled and dependable transportation leaders. But I had never encountered a lead driver as unprepared—or as unprofessional—as the one assigned to this charter. Out of respect and professional courtesy, I will not identify either the individual or the company. There had been rumors that the Jets demanded buses painted in green and white. That simply wasn't true. Niagara Scenic Tours' fleet is primarily royal and navy blue, and color was never the issue.

The real issue was hesitation—hesitation to fully move on from a long-standing relationship with their former motorcoach provider. On Thursday, November 16, I attempted to contact the assigned lead driver to coordinate logistics and confirm the plan. My goal was simple: align both companies, confirm the route, and ensure every driver had the same information. That conversation never happened. It was a missed opportunity—one that would soon create entirely avoidable problems.

Why NFL Charters Leave No Room for Guesswork

In NFL charters, planning is not optional. Communication is not optional. There is no room for improvisation. Earlier that season, Erie County Sheriff Sergeant Warren Luick and I had already agreed on the safest and most efficient route for this hotel drop. Despite my attempt to share this plan, the lead driver chose to disregard it. The unspoken message was clear: **Follow. Don't question**. But leadership requires more than being first in line. The lead driver never briefed his own team. I personally had to direct Bus 7—the equipment bus—into proper position at the airport. (For reference: team buses stage on the left side of the aircraft, the equipment bus on the right by the cargo bay. Once loaded, the equipment bus goes straight to the stadium while the others go to the hotel.) These are basics. And basics matter.

When One Wrong Turn Creates a Cascade

We left the airport smoothly—until we reached Goodell Street. The lead escort continued straight and turned right onto Edward Street. Three escort vehicles behind him went left, their job being to get out in front of the motorcade before it came down Delaware Avenue. The plan was clear. But the lead driver of the motorcade turned left instead of right. He followed the wrong escort. And the entire motorcade followed him. It was a costly mistake.

Shea's Performing Arts Center had just let out **Menopause The Musical**, and Pearl Street was suddenly choked with cars and pedestrians. Despite prior warnings about this exact scenario, the lead driver had ignored them. Now Erie County deputies had to step out of their vehicles and manually control traffic—clearly frustrated, but still professional. Despite everything, we delivered the New York Jets safely to their hotel. After a final inspection, I notified Mari Jo Kohler that everything was clear. We said our goodbyes and departed. But the lesson lingered.

A Lesson for Anyone in Customer Service

Teamwork isn't a slogan; it's the difference between chaos and coordination. I truly believe that the carrier's management would never have approved the lack of professionalism displayed that day. Niagara Scenic Tours was brought in to support the operation—not rescue it. I don't share this story to criticize. I share it to underline a truth: **preparation, communication, and teamwork are what keep people safe.**

Since then, that motorcoach company has permanently closed its doors. Leadership matters. And while no one is born with all the qualities of a great leader, they *can* be developed. A mature, well-seasoned leader strives to grow in:

- Adaptability
- Communication
- Accountability
- Approachability
- Conflict resolution
- Confidence balanced with humility
- Continuous learning
- Decisiveness
- Delegation
- Empathy
- Inclusiveness
- Integrity
- Problem-solving
- Vision
- And above all: **Team cooperation**

Growing Into the Qualities that Define Excellence

That season, I had hoped to drive for the Jets for three personal reasons: Garrett Wilson, Jeremy Ruckert, and Jalyn Holmes—all proud Ohio State Buckeyes, like my son. As it turned out, they were assigned to my bus. So was quarterback Zach Wilson. It was an honor to serve them.

The Jets opened the 2023 season with a dramatic overtime win over the Bills on September 11, 22–16. But on November 19, 2023, the Bills returned the favor with a decisive 32–6 victory. Looking ahead, my goal was simple: to do my part in helping Niagara Scenic Tours earn the Jets' full confidence—by showing, not telling, what true professionalism, preparation, and safety look like. Because in this business, excellence isn't promised. It's proven—one trip at a time.

CHAPTER FORTY-SEVEN

THE DALLAS COWBOYS

A High-Stakes December Showdown

On Sunday, December 17, 2023, the Dallas Cowboys arrived in Buffalo for a pivotal late-season matchup loaded with playoff implications. Both teams were riding emotional highs: the Cowboys were fresh off a commanding 33–13 victory over their archrivals, the Philadelphia Eagles, while the Buffalo Bills were surging after a dramatic 20–17 upset of the Kansas City Chiefs. Confidence was high. Momentum was real. And the stakes couldn't have been higher.

A Conflict of Schedules

Each year, our CEO, Mr. K. Fisher, hosts his annual Christmas party at his home—a special occasion I traditionally attend as a driver, shuttling family and friends between properties. This year, the party fell on Saturday, December 16—the same day the Cowboys were scheduled to arrive in Buffalo. Because of that commitment, I couldn't lead the arrival operation. Naturally, that caused some understandable anxiety for our dispatcher and driver-assignment coordinator, Mary Schumacher.

Not enough can be said about Mary. She is the complete package: dispatcher, over-the-road driver, NFL team fill-in, and master cook. She is steady under pressure, sharp in her judgment, and unmatched in her dedication to service. In my years at Niagara Scenic Tours, she is the best I've ever seen. It is both an honor and a joy to serve alongside her.

On game days, when our team tailgates, Mary elevates the moment with her homemade baked goods—lemon meringue pies, apple pie bars, and more. But beyond that, her professionalism is so trusted that her opinion could easily influence hiring and termination decisions. She is that respected. NFL assignments are highly coveted. Fairness in scheduling always matters. And when the usual lead operator is unavailable, it puts pressure on the whole system.

That's why I've long proposed creating four permanent backup operators trained directly under my supervision—so that no matter what, operations continue seamlessly. A true customer service specialist doesn't just perform well. He makes sure the next person is ready to perform just as well.

Choosing A Leader in My Absence

For the Cowboys' arrival, I recommended Operator David Cercone as lead driver. David is one of the most reliable and personable drivers in our fleet—professional, observant, and calm under pressure. We've worked closely for years, and I trusted him completely. On Tuesday, December 12, 2023, David reached out to the Cowboys' Director of Team Operations, Craig Glieber, and looped me into the text thread. Their exchange was smooth and professional—exactly how these things should be done. David informed Mr. Lieber that he would lead Saturday's airport-to-hotel operation and that I would resume my role as lead driver for game-day operations.

A Smooth Arrival

On Saturday, December 16, at 5:30 p.m., American Airlines Flight #9748 touched down in Buffalo carrying the Dallas Cowboys. David led the motorcade with precision. The team arrived safely and on time. Afterward, he called me to report that everything went smoothly and thanked me for the recommendation. David is a consummate professional. As a public-school teacher in Bradford, Pennsylvania, he brings exceptional communication skills and sound judgment under pressure—qualities that serve him just as well on the road as in the classroom. The next day, I resumed my duties.

A Personal Courtesy—And A Disqualification

That Sunday morning, I met Mr. Glieber in person—a distinguished, observant, and highly professional gentleman. Rain was in the forecast, so I brought an extra umbrella for him, just in case. He appreciated the gesture and made sure to return it before departure—a small exchange that says a lot about mutual respect.

As we prepared to depart for Highmark Stadium, one of the operators assigned to Bus 7 approached me with a question. After answering him, I noticed he wasn't wearing the Cowboys hat issued by Mr. Glieber. "Where's your hat?" I asked. "I'm a Bills fan. I don't do that," he replied. I had to be direct. "When we drive for NFL teams—including our own Buffalo Bills—we are not fans. We are professionals. This team is paying your salary today. Wearing the hat isn't mandatory, but it is a professional courtesy. If that's not acceptable to you, this will be your last NFL assignment under my leadership."

Unbeknownst to him, Mr. Glieber had overheard the exchange. After the driver walked away, I apologized and expressed my disappointment. Mr. Glieber nodded and said, "I'm impressed. I appreciate your high level of professionalism and the cooperation you expect from your drivers." I reported the incident to the company. The operator effectively disqualified himself from future NFL assignments.

Champions in Triumph and Defeat

Moments later, a ripple of excitement moved through the fans. Out walked Dak Prescott, followed by Stephon Gilmore and then CeeDee "Cedarian" Lamb. We exchanged nods and waves before they boarded Bus 2. But the afternoon belonged to Buffalo. The Bills dominated from start to finish, defeating the Cowboys 31–10. One team celebrated. One team absorbed the loss. But both organizations handled the moment with the dignity and composure befitting champions.

A Word About the Dallas Cowboys

What stood out to me most about the Dallas Cowboys was their kindness and respect from the moment they arrived. From head coach Mike McCarthy to the newest staff member, they carried themselves with professionalism and humility. No egos. No attitudes. Just good people who understood the value of treating others well. They reminded me that greatness isn't measured only in wins and losses—but in character. For that, I hold the Dallas Cowboys in the highest regard.

A Courteous Departure

After the game, we arrived at the airport. The Cowboys stepped off the buses, climbed the stairs to their aircraft, and prepared for departure. As they boarded, it felt as though they were riding off into a vast, open pasture of sky—heading home with our respect and our best wishes for a safe journey.

CHAPTER FORTY-EIGHT

THE NEW ENGLAND PATRIOTS

A Standard You Don't Forget

Sunday, December 31, 2023—Week 17 of the NFL season—brought the New England Patriots to Buffalo. It was also the first and only time I had the privilege of working with their Director of Operations, Alec Kerr. I didn't know then that it would be a one-time encounter, but I'm grateful it happened. Everything about Alec was warm, steady, and honorable. Some people extend a handshake that feels like a damp mop; others carry themselves with the quiet grace of royalty. Alec was the latter.

Young—perhaps the youngest Director of Operations I had ever met—he carried himself with the polish of a seasoned executive. When he stepped onto the bus at the hotel for our airport pickup, he was dressed in a sharp navy two-piece suit, crisp white shirt, red tie, and black shoes. He looked like a Wall Street investment banker on his way to close a major deal. But what stood out even more than his appearance was his demeanor. His professionalism, humility, and warm personality made him the complete package. Our communication leading up to the Patriots' arrival only reinforced that impression.

When Respect Goes Beyond the Itinerary

What struck me most about Alec Kerr was this: he was the only Director of Team Operations all season who personally texted me to let me know he and the team made it home safely. That small gesture says more about a person's character than any résumé ever could. The text thread from that week—one I'll always cherish, but never print—says it all: professional, respectful, and at times, even personal.

There was only one negative moment that weekend. Again, one of my drivers refused to wear the Patriots hat. I reported the issue to the company, and the operator was disqualified from future NFL assignments. I was beginning to wonder if someday I would have to drive all the buses at the same time. Even so, the charter itself went exceptionally well—and Alec made sure leadership knew it.

Alec Kerr's Email to the Company
Monday, January 1, 2024 – 11:57 AM
To: Hadley Bos-Fisher
Subject: Thank you!

Hadley,

I hope all is well and your New Year is off to a great start! I just wanted to send an email voicing
how great Tommy and his crew were this weekend. Tommy exemplified true professionalism throughout our trip. How he and his crew efficiently and effectively communicated on the fly did not go unnoticed.

All the best,

Alec

The company forwarded that email to every operator on the charter. The next day, January 2, 2024, I texted Alec:

"Good day, Alec!

The company shared your evaluation with the drivers. Thank you for taking the time to write such uplifting words. Your kindness is appreciated more than you know…

God bless!"

That weekend, the Buffalo Bills defeated the New England Patriots, 27–21. But the real victory for me had nothing to do with the scoreboard. It was the professionalism. The mutual respect. The simple human decency shared between two men just trying to do their jobs the right way. Alec Kerr left an impression I will never forget.

CHAPTER FORTY-NINE

THE PITTSBURGH STEELERS

JANUARY 15, 2024 — AFC Wild Card Game

The Storm That Changed Everything

The AFC Wild-Card showdown between the Buffalo Bills and the Pittsburgh Steelers on January 15, 2024, was destined to be unforgettable—but not only for what happened on the field. A massive winter storm barreled toward Buffalo that weekend, forcing the NFL to take a rare and unprecedented step: delaying a playoff game. On Saturday, January 13, after consulting with the Bills organization, New York State officials, and Erie County authorities, the league rescheduled the matchup—originally set for Sunday at 1:00 p.m.—to Monday at 4:30 p.m.

Governor Kathy Hochul confirmed the decision at a Buffalo press conference, explaining that she had spoken directly with NFL Commissioner Roger Goodell about the dangerous conditions. "Given the hazardous weather expected this weekend," she said, "we've worked closely with emergency crews, Bills' leadership, and the NFL to reschedule the game." Meteorologists warned of heavy lake-effect snow, sustained winds of 20–30 mph, and gusts approaching 50 mph. Travel for the 70,000 fans headed to Highmark Stadium would be perilous. And the memory of the deadly Christmas 2022 blizzard—one that claimed 47 lives—hung over every decision.

Preparations and Tough Calls

Governor Hochul declared a state of emergency, activated the National Guard, and deployed utility crews for the anticipated outages. A travel advisory took effect at 9 a.m. Saturday, followed by a full travel ban at 9 p.m. The Steelers, anticipating complications, adjusted their plans and moved their flight to Sunday instead of Saturday. There was even a brief discussion of relocating the game to a neutral site—Mercedes-Benz Stadium in Atlanta—but the Governor successfully argued for a one-day delay instead. Had the Steelers remained on their original schedule, their Saturday arrival would have been routine. But their new Sunday itinerary placed my drivers and me directly in the path of the storm's peak fury.

The Drive into the Heart of the Storm

Normally, the drive from my home to work takes 20–25 minutes. That day, knowing the magnitude of what lay ahead, I left two hours early. The weather near my home was manageable, but as I approached downtown Buffalo, conditions deteriorated quickly. I urged my drivers to do the same—leave early, go slow, and stay safe.

Pittsburgh had reserved six buses for their visit, but one of my drivers, Niles Hardy, was completely snowed in. With no replacements available, we rolled with five. From Buffalo to Hamburg—where Niagara Scenic Tours is headquartered at 5175 Southwestern Boulevard—the storm intensified. Road closures were mounting by the hour.

Route Closures and a Police Assist

The Skyway, Buffalo's elevated route to the Southtowns, was closed—as it always is in severe weather. My alternate route via Ohio Street was also shut down. A Buffalo police officer stationed there listened as I explained why I was traveling during the ban. Instead of turning me away or issuing me a citation, he offered a lifeline:

"Try South Park Avenue."

Traffic was heavy, but I knew that if I could reach Lake Avenue, I could reconnect with Route 5—the same route Ohio Street would have carried me to. What I didn't know was that the most dangerous moment of my day was still ahead.

The Near-Miss at the Guardrail

As I crept along Route 5, the storm unleashed its full fury. Blinding snow. Howling winds. Visibility near zero. The snowbanks carved by plows were my only guides. Then, near the Ford Stamping Plant, my vehicle suddenly came to a dead stop. I tried rocking it free—reverse, drive, reverse—but the wheels spun uselessly. Thinking I was buried in a drift, I stepped into the storm to investigate. To my surprise, there was barely any snow buildup at all. I walked to the front—and felt a jolt of fear.

In the whiteout, I had drifted and wedged the front end of my vehicle against the guardrail. If not for that guardrail, I would have slid down the embankment to the lower roadway. A chill ran through me that had nothing to do with the temperature. Carefully, I backed off the rail, corrected my alignment, and crept forward—moving only during the brief moments when the wind paused and visibility returned. When I finally reached the yard, relief washed over me. All my remaining drivers had made it—except the one still buried at home. Now came the pressing question:

> **How do you pick up the Pittsburgh Steelers in a blizzard like this?**

The Rescue Convoy: Plows, Police, And Purpose

The answer: with flashing lights, roaring engines, and teamwork. We were joined by the New York State Highway Authority and our trusted Erie County Sheriff escorts assigned to NFL operations. The Highway Authority dispatched three massive snowplows to guide us from the yard to the airport. Following their illuminated blades through the swirling whiteout made the impossible feel almost effortless. Kudos to the New York State Highway Authority. Thank you for your service.

Once the team boarded the buses, those same plows and police escorts led our convoy safely to the Steelers' downtown hotel. Despite the chaos outside, the mood on the bus was relaxed and upbeat.

A Moment with Coach Mike Tomlin

The winner of the Bills–Steelers game would advance to the next round in Baltimore. Coach Mike Tomlin, seated just to my right, radiated confidence. "Shit, we should be playing this game today," he said with a grin. "By next week, we'll be on our way to Baltimore!" The staff nearby laughed in agreement. Outwardly, I stayed composed. Inwardly, I thought, "Coach…first of all, you talk just like we did in the hood. And secondly, regarding Baltimore, have you forgotten your last visit to Buffalo? 38–3." It was playful, competitive banter—the kind that keeps football alive even in the middle of a blizzard.

But what struck me most was how naturally Mike Tomlin moved between worlds. One moment, he could speak with the rhythm and grit of the streets, and the next rise effortlessly into the realm of statesmen—comfortable in rooms where leaders and kings sit. His authenticity wasn't crafted. It was lived.

And I respected him for it. After the hotel drop-off, the plows escorted us back to the garage. We thanked them, and they saluted before disappearing once more into the storm.

Game Day: Buffalo's Answer

The next day, under the bright lights of Highmark Stadium—and with mountains of snow piled throughout Orchard Park—the Bills delivered their reply: **Buffalo 31. Pittsburgh 17.** After the game, we transported the Steelers back to the airport, wished them a safe flight, and said our goodbyes. Buffalo was headed to Baltimore.

A Weekend I'll Never Forget

Another storm had passed. The roads were clear again. But that weekend wasn't just about football. It was about endurance. It was about judgment. It was about the razor-thin line between chaos and control. January 15, 2024, wasn't merely a playoff game. It was a test of resilience—Buffalo's, mine, and everyone involved. A storm I'll never forget. A game I'll always remember.

CHAPTER FIFTY

THE KANSAS CITY CHIEFS

The 2024 AFC Championship Visit to Buffalo

The road to Super Bowl LVIII ran straight through Orchard Park. For the Buffalo Bills and the Kansas City Chiefs, no stage could have been heavier with history, heartache, and consequence. After years of near-misses, unforgettable duels, and playoff drama that had rewritten NFL folklore, the league's most compelling modern rivalry returned to center stage—this time with a Super Bowl berth on the line.

Kansas City arrived carrying both the burden and the confidence of a dynasty. With Patrick Mahomes commanding the huddle, Andy Reid orchestrating every detail, and veterans like Travis Kelce and Chris Jones anchoring a battle-tested core, the Chiefs were built for January. Cold weather. Hostile environments. Deafening crowds. Crushing pressure. This is where they had lived—and thrived. But Buffalo was no longer the same team from prior showdowns. With a recalibrated roster, a locked-in Josh Allen, and a defense rising to every challenge, the Bills stood one win away from their first Super Bowl appearance since the early 1990s.

Highmark Stadium—already famous for its seismic noise—was ready to become something even more ferocious. The storylines were irresistible. Mahomes vs. Allen—the defining quarterback rivalry of a generation. Andy Reid was returning to Buffalo—the city where his coaching journey began. Sean McDermott aimed for the breakthrough Bills fans had long believed was overdue. Both teams were built for moments like this. Explosive offenses. Punishing defenses. Coaching staffs that treat game planning like chess.

Every possession would matter. Every mistake would tilt the emotional balance of an entire region. This wasn't just a game. It was legacy versus legacy. Heartbreak versus redemption. On Championship Weekend, all roads led to

Buffalo. The weather was fierce. The crowd was volcanic. And the stakes were as historic as they come.

A Buffalo Connection Inside a Championship Organization

My point of contact with the Chiefs was Mitch Reynolds—a man whose résumé speaks for itself. With a long history in football operations—team travel, logistics, scheduling, and training camp management—Mitch joined the Chiefs in 2011 after working multiple training camps and a season with the Buffalo Bills. Over time, he rose to Senior Director of Team Operations, becoming Kansas City's primary contact for multiple Super Bowls and international games. Twice, he was honored as **NFL Travel Director of the Year** (2013 and 2017).

Early that week, I sent Mitch a text introducing myself and assuring him that the Chiefs would receive the highest level of professionalism, safety, and service during their stay in Buffalo. His response was soft, courteous, and warm—so much so that I genuinely looked forward to meeting him in person. Through our exchange, we finalized Kansas City's itinerary.

Two Buffalo Natives, One Instant Bond

I picked Mitch up at the hotel for the short trip to the airport. Because we had already built rapport through text, our first in-person meeting felt natural—relaxed, genuine, unforced. These drives are often where I learn about an operations lead—and where they learn a little about me. What I didn't expect was the immediate connection that formed the moment Mitch told me he was a native of **Elma, New York**, just minutes outside Buffalo.

I'm a Buffalo man myself, born and raised, and that shared hometown thread stitched the conversation together instantly. No ego. No pretense. Just two men cut from the same cloth. Though Mitch had booked a hotel room for professional reasons, he chose instead to stay at his parents' home in **Boston, New York**, also just minutes from Buffalo.

That detail spoke volumes. Here was a man operating at the highest level of the NFL—yet still grounded, family-centered, and anchored to the place where his story began. He also had connections to two respected regional universities: **Canisius and Cortland**. Learning that only deepened our sense of shared identity. In this business, I meet everyone from rookies to Hall of Famers. But people like Mitch Reynolds stand out—not because of titles, but because of heart.

A Championship Team Touches Down in Buffalo

On Saturday, January 20, 2024, United Flight #2543 touched down in

Buffalo. This would mark the first time Patrick Mahomes and the Chiefs played in Buffalo against Josh Allen in the postseason—a moment NFL fans had anticipated for years. As the players stepped off the plane, Coach **Andy Reid** immediately stood out. What a privilege it was to drive for him. Reid is everything people say he is: humble, soft-spoken, gracious, and radiating calm. His presence alone settles the chaos of a championship weekend.

"Welcome to Buffalo, Coach," I said. "It's a pleasure to be here. Thank you," he replied—sincere as always. Moments later came Mahomes, Kelce, and Isiah Pacheco. Kelce responded warmly. Pacheco nodded respectfully. Mahomes didn't respond. For a moment, a thought crossed my mind, "Is this some lingering echo of the 2017 draft trade that sent Buffalo's pick to Kansas City and eventually set both franchises on their current paths?"

I dismissed it immediately. This was playoff football. Mahomes was locked in. Focused. Blocking out everything that wasn't the mission. Once the bags were loaded, we headed for the hotel. The weather wasn't cooperative, but we made the trip safely—another quiet testament to preparation and professionalism on both sides.

A Bitter Ending for Buffalo

The AFC Championship was unforgiving. The temperature dropped. The wind tightened. And Buffalo's season ended in heartbreak: **27–24**. With 2:51 remaining, the Bills had the ball at Kansas City's 27-yard line. Three plays later, with everything on the line, Tyler Bass attempted a 44-yard field goal to tie the game. He missed. For many fans, the pain rivaled the wound of the infamous "13 seconds" game. Once again, Kansas City found a way. And once again, Buffalo was left with questions and heartache.

Two Handshakes, One Hug, and a Flight into the Clouds

After the game, the ride to the airport felt like a quiet decompression from the intensity of the night. At the terminal, Coach Reid and I exchanged a firm, respectful handshake. Mitch and I shared a warm, brotherly hug—two Buffalo men who had crossed paths through football, professionalism, and mutual respect. I wished them well and a safe journey home. Moments later, their aircraft lifted into the winter clouds—carrying a championship-bound team toward the next chapter of its legacy.

CHAPTER FIFTY-ONE

2023 OPERATOR OF THE YEAR

A Day I'll Never Forget

On Wednesday, December 13, 2023, our company held its annual safety meeting and luncheon. I couldn't be there in person because I was on the road, so I joined by Zoom—listening in from the driver's seat between assignments. That day, Buffalo City Hall—led by the one and only Annette Reid—had booked a trip to the Toronto Eaton Centre. And if you know Annette, you already know that trip was going to run like a military operation mixed with a comedy show.

Annette is the most no-nonsense, straight-shooting, and unintentionally hilarious group leader you could ever serve. She tells her passengers, "If you're not on the bus when it's time to pull out, plan to get home by Uber," and she doesn't blink when she says it. And trust me—she means it.

In the middle of that busy day, as I listened through the Zoom session, the company announced the very first **Operator of the Year Award**. And then they called my name. As I move into the later chapters of my career, being selected as the inaugural recipient of such a meaningful honor felt like a full-circle blessing. It was humbling. It was emotional. And I remain forever grateful. Among other keepsakes, Niagara Scenic Tours presented me with a blazer embroidered:

"Niagara Scenic Tours — 2023 Operator of the Year."

I want to sincerely thank all my fellow operators for your vote. I wish there was a way we could share this award, because every one of you is just as deserving. This job has never been about one person. It's about early mornings and long nights. It's about watching out for each other. It's about taking pride in doing things right—even when nobody's watching. If my name is on this award, it's only because I stand on the shoulders of great teammates.

TRAVEL NFL PARTNER OF THE YEAR PROGRAM

What It Really Means

The phrase "NFL Travel Partner Program" isn't one single, official program. It's an ecosystem—a network of trusted partners who keep both fan travel and team logistics moving smoothly. Companies like **On Location** design premium, officially licensed travel experiences. NFL teams rely on airlines, hotel chains, ground transportation providers, and in some cases, team-owned aircraft. Some organizations—like the New England Patriots—even fly on their own branded planes. Together, these partners form the unseen backbone of the NFL travel world—making sure fans have unforgettable experiences and teams move with precision, safety, and reliability.

A Moment of Honor: 2023 Travel Partner of the Year Nomination

As the 2023 season drew to a close, I received a recognition that caught me completely off guard, a nomination **for Travel Partner of the Year**. In a world where excellence is often measured by numbers and trophies, this one touched me differently. It represented the unseen miles—the dawn departures, the late-night airport runs. The quiet moments of getting every detail right. To be nominated by the very teams and professionals I serve was more than an honor—it was a reminder that consistency and humility never go unnoticed. I wasn't chasing applause. But somehow, it found me. The nominees (listed alphabetically) were:

- ATLAS AIR
- Bill Harpole, Transportation Charter Management
- Bill Thompson, Grey Line of Tennessee
- Charter Pro
- Danielle Derkacz, Marriott International
- Dingman Group
- Echo AFC Transportation
- Gold Coast Tours
- Gretchen Wiseman, Seattle Marriott Bellevue
- Julie Spaziano, The Westin Philadelphia
- Lindsay Kittrell, Marriott International
- Matt Goldberg, Delta Airlines

- Maya Rhodes, Marriott International
- Micaela Ward, Royal Coach Tours
- Nichole Quinn, Detroit Troy Marriott
- Rebecca Donahue, The Westin Philadelphia
- Storer Coachways
- **Tommy Seay, Niagara Scenic Tours**
- United Airlines
- Virgin Airlines

Seen, Trusted, And Grateful

To all the Directors of Team Operations and coaches who nominated me—thank you. When I first started as a motorcoach operator, I never imagined something like this. I just tried to do things the right way—even when no one was keeping score. Thank you for the conversations we shared on the way to the airport, the hotel, and the stadium. Those moments—brief as they were—meant more than you know. What touches me most is this:

> You saw me.
> Not just as a driver.
> Not just as logistics.
> But as a person.

You saw the care. The preparation. The consistency. The pride. This recognition doesn't belong to me alone. It belongs to every early morning, every late night, every careful mile, and every quiet responsibility that comes with doing this job right. Over the years, I've learned this work is about more than transportation. It's about **trust**. And for a short while, I get to be part of some of the most important days in people's lives.

Gratitude to Those Who Paved the Way

No one gets here alone. I think about the leaders who sharpened me, the dispatchers who trusted me, the mechanics who kept my wheels turning, and the passengers who shared stories, laughter, and silence along the way. Every mile taught me something. Every team shaped me. Every year prepared me. These honors belong to everyone who walked even a small part of this road with me.

The Road Ahead

As I approach the closing stretch of my career, I don't see these recognitions as a finale. I see them as **confirmation**. That the work mattered. That the journey meant something. That there is still purpose in every mile I have left to drive. If anything, they inspire me to finish even stronger—with more patience, more humility, more gratitude, and more of that **Priority One** mindset I've carried since the first day I put on a uniform. Because at the end of the day—whether you're transporting dignitaries, NFL teams, or a bus full of schoolchildren—the mission is always the same:

> **Give people your best.**
> **Treat them with dignity.**
> **Send them home with a good story to tell.**

CHAPTER FIFTY-TWO

2024 NFL SEASON

ROOKIES AND TRYOUTS

Arrival: Stars in the Making

The 2024 rookie class and the Buffalo Bills' tryout players felt different from every group that came before them. By far, they were the most personable—open, respectful, and genuinely appreciative of every moment. On Thursday morning, May 9, 2024, at exactly 10:15 a.m., I pulled into Buffalo Niagara International Airport to greet these young men—stars in the making—ready to be transported to the Bills Training Center. You could feel it immediately. There was excitement in the air, but also humility. These players knew nothing was guaranteed. Every rep, every interaction, every impression mattered.

Off The Field: Bowling Night in West Seneca

After practice on May 17, 2024, I had the pleasure of driving the rookies and tryout players to Strikers Lanes on Michael Road in West Seneca. It was a rare chance to see who they were away from the field—no pads, no playbooks, just competition, laughter, and camaraderie. What followed surprised me. Many of these young men could really bowl.

Especially cornerback **Keni-H Lovely**, whose bowling ball stuck the pins with such force it felt like the lanes were under attack. Strike after strike—the pins didn't stand a chance. Watching them relax, joke, and compete revealed something special: chemistry, confidence, and character.

The Draft Picks

Among those in attendance were the Bills' 2024 draft selections:

• Keon Coleman, WR – Florida State (Round 2, No. 33 overall)
• Cole Bishop, S – Utah (Round 2, No. 60)
• DeWayne Carter, DT – Duke (Round 3, No. 95)
• Ray Davis, RB – Kentucky (Round 4, No. 128)
• Sedrick Van Pran-Granger, C/G – Georgia (Round 5, No. 141)
• Edefuan Ulofoshio, LB – Washington (Round 5, No. 160)
• Javon Solomon, DE – Troy (Round 5, No. 168)
• Tylan Grable, T – UCF (Round 6, No. 204)
• Daequan Hardy, CB – Penn State (Round 6, No. 219)
• Travis Clayton, G – International Player Pathway (Round 7, No. 221)
Each carried themselves with professionalism well beyond their years.

The Tryouts and the Hopefuls

Also present were the minicamp tryouts and free agents—players fighting for a dream. Some were local. Some came from far away. All were hungry. Syracuse. Buffalo. Kansas. Clemson. Troy. Pittsburgh. Boston College. Monmouth. Rutgers. Arkansas. Even pro lacrosse backgrounds were represented. Then there were the undrafted free agents—including names that already carried weight, like **Frank Gore Jr.**—each one chasing the same opportunity, hoping this moment would change everything.

Faith, Family, And Character: Xavier Johnson

One player, in particular, stood out to me: **Xavier Johnson**, wide receiver. Yes—he's an Ohio State Buckeye, which already earned him points with me. But what truly impressed me was his faith, his manners, and the quiet strength he carried with him. You could tell immediately that his upbringing mattered—that talent alone wasn't what shaped him. Xavier is also a close friend of fellow Buckeye **Jalin Marshall**, a 2016 undrafted free agent with the New York Jets. Jalin once trained our grandson, **Jayden**, in Cincinnati—training that ultimately helped him earn a full scholarship to **West Point**.

In December 2025, Army Head Coach **Jeff Monken** flew to Ohio to spend time with Jayden and the family at the house. Life has a funny way of connecting dots. I was disappointed when the Bills released Xavier, but grateful when the **Houston Texans** gave him another opportunity. That's the NFL. Doors close. Others open. And character determines what happens next.

A Small Gesture, A Big Meaning

That evening, there was pizza and chicken wings laid out for the players. Without hesitation, they invited me to help myself. It was a small gesture—but it spoke volumes. Respect goes both ways. And these young men understood that.

A Surprise Assignment: Coach McDermott

On May 31, 2024, I was assigned to transport what I assumed would be players to **Houghton University**. Instead, **Coach Sean McDermott** walked toward the bus—followed by his entire coaching staff. As he approached, I said, "Coach, this is my second time driving for you." He stopped and smiled. "When was the first?" "When I drove you and the team down Jefferson Avenue after the Tops Market mass shooting," I said. "You asked me if I would teach your kids how to drive." We both burst out laughing. He shook my hand and stepped onto the bus.

Closing: Service, Pride, and the Buffalo Way

Moments like that remind me why this work matters. It's always an honor—and a joy—to drive for the Buffalo Bills. Through triumph, tragedy, rookies, veterans, and coaches alike, we'll always be there when they call. That's the Buffalo way.

CHAPTER FIFTY-THREE

THE ARIZONA CARDINALS

A First-Class Arrival

In the modern NFL, only two franchises operate their own private aircraft: the New England Patriots and the Arizona Cardinals. The Patriots fly two Boeing 767-300ERs. The Cardinals travel aboard a Boeing 777-200ER—a flying statement of preparation, precision, and organizational pride.

I paused to take a snapshot. During the opening week of the 2024 season, construction on the runway at Buffalo Niagara International Airport required a logistical pivot. As a result, the Arizona Cardinals—along with the Jacksonville Jaguars—used Niagara Falls International Airport for both arrival and departure. It was a small change on paper, but one that required flawless execution behind the scenes.

Setting the Tone

On Tuesday, September 3, 2024, I connected with **Dan O'Brien**, the Cardinals' Manager of Football Operations. Dan is a distinguished gentleman, but what truly defines him is his warmth and calm professionalism. From our first exchange, the tone was set: clear communication, mutual respect, and a shared commitment to getting everything right. Most NFL teams arrive the day before kickoff. The Arizona Cardinals, like the San Francisco 49ers and Denver Broncos, chose a different approach—extending their stay to three days and departing after Sunday's game. The itinerary was finalized. The details were locked in. All that remained was execution.

Touchdown in Niagara Falls

At 8:30 p.m. on Friday, September 6, 2024, the Arizona Cardinals touched down at Niagara Falls International Airport. Six buses were staged and waiting—lined up with purpose and precision. One of the fascinating things about this job is how easily even the biggest stars blend in. Unless a player draws attention to himself, he's just another professional heading to work.

I can't recall which bus **Kyler Murray** boarded, nor where my favorite Cardinal, **Marvin Harrison Jr.**—an Ohio State Buckeye—was seated. They may very well have been on mine. The one face I recognized immediately was **Head Coach Jonathan Gannon**. With Coach Gannon seated across from me in the front row, the motorcade rolled out smoothly, delivering the team safely to their hotel.

Game Day in Buffalo

Sunday, September 8, 2024. A 1:00 p.m. kickoff. Season opener. Arizona Cardinals versus Buffalo Bills. As always, when these two teams meet, the game is electric. Every drive felt urgent. Every play carried consequence. The Cardinals fought hard, but when the clock hit zero, the Bills emerged with a **34–28 victory**.

Class to the very End

Win or lose, character always reveals itself in the final moments. The Arizona Cardinals carried themselves with professionalism from start to finish—organized, respectful, and composed. At the airport, handshakes were exchanged. Safe travels were wished. Another chapter quietly closed. Serving the Arizona Cardinals was a pleasure in every sense of the word. As their aircraft lifted into the night sky, it reminded me why I take pride in this work: executing the details, honoring the people, and being part of moments that most will never see.

CHAPTER FIFTY-FOUR

THE JACKSONVILLE JAGUARS

Week Three Under the Lights

Week 3 of the NFL season brought a Monday night showdown to Buffalo. These primetime games always carry a different kind of electricity—brighter lights, tighter schedules, and zero room for error. On September 17, I connected with **J.K. Lacosta**, the Jacksonville Jaguars' Senior Manager of Team Logistics. As is customary, our first interaction was brief, cordial, and professional—the calm before a very busy storm.

First Impressions Matter

On Sunday, September 22, at exactly 1:55 p.m., I picked up Mr. Lacosta at the hotel—right on schedule. From the moment we met, it was clear he was a character in the best sense of the word. Tall, fit, well-groomed, articulate, and occasionally animated, he carried himself with confidence and professionalism—balanced perfectly by a sharp sense of humor that made conversation effortless. At 4:07 p.m., the Jaguars touched down at Niagara Falls International Airport. Head Coach **Doug Pederson** took a seat directly across from me for the ride back to the hotel. The trip was smooth, uneventful, and exactly how it should be—quiet competence doing its job in the background.

Earning Trust, One Mile at A Time

During that first transport, Mr. Lacosta introduced me to **Brandon Roth**, the Jaguars' Senior Manager of Team Operations, who would become my primary point of contact. Brandon's demeanor was noticeably different—more reserved, more guarded. It didn't take long to understand why. Before arriving in

Buffalo, the Jaguars had experienced a major failure with another motorcoach carrier. The buses had shown up **an hour late**. In this business, punctuality isn't a preference—it's a requirement. I looked him in the eye and said with complete confidence:

> **"Sir, we don't possess any elements of incompetence or unprofessionalism."**

Those words weren't bravado. They were a promise. Over time—mile by mile—his initial tension faded. In its place grew trust, the kind that only forms when expectations are consistently met.

A Familiar Face in New Colors

Game day arrived—**Monday, September 23, 2024**. As the Jaguars began filtering out of the hotel and boarding the buses for Highmark Stadium, I caught sight of a familiar face that stopped me cold. "Gab… is that you?" I asked. He turned, smiled, and said, "Yeah, that's me," as he shook my hand. It was **Gabriel Davis**. I knew he had parted ways with the Buffalo Bills, but I hadn't realized he'd landed in Jacksonville. (In 2025, he would rejoin the Bills.)

Calm, soft-spoken, and respectful, he carried himself exactly as Buffalo fans remembered. I thanked him for what he gave to the city—for the big catches, the clutch moments, and the memories that don't fade. Gabriel had spent four seasons with the Bills after being selected in the fourth round of the 2020 NFL Draft, remaining through the 2023 season before signing with Jacksonville in 2024. With a nod and a quiet smile, he boarded the bus.

A Quarterback Raised Right

Another moment that stayed with me came courtesy of Jacksonville's star quarterback, **Trevor Lawrence**. He stepped out of the hotel looking every bit the part—polished, composed, and carrying himself with a courtesy that spoke volumes about his upbringing. King Solomon once wrote:

> "Train up a child in the way he should go: and when he is old, he will not depart from it."

Standing there, watching Trevor move with humility and grace, those words felt alive. Tall as a tower and dressed in a light brown, sugar-colored, slim-fit designer suit, he carried himself with quiet confidence. I welcomed him to Buffalo and told him how proud I was of his accomplishments—not just in the NFL, but going all the way back to his college days. I told him I'm a Buckeye fan and the proud father of a full-scholarship swimmer at **The Ohio State University**—but I also made sure he knew this:

He's my favorite Clemson player.
Yes—even above Sammy Watkins.

He looked genuinely surprised—maybe even a little honored—to hear that from a Bills fan. I smiled and added, respectfully, that when it comes to **Josh Allen**, he'd still have to take a back seat.

A Long Night's End

The Jaguars arrived in Buffalo riding a wave of confidence, having enjoyed success against the Bills in recent years. But that Monday night belonged entirely to Buffalo. The Bills dominated, winning **47–10**. After a loss like that, most teams want out of town as fast as possible. Unfortunately for Jacksonville, that wasn't in the cards. Their aircraft developed a mechanical issue and was grounded.

The team remained at the stadium until a replacement plane arrived from Miami. At **2:00 a.m. Tuesday morning**, we transported the Jaguars back to Niagara Falls International Airport. By the time our shift finally ended at **5:00 a.m.**, exhaustion had fully set in. Burned out would be an understatement. Still—as always—it was worth it. Another long night. Another job done right.

CHAPTER FIFTY-FIVE

THE TENNESSEE TITANS

A Franchise In Transition

After six seasons at the helm, the Tennessee Titans parted ways with head coach **Mike Vrabel** in January 2024, turning the page and ushering in a new era under **Brian Callahan**. By Week 7 of the 2024 NFL season, the Titans arrived in Buffalo carrying the weight of transition—a team in the early stages of rebuilding, standing at **1–4**, while the Buffalo Bills sat confidently at **4–2**. On Wednesday, October 16, 2024, I reached out to **Luke Morrow** of the Titans' operations staff, who promptly introduced me to **Nick Hardesty**. From our very first exchange, both gentlemen proved to be professional, organized, and easy to work with. We reviewed the Titans' itinerary in detail, making sure every moving piece was aligned well before wheels ever touched the ground.

Arrival In Buffalo

The Titans landed at Buffalo Niagara International Airport on **Saturday, October 19, 2024, at 5:00 p.m.** Six buses were staged and ready to accommodate the players and staff. As is customary, I extended a warm welcome to Coach **Brian Callahan**. He returned the greeting with the quiet confidence of a leader still finding his footing, then boarded the bus for the short ride to the team hotel. The trip from the airport unfolded exactly as it should—safe, smooth, and comfortable. Interaction with the team was minimal, but their demeanor spoke volumes. Even in the middle of a rebuilding season, everyone carried themselves with professionalism, respect, and dignity—traits that never go unnoticed behind the scenes.

Game Day at Highmark Stadium

Sunday, **October 20, 2024**, brought game day in Orchard Park. The Titans boarded the buses bound for Highmark Stadium, ready to compete. With **Mason Rudolph** under center, Tennessee gave its best effort—but Buffalo controlled the afternoon. The Bills emerged with a decisive **34–10** victory.

A Quiet Departure

After the game, we transported the Titans back to the airport. There were no long speeches. No lingering moments. Just handshakes, exchanged well-wishes, and mutual respect on both sides. Shortly thereafter, the team boarded their aircraft and headed home—continuing a season still searching for its footing. As of **December 19, 2025**, the Titans stood at **2–12**, a clear reflection of a franchise still in transition. But records tell only part of the story. What remained consistent throughout their visit to Buffalo was their professionalism and dignity—qualities that endure even in the most difficult seasons.

CHAPTER FIFTY-SIX

THE MIAMI DOLPHINS

A Familiar Connection

On Wednesday, November 2, 2024, I connected once again with Nate Hammett, the Miami Dolphins' Senior Manager of Team Operations. Seeing Nate is always a pleasure, and working alongside him is consistently smooth, professional, and genuinely enjoyable. Some relationships in this line of work feel purely transactional; this one never does. It's built on trust, mutual respect, and shared experience. Driving for Coach Mike McDaniel and his coaching staff remains an honor and a privilege—one I never take lightly.

Arrival In Buffalo

On Saturday at 4:30 p.m., the Dolphins touched down at Buffalo Niagara International Airport aboard Atlas Air Flight #8086. The routine unfolded with the kind of practiced precision that only comes from repetition and preparation. As had happened the last time Miami came to Buffalo, Coach McDaniel took a seat directly across from me. Quiet, focused, and observant, he carried the calm presence of a coach who always seems to be thinking a few plays ahead—already living in the next series before the current one has even ended.

A Game of Inches

The game itself was a thriller—tight, intense, and balanced on a razor's edge. Although the Dolphins came up short, they played exceptionally well. The Bills prevailed 34–31, but this was a contest that could just as easily have gone Miami's way. In football, games like that often come down to one moment, one misstep, one break in rhythm. This one was no different.

After The Final Whistle

Following the game, we returned to the airport to prepare for departure. A long line at the security checkpoint slowed things down, but it also created an unexpected moment—one of those brief windows where the walls between roles come down just enough for simple human connection. I found myself chatting with Tyreek Hill (#10) and Marcus Maye (#26). Interacting with players often comes more naturally than with coaches, and this exchange was easy, relaxed, and respectful.

A Moment of Perspective

Earlier in the season, on September 8, 2024, Tyreek Hill's highly publicized traffic incident involving Miami-Dade police officer Danny Torres had dominated headlines nationwide. Like many others, I had my own thoughts about the situation. But meeting Tyreek face-to-face offered a kind of perspective that headlines alone never can.

He was soft-spoken, intelligent, and respectful—the kind of presence that makes you pause and reconsider how quickly public narratives are formed. In that moment, it became clearer why the Miami Dolphins stood by him as they did. While no inappropriate behavior should ever be condoned—by anyone, under any circumstances—the incident also brought attention to the officer's own history of misconduct-related suspensions.

In truth, it appeared to be a bad day for both men, magnified by fame, authority, and public scrutiny. The whole episode was a reminder of how human we really are. I appreciated the conversation with Tyreek. It offered understanding without the need for explanation.

Parting Ways

As we said our farewells, the mutual sentiment was clear: it's always a pleasure serving the Miami Dolphins. Respect was exchanged. Handshakes were genuine. And once again, professionalism carried the day. Another chapter closed—not just of football logistics, but of the quiet human moments that unfold behind the scenes, long after the final score is written. And that, in many ways, is what this entire journey has always been about—not just the miles, the schedules, or the assignments, but the people. The brief conversations. The shared spaces. The small moments of understanding that remind us we're all carrying more than the world ever sees.

CHAPTER FIFTY-SEVEN

THE KANSAS CITY CHIEFS

Uncertainty, Doubt, and a Season Rewritten

As the 2024 season approached, uncertainty hung heavily over Buffalo. Bills fans watched as six of the team's eight captains were released, including star wide receivers Stefon Diggs and Gabriel Davis. To the outside world, the roster looked depleted. Analysts and experts were quick to declare the window closed. What they didn't see coming was a late-season collision with destiny—one that would bring the Kansas City Chiefs back to Buffalo in a rematch loaded with championship implications.

A Familiar Rival Returns

The November 17, 2024, showdown between the Buffalo Bills and the Kansas City Chiefs was more than just another game. It was a rematch of their January 24, 2024, AFC Championship playoff battle—two heavyweights meeting again, with pride, positioning, and momentum on the line. My primary contact with the Chiefs was Andrew Schnoebelen, who introduced me to Brock Baumert, the Chiefs' Director of Team Operations. Both men were professional, organized, and genuinely enthusiastic about their visit to Buffalo—qualities that have come to define Kansas City's traveling operation.

Class, Consistency, And Coach Reid

This trip also marked a noticeable shift in my interaction with Head Coach Andy Reid. During our first encounter, our exchange had been limited to a polite greeting. This time, Coach Reid stopped, smiled, and shook my hand. It was a small gesture, but one that spoke volumes. Andy Reid is the embodiment of class in the NFL—an ambassador among coaches whose professionalism quietly sets the standard. The ride from the airport to the hotel was smooth and uneventful, just the way a well-run operation prefers it.

A Champion steps off the Bus

The highlight of the visit came when we arrived at the hotel. As I stepped off the bus, I reminded the team to watch their footing while we began unloading the luggage. I didn't even have to see him step off the bus to know Patrick Mahomes had arrived. The reaction said it all. A small group of fans had gathered nearby, and the cheers erupted instantly—especially from the ladies, who made their excitement unmistakably clear.

With a grin, I deliberately grabbed Patrick Mahomes' bag and set it down with the rest of the team's gear. Playing it completely straight, as he reached for it, I said, "Mr. Mahomes, don't flatter yourself. They react that way every time I show up. There's your bag, sir." For a brief moment, he looked genuinely stunned—like he was still deciding whether he'd heard me correctly. Then the champion in him surfaced. He smiled, nodded, and calmly replied, "Nice play." It was a perfect moment—lighthearted, respectful, and genuine. Often misunderstood, Patrick Mahomes is not just an elite competitor; he's a warm, approachable individual whose confidence never overshadows his humility. Love you, Pat!

Game Day: Buffalo Delivers a Statement

On game day, November 17, 2024, the Buffalo Bills delivered a defining performance, handing the Kansas City Chiefs their first loss of the season with a 30–21 victory at Highmark Stadium. Josh Allen led the charge, throwing for 262 yards and delivering the game's signature moment—a fearless 26-yard touchdown run on 4th-and-2 with just over two minutes remaining. The play sealed the outcome and sent the stadium into a frenzy.

James Cook powered the ground game with two rushing touchdowns, while Curtis Samuel added a crucial receiving score. Patrick Mahomes and tight end Noah Gray kept Kansas City competitive, but Buffalo's balanced offense and timely defensive stops proved too much. The win lifted the Bills to 9–2 and brought the Chiefs' pursuit of an undefeated season to a halt.

Respect in Defeat

The loss was disappointing for Kansas City, but their character never wavered. From top to bottom, the Chiefs carried themselves with professionalism, dignity, and class—traits that define elite organizations. When it comes to measuring excellence beyond the scoreboard, the Kansas City Chiefs remain among the NFL's finest. Once again, we wished them a safe journey home, watched them board their plane, and then—just like that—they were gone, disappearing into the clouds. Another chapter written. Another standard upheld. Another reminder of what excellence looks like on both sides of the field.

CHAPTER FIFTY-EIGHT

THE SAN FRANCISCO 49ERS

A Long Road Back to Buffalo

Before Week 13 of the 2024 NFL season, the last time the San Francisco 49ers had played the Buffalo Bills in Buffalo was October 16, 2016—a lopsided 45–16 Bills victory. Buffalo had won the previous three meetings, and the 49ers arrived this time intent on changing the narrative. But before they could line up against the Bills, they would have to confront something far less predictable than any opponent: a Western New York winter at full force.

Nature Takes the Field First

In late November and early December of 2024, a powerful, multi-day lake-effect snowstorm engulfed the Buffalo region. Arctic air surged across the warmer waters of Lake Erie and Lake Ontario, forming a slow-moving, highly concentrated snow band that stalled over Western New York. In some areas, snowfall totals reached several feet. Whiteout conditions became common. Roads vanished beneath blowing snow. Major highways—including critical stretches of the Thruway—were shut down entirely.

Communities were paralyzed. Snow fell at rates of several inches per hour. Emergency declarations followed. Holiday travel plans dissolved in real time. It quickly became one of the defining early-season storms of the 2024–25 winter—remembered not only for its intensity, but for its persistence and the way it tested everyone who had to move through it.

Choosing The Road Home

It was Thanksgiving weekend, and my family and I had spent the holiday in Ohio. With storm warnings intensifying by the hour, we decided to leave on Friday instead of Saturday. Experience has taught me to respect weather forecasts—especially in this part of the country. A replacement lead driver for the 49ers had already been arranged. Since both David Cercone and I were unavailable for the airport arrival, I recommended Henry Jasinski—an operator I personally trained from the ground up to be a professional motorcoach driver. Henry would bring the team from the airport to the hotel, and I would step back in on game day.

We left early, hoping to beat both the storm and nightfall. Things held steady until Ashtabula, Ohio. From there, conditions deteriorated rapidly. Roads grew slick. Visibility shrank. Mile by mile, the journey became more dangerous. As we pushed eastbound on the Thruway—eventually shut down entirely—the true severity of the storm revealed itself.

The hardest part was seeing the cars scattered off the roadway, buried in ditches. Many were only visible by the faint glow of snow-covered headlights. Without that light, no one would have known they were there. What should have been a six-hour drive stretched into nearly twelve—every mile earned.

Then, just outside of Buffalo, something changed. As we reached Irving, New York, the snow began to ease. The wind relaxed its grip. The road ahead slowly came back into view. It felt like crossing an invisible line—one final reminder of how quickly conditions can shift in Western New York.

Arrival in the Storm

On Friday, November 29, 2024, at approximately 11:00 p.m., the San Francisco 49ers arrived in Buffalo aboard United Airlines Flight 3818. The team required seven buses to meet their transportation needs. Despite the conditions, Henry Jasinski delivered the team safely to the hotel and kept me informed throughout the process. Knowing that Henry was behind the wheel—someone I had personally trained and trusted—gave me complete confidence. He handled the assignment with professionalism, composure, and precision—exactly what's required when conditions are at their worst.

Game Day Connections

On Sunday, December 1, 2024, I met Chase Fisher in person for the first time after several phone conversations leading up to the visit. Even before we met face-to-face, his professionalism, kindness, and attention to detail were evident. Meeting him in person only confirmed what I already knew. Chase extended a breakfast invitation to the drivers through his assistant, Amanda Hilman—a thoughtful gesture that didn't go unnoticed and wasn't declined by anyone. In this line of work, those small moments of appreciation mean more than people realize.

Serving The Standard

As the team boarded the buses for the stadium, Coach Kyle Shanahan—son of the legendary Mike Shanahan—and quarterback Brock Purdy rode on Bus 1. It was an honor to serve them. Both men carry themselves with quiet confidence and professionalism. They are exceptional at their craft, but just as importantly, they lead with character. In an environment built on pressure, preparation, and performance, that combination matters. The San Francisco 49ers are fortunate to have them at the helm.

A Message Delivered—With A Smile

I had a brief moment to connect with Purdy and pass along a message. Earlier that week, several delightful women from the East Aurora Seniors group—one of my regular clients—asked me to do them a favor. I assured them that if the opportunity presented itself, I would do my best. When I asked what the message was, they smiled and said, "When you drive for the 49ers, tell Brock Purdy he's a dream—and we'd date him anytime."

For a split second, I considered telling them they needed to get themselves to church—fast. Instead, I laughed and replied, "I'll see what I can do." On game day, as Brock placed his bag into the luggage bay, I told him how proud I was of what he had accomplished. Compliments tend to get a person's attention. Then I added, "Sir, you have some eighty-year-old secret admirers in East Aurora, New York, who are interested in dating you." We both laughed. He shook his head and said, "Tell them I'm flattered." Mic drop. Brock has a fantastic personality.

The Final Chapter

The 49ers battled hard, playing with toughness and resolve—true gladiators in harsh conditions. But on this day, they ran into a Buffalo team that controlled the game, and the Bills won 35–10. At the airport, I shared one final warm exchange with Chase, thanking him for his professionalism, kindness, and mutual respect. We shook hands, said our goodbyes, and soon after, the team boarded their plane, lifted off, and disappeared into the clouds, bound for home. It was my first time driving for Chase Fisher and the San Francisco 49ers—and it was an honor from start to finish.

CHAPTER FIFTY-NINE

THE NEW ENGLAND PATRIOTS

A Familiar Rival Returns Home

After a demanding two-game road trip, the Buffalo Bills finally returned to familiar ground, preparing once again to host one of the NFL's most storied franchises—the New England Patriots. Rivalry games like this carry history in their bones, and even in rebuilding years, the Patriots never arrive quietly.

First Contact

On Wednesday, December 18, 2024, I connected with Football Operations Assistant, Sarah Jackson, my primary point of contact for the Patriots. Our exchange was pleasant and professional—the kind that signals mutual respect from the start. Alec Kerr, whom I had worked with the previous season, had since moved on to another opportunity. I wish him good health and success in all his endeavors.

Seven Buses, One Plan

Saturday, December 21, began like so many NFL weekends. After picking up Sarah at the team hotel, we joined the rest of the motorcoaches at the airport. The Patriots had reserved seven buses. No two NFL teams operate the same way, and adapting to each Director of Operations' preferences is part of the craft. Sarah was precise—polite, professional, and intensely focused on execution. On game day, as law enforcement escorts guided us toward the stadium, she stepped to the front of the coach and gave driving instructions, asking me to tighten the gap between my bus and the lead escort.

Over Forty Years at the Wheel

With calm reassurance, I let her know I had over forty years of motorcoach experience and that her team's safety would always be Priority One. I maintained my traveling distance. Coming over from the Indianapolis Colts, this was Sarah's first year with the Patriots, and her approach reflected a true servant's heart. She wanted everything done right—for the team, the staff, and the entire organization. She poured herself into the job. Had she known that she and I were, in many ways, the most important "celebrities" on the bus, she might have relaxed just a bit. But that wasn't her style—and that was exactly what made her special. Her passion was second to none, and I couldn't help but admire it.

Another familiar face, Mike Grady, also served as a point of contact. One conversation was all it took to know—this was not his first rodeo. When the Patriots' aircraft touched down, its tail proudly displayed six Super Bowl championships. It was impossible not to think of the former offensive commander who helped earn them—Tom Brady.

A New Chapter on the Sideline

With Bill Belichick gone, the Patriots had turned the page, naming Jerod Mayo as head coach. Mayo's résumé speaks for itself—eight seasons as a Patriot, a 2008 first-round pick, Super Bowl champion, two-time Pro Bowler, and seven-time team captain. Leadership was never the question. Still, his rookie season as a head coach was a baptism by fire. A talent-thin roster and an inexperienced coaching staff made success difficult to manufacture. Notably, Coach Mayo rode on Bus 2—an unusual choice that didn't go unnoticed. The ride to the hotel, however, was smooth and uneventful.

Building for Tomorrow

The Patriots were clearly in rebuilding mode, but there were signs of hope. Young quarterback Drake Maye stood out as a promising foundation for the offense—a player the franchise could grow around.

Sunday's Statement

On December 22, 2024, the Patriots entered the game at 3–11, while the Bills stood strong at 11–3. Records meant little once the ball was kicked. New England played with grit, discipline, and heart, pushing Buffalo to the final whistle before falling by a single field goal, 24–21. The loss didn't tell the full story. What the Patriots showed that afternoon—their character, resolve, and emerging identity—sent a quiet message to the rest of the league: **"We're back."**

Into the Clouds

After the game, we transported the team back to the airport. The Patriots stepped off the buses, passed through security, boarded their aircraft, and disappeared into the clouds—heading home, still rebuilding, but clearly moving forward.

CHAPTER SIXTY

THE NEW YORK JETS

A Late-Season Sunday in Buffalo

On Sunday, December 29, 2024, the New York Jets endured their twelfth loss of the season, falling 40–14 to the Buffalo Bills. By the time the calendar flips to late December, the stakes are often less about playoff positioning and more about professionalism—how a team travels, prepares, and conducts itself, even when the season has been unforgiving.

Because Christmas fell on a Wednesday that week, I reached out a bit later than usual. On Thursday—just two days before the Jets' arrival—I connected with Director of Operations Aaron Degerness and Assistant Director of Operations Mari Jo Kohler. We reviewed the work order together, confirmed the details, and locked everything in. Smooth. Efficient. To the point. Exactly how it needs to be.

Arrival Day: First Impressions Matter

The Jets had reserved seven buses for their visit. On Saturday, December 28, at 1:40 p.m., I picked up Mari Jo at the hotel. She was accompanied by Alyssa LaBelle, a seasonal intern with the Football Operations staff, whom she introduced with obvious pride. At the time, Alyssa was still in training, and that small moment said a lot about Mari Jo—leadership that doesn't just manage, but teaches, invests, and prepares the next generation.

At 3:25 p.m., United Airlines Flight #3810 touched down at Buffalo Niagara International Airport. One by one, the Jets descended the aircraft steps and boarded our buses, the familiar choreography of arrival unfolding just as it always does—smooth, efficient, disciplined, and precisely timed. A quiet ballet of logistics that only looks effortless when everyone does their job right.

Earning Trust, The Right Way

Every NFL team matters to Niagara Scenic Tours, but the Jets held a unique place in our lineup. They were the only NFL team we had not previously secured, largely out of loyalty to a long-time motorcoach provider. However, after experiencing unprofessional conduct the year before—and hearing consistent feedback about our level of service—the Jets decided to come on board with us. We knew what that meant. This wasn't just another assignment. This was an audition. And we delivered. During the hotel drop-off, I caught Mari Jo in my peripheral vision, watching our every move with an eagle eye. After completion, we did our routine bus check to ensure nothing had been left behind. I sent her a quick text update. Her response said it all:

"Thanks, Tommy! You guys are great!"

For a first visit, that was more than encouraging—it was confirmation that trust was already being built.

Game Day Energy and a Bus Full of Laughter

The New York Jets were, without question, the most animated team I worked with all season. On game day, Buses 1, 5, and 6 were scheduled to depart the hotel at 10:00 a.m. As players and staff trickled out and boarded, I stood outside chatting with James Williams, the hotel's security chief. Suddenly, a booming voice erupted from my bus. "**Yo, driver!**" It was so loud it felt like an earthquake. "Yes, sir—everything okay?" I called back. "**Heat!**" he shouted. I stepped onto the bus. About a dozen team members were already seated. "You guys need more heat?" I asked, trying to clarify. "**No! It's hot as hell in here!**" they yelled in perfect unison.

The staff member who had started it all—whose name I never did catch—took center stage. "Are you on the Buffalo Bills' payroll?" he asked. "You're trying to dehydrate us so we can't play! Yeah, you're wearing our hat, but I think you're an impostor!" I laughed and fired back, "No sir—I'm a Jet this weekend." The entire bus exploded with laughter and applause. With the mild December weather, the heat wasn't needed anyway. I shut it off as I exited, the mood light and the energy high.

Familiar Faces and Quiet Respect

Wide receiver Garrett Wilson is my favorite Jet—strictly because he's a Buckeye—but I didn't get the chance to connect with him on this visit. I did, however, reconnect with quarterback Tyrod Taylor, whom I had worked with during his time with the 2023 New York Giants. When you see players and coaches often enough, you stop being just another driver. You become a familiar face. And that familiarity opens the door to genuine moments. Enough can't be said about Tyrod Taylor—his manners, character, and professionalism stand out in a league full of talent. Wherever life takes him next, I wish him nothing but success.

A Professional Goodbye

It was truly a pleasure serving the New York Jets, and I looked forward to doing it again the following season. At the airport, we exchanged goodbyes—routine, but respectful. The team retrieved their luggage, passed through security, boarded their aircraft, and soon disappeared into the atmosphere. Another chapter closed. Another relationship built the right way.

CHAPTER SIXTY-ONE

THE DENVER BRONCOS

Passing the Torch

The Denver Broncos made a bold statement that season. Moving on from Russell Wilson, they placed their future in the hands of rookie quarterback **Bo Nix**, selected 12th overall in the 2024 NFL Draft. Nix responded with poise well beyond his years, guiding Denver to a 10–7 regular-season record and a Wild Card berth. That January, the Broncos arrived in Buffalo with one clear objective: knock out Josh Allen and the Buffalo Bills and keep their postseason hopes alive. It was a tall task—and one that history has shown is never easy in Western New York.

The Calm Behind the Clipboard

On Tuesday, January 7, 2025, I reached out to Josh Brunning, the Broncos' Director of Team Operations. It was our third time working together, and that familiarity brought an easy rhythm. We reviewed the itinerary, confirmed every detail, and moved forward with quiet confidence. Josh carries himself with a gentle professionalism that puts everyone at ease. When he's in charge, things don't just get done—they fall into place.

Arrival In Buffalo

On Friday evening, January 10, at 7:00 p.m., I stopped by the hotel, picked Josh up, and joined the rest of the motorcade at the airport. At 9:15 p.m., Atlas Air Flight #8248 touched down in Buffalo, delivering the Denver Broncos into the cold January night. Seven buses stood staged and ready. The transfer from the airport to the hotel went smoothly. As Coach Sean Payton approached,

I welcomed him back to Buffalo. He smiled and replied, "Thank you. I'm glad to be back." I took his bag, placed it in the luggage bay, and watched as he boarded the bus—another familiar chapter beginning.

Business As Usual

The Broncos always arrive two days before game day. Saturday would be dedicated to practice—either at Highmark Stadium or a nearby university—fine-tuning details and preparing for the challenge ahead. On Sunday, January 12, 2025, the team boarded the buses for Highmark Stadium. The Broncos fought like warriors, but the Bills proved too much on that day, securing a 31–7 victory. Despite the loss, Denver's trajectory was unmistakable. This was a team rebuilding with purpose. That belief would soon be validated. By Week 14 of the 2025 season, the Broncos sat atop the AFC as the No. 1 seed at 12–2, while the Bills followed closely at 10–4.

A Quiet Exchange

I don't recall Bo Nix riding my bus from the airport to the hotel, but he did ride with me from the hotel to the stadium. Our interaction was brief, yet telling. "Good day, Mr. Nix. Have a great game," I said. "Thank you. I appreciate that," he replied, offering a bright, warm smile before taking his seat. It doesn't take a long conversation to recognize a meek and quiet spirit. Bo Nix carries himself with humility and grace. He comes from good stock, and I'm certain his parents are very proud—not just of the player he's becoming, but of the man he already is.

Into the Clouds

After the game, we transported the Broncos back to the airport. Goodbyes were exchanged. Hands were shaken. Safe travels were wished. One by one, they boarded their plane, lifted off, and disappeared into the clouds—leaving Buffalo behind, but carrying their promise with them into the seasons ahead.

CHAPTER SIXTY-TWO

THE BALTIMORE RAVENS

A Reckoning in January

The January 19, 2025, AFC Divisional Round between the Baltimore Ravens and the Buffalo Bills was the kind of game that tightens your chest and refuses to let go. Every snap carried weight. Every moment felt borrowed. The Bills survived—barely—escaping what could have been another crushing postseason heartbreak.

The memory of Week 4 still lingered. Back on September 29, 2024, under the bright lights of prime-time television, the Ravens had dismantled the Bills in Baltimore, snapping Buffalo's winning streak with a commanding 35–10 victory. That night belonged entirely to the Ravens, and it gave them plenty of confidence as they arrived in Buffalo for the rematch.

First Impressions Matter

Earlier that week, I connected with Dan Parsons, the Ravens' Director of Team Operations. It was my first time working with Baltimore, and Dan's warm demeanor and professionalism immediately stood out. He made it easy for us to do what we do best—serve. That said, the Ravens' travel instructions were unlike anything we'd encountered before. Some details were awkward, even puzzling—especially one request that left our whole staff scratching their heads: covering clocks. In an era where everyone wears a watch or carries a phone with a crystal-clear digital display, the urgency to obscure clocks was a mystery. I asked questions, but never received an explanation that truly satisfied my curiosity. Still, our role is not to question—it's to execute. And execute we did.

Arrival of The Ravens

On Saturday, January 18, 2025, at 1:30 p.m., I arrived at the hotel to pick up Mr. Parsons, then headed to the airport to meet the rest of the fleet. Atlas Air Flight #8054 touched down right on time at 4:00 p.m. As the Ravens began descending the aircraft steps, one familiar figure made his way toward my bus—Head Coach John Harbaugh. We locked eyes, exchanged smiles, and shook hands as I welcomed him to Buffalo.

He took a seat directly across from me, calm and composed. When we arrived at the hotel, Coach Harbaugh did something I had never witnessed before. Before stepping inside, he raised both fists into the air and shouted to the fans, "**Go Ravens!**" The crowd roared back in unison, their energy echoing through the cold Buffalo air. In that moment, Coach Harbaugh earned what I proudly call **The Team Spirit Award**.

A Brief Encounter with Greatness

Just as we were preparing to depart the airport, one final player approached, causing a short delay. Meanwhile, my driver on Bus Two was struggling with his radio channel selection and asked for help. I quickly programmed the unit and turned back toward my bus. That's when I crossed paths with the Ravens' star quarterback. "Brother Jackson, welcome to Buffalo, sir," I said. "Thank you—and I'm glad to be here," Lamar Jackson replied, his words sincere and his smile unmistakably genuine. There was no edge. No animosity. Just warmth. As we passed each other, I couldn't help but notice Lamar holding up his pants as if gravity itself were testing him. I chuckled to myself:

> "Bro, I don't really need my belt. You can borrow it until we get to the hotel."

A Class of their Own

Josh Allen and Lamar Jackson both emerged from the historic 2018 NFL Draft—alongside Baker Mayfield, Sam Darnold, and Josh Rosen. As of 2025, Allen and Jackson remain the only two still with the teams that drafted them. Many players return to cities that passed them over, fueled by resentment. Lamar Jackson isn't wired that way. He is, without question, one of the friendliest and most respectful players in the league. For that, he earns my **Most Vibrant Personality Award**. The ride from the airport to the hotel was smooth. At drop-off, I stepped off the bus, followed by Coach Harbaugh and his wife—class and dignity personified.

Sunday Morning Hospitality

On game day, January 19, we returned to the hotel to transport the team to Highmark Stadium. Not all teams invite the drivers to breakfast—but the Ravens did. What awaited us was nothing short of royal. The hotel laid out a spread worthy of champions. Though we never sit down with the team, we filled our plates and returned to the buses, grateful for the gesture. Moments like these remind you that respect goes both ways. Working alongside hotel security, Chief James Williams, and Chief Marlon Hall, was, as always, seamless.

A Game That Felt Like War

Highmark Stadium was electric. The clash between the Bills and Ravens unfolded like warfare. Baltimore struck first and looked poised to finish the job—until momentum shifted. Carelessness crept in. Two turnovers gave the Bills life. With 8:50 remaining in the fourth quarter, Buffalo led 24–19. On 2nd-and-11, Lamar Jackson delivered a dart to Mark Andrews at the Bills' 43-yard line. Then, the unthinkable. Andrews fumbled. The third turnover. Tyler Bass capitalized with a field goal, pushing the Bills ahead 27–19 with 3:31 left. Still, the Ravens refused to fade quietly. Lamar led a relentless drive that ended in a touchdown, pulling Baltimore within two points—27–25—with 1:33 remaining. Everything hinged on the conversion.

Inches from Immortality

Mark Andrews lined up just off the line, drifting into open space at the goal line. Lamar fired a perfect pass—right into Andrews' hands. And then… heartbreak. The ball hit the turf. For the second time in the game, Andrews couldn't secure it. The Bills recovered the onside kick, drained the clock, and in one dramatic exhale, ended the Ravens' season.

Dignity in Defeat

The bus ride back to the airport was quiet. Heavy with disappointment. Understandably so. Yet even in devastation, the Ravens carried themselves like champions. Coach Harbaugh shook my hand and thanked me for our service. "It was an honor to serve you and the mighty Ravens, Coach," I told him. "I hope to do it again. Stay safe, and God bless you and the Ravens." With that, he passed through security, boarded the plane, and disappeared into the night—another chapter written, another season concluded, and respect earned on both sides.

CHAPTER SIXTY-THREE

2025 NFL SEASON

THE NEW YORK GIANTS

A Familiar Rival Returns to Buffalo

The Buffalo Bills opened the 2025 NFL preseason at home against the New York Giants—their lone preseason game at Highmark Stadium. The matchup carried echoes of the past. The last time these teams met in Orchard Park, on October 15, 2023, the Bills escaped with a gritty 14–9 victory. This time, the stakes were lighter, but the atmosphere—and the memories—were very real.

On August 6, 2025, I reached out to **Jeff Conroy**, the Giants' Director of Team Operations. Having worked with Jeff before, there was an immediate sense of trust and rhythm. He possesses a rare balance—genuinely friendly, yet relentlessly professional. His expectations are precise, his standards high, and his respect for the people executing the work never goes unnoticed. When someone cares that deeply about doing things right, it elevates everyone around them.

Arrival Day: Precision and Preparation

On August 8, at 1:15 p.m., I picked up Mr. Conroy at the team hotel, and together we joined the rest of our buses at the airport. Seven buses were required for the Giants' arrival, though only six would be needed on game day. Shortly after 3:00 p.m., United Airlines Flight #3817 touched down at Buffalo Niagara International Airport. As the Giants disembarked, it became clear this was not just another preseason trip—there were familiar faces woven into this new roster.

Devin Singletary: A Reunion Years in the Making

The first player to board my bus stopped me in my tracks. **Devin Singletary**. I hadn't realized the Giants had acquired him, though in hindsight, it made perfect sense. Devin once thrived under Brian Daboll during Daboll's tenure as the Bills' offensive coordinator. Drafted by Buffalo in the third round of the 2019 NFL Draft, Singletary's journey had come full circle—just in a different uniform.

During his rookie season, I regularly drove Devin and other draftees to practice. That 2019 class included names like **Ed Oliver**, **Cody Ford**, and **Dawson Knox**—players who not only became stars, but also pillars in their communities. Devin always stood out for his humility, his manners, and his quiet professionalism. It took me a second to register who was approaching my bus, smiling. "Devin!" I said. "Yep!" he replied. We shook hands, shared a hug, exchanged a few words, and he boarded.

Superstars don't always look the part—and some who look the part aren't superstars at all. On game day, Devin wore yellow sweatpants with a few holes, a matching pullover, and sneakers—no flash, no fuss. Just Devin being Devin.

A Meaningful Moment at Highmark Stadium

As the team arrived at Highmark Stadium and began unloading, I noticed something as Devin stepped down from the bus. Across the crest of his pullover, the word **ARMY** stood out boldly in black letters. Knowing Devin graduated from Florida Atlantic University, I asked him about it. "One of my relatives attended ARMY," he said proudly. I smiled. "That's special. My grandson, Jayden, is a wide receiver at Lakota East High School in Ohio. ARMY at West Point gave him a full scholarship—he'll be attending in 2026." Devin's face lit up. "That's wonderful. Good luck—and enjoy the ride." And just like that, he disappeared through the security checkpoint, headed toward the locker room—another small moment that somehow felt bigger than the game itself.

Captain Wilson takes the Lead

Another familiar figure followed soon after—Quarterback **Russell Wilson**. With his trademark platinum smile and a calm, regal presence, Russell placed his bag in the luggage bay, shook my hand, and immediately began recalling details from our last encounter. Hearing him recount previous conversations caught me off guard in the best way. It was humbling—and meaningful—to know those moments stayed with him.

Russell always rides on Bus 1. Over the Giants' two-day stay, he never boarded without first shaking my hand—even if I wasn't standing at the door. He'd stow his gear, then seek me out. There are handshakes you forget instantly. And then there are handshakes that tell you everything you need to know about a person. Russell's is firm, intentional, and grounded, with steady eye contact. A leader's handshake. From that point forward, I called him **Captain Wilson**. Riding alongside him was his student and future starting quarterback, Jaxson Dart—quietly absorbing everything.

Brian Daboll: Home is where the Heart is

The most familiar face of all belonged to Head Coach **Brian Daboll**. Born in Welland, Ontario—just across the border—Daboll has deep roots in Western New York. A graduate of St. Francis High School in Athol Springs and the University of Rochester, he's a true local son with dual citizenship and lifelong ties to the region.

Welland itself is a place where history flows alongside the Welland Canal, linking Lake Erie to Lake Ontario. It's a city shaped by water, rail, and resilience—much like Daboll himself. Let me be clear: **Brian Daboll is a funny man.** He stepped off the plane empty-handed, his belongings clearly handled by staff, and approached the lead bus like he was walking into his own house. I welcomed him home. He smiled, shook my hand, thanked me, and took his seat directly behind me.

As I buckled in, he leaned forward and said, knowing the intensity of Bills Mafia, "Are you going to be okay wearing that hat?" I didn't miss a beat. "Coach, we're Giants for the weekend—and there's nothing anybody can do about it." The nearby seats erupted in laughter and cheers.

Game Day and a Daboll Celebration

The Bills rested most of their starters, including Josh Allen. The Giants took full advantage, winning the preseason contest 34–25. After the game, as the team prepared to head back to the airport, Coach Daboll finally appeared—though not in any rush. Instead of boarding the bus, he sat comfortably on a shuttle cart, puffing on a massive cigar like he just won the Super Bowl, chatting like a man with nowhere else to be. Despite the smoke-free zone, no one dared say a word. Next, he wandered over to the field supply building, greeting familiar faces, moving about as if he owned the place.

At one point, he approached two of my drivers on Buses 2 and 4—David Cercone and Niles Harding. He thanked them personally and shared a laugh. David joked, "Coach, I wish you had another one of those cigars." Daboll replied, "I wish I did, too—so we could share it." David doesn't even smoke. For that moment alone, Brian Daboll earned my personal honor:

The Most Courageous and Animated Award.

Faces that Complete the Day

Two other personalities made the day unforgettable. **Billy Buffalo**—the eight-foot guardian spirit of the Bills—and **Sally Cataldo**, one of Highmark Stadium's directors, who manages the tunnel and bus docking areas with grace and authority. Sally is the heartbeat of that space. She looks out for everyone—drivers, staff, and security alike. From donating cookies and desserts to keeping coffee flowing, she supports our tailgate like family. Once, she introduced me to her mother, and instantly, I understood where Sally got her warmth. I told her mother that it was an honor to meet someone so kind. She smiled, looked at her daughter, and said, "I love him already."

Final Thoughts

Eventually, the Giants prepared to board their flight. We said our farewells, and they disappeared into the sky. Football has a way of bringing life full circle. Old connections resurface in new uniforms. Familiar smiles appear where you least expect them. And home somehow feels like home—even when you're on the other sideline. The Giants' visit to Buffalo wasn't just another preseason stop. It was a collection of moments that proved the NFL is as much about relationships as it is about competition.

And as I watched those planes lift off into the late summer sky, I couldn't help but realize something: seasons don't just change on the field. They change in life, too. The faces, the uniforms, the destinations—they're always changing. But the purpose never does. Somewhere ahead, there are new stadiums, new stories, and new chapters waiting to be written. And as always, I'd be right there in the driver's seat—ready for whatever came next.

CHAPTER SIXTY-FOUR

THE BALTIMORE RAVENS

A Rematch Under the Lights

On Sunday night, September 7th, the Baltimore Ravens returned to Buffalo for a prime-time rematch against the Bills on **Sunday Night Football**. The memory was still fresh. Just eight months earlier, on January 19, 2025, the Bills had ended Baltimore's Super Bowl hopes in the AFC Divisional Round. That loss lingered. The Ravens arrived in Buffalo with one clear purpose: revenge.

Reconnecting with Dan Parsons

On Wednesday, September 3rd, I reconnected with **Dan Parsons**, the Ravens' Director of Team Operations. Our reunion was cordial and efficient. Dan is a straight shooter—quiet, composed, and always professional. I've never seen him smile, but he carries himself with a calm confidence that sets the tone. Together, we reviewed the itinerary and fine-tuned every detail, making sure nothing was off-key before the Ravens touched down in Buffalo.

A Weather Delay and a Coach's Character

The Ravens were scheduled to arrive on Saturday, September 6th, via Atlas Air Flight #8054 at 4:00 p.m. Severe weather in Baltimore delayed the flight until 7:15 p.m. When they finally arrived, seven buses were staged and ready. As players began stepping off the plane, I walked toward the aircraft just as Head Coach **John Harbaugh** descended the stairs. Our eyes met, and we exchanged smiles. He chose to carry his own medium-sized travel bag onto the bus—an understated detail, but a telling one.

I took the moment to tell him that I had written a complimentary passage about him in my book, highlighting the pride and enthusiasm he showed while representing the Ravens during their January visit. I also mentioned that I had honored him with what I called **"The Team Spirit Award."** His face lit up. "I love it! That's really great!" he said. What happened next confirmed everything I believed about him. After boarding the bus, Coach Harbaugh unexpectedly stepped back off.

I assumed he had forgotten something on the plane. Instead, he walked over to the fence separating a group of Ravens fans from the tarmac. He lingered there, laughing and talking with them, patiently allowing selfies to be taken through the fence—fans turning their backs to him just to make sure he was in the shot. In all my years, I had never seen a head coach get off the bus once boarded—until that moment. That's when I fully understood why Coach Harbaugh is loved and respected not only by his players, but by Ravens fans everywhere.

Arrival, Game Day, and a Dominant Force

The transport from the airport to the hotel was smooth, safe, and punctual. Lamar Jackson, as he had before, rode on Bus Two. I wasn't sure which bus Derrick Henry boarded—but once the game kicked off, his presence was impossible to miss. On Sunday, the Ravens delivered a football lesson. Henry punished Buffalo's defense, racking up 169 rushing yards. Dating back to October 7, 2018, through September 7, 2025, he had faced the Bills seven times—amassing 727 yards on 125 carries with 11 touchdowns. The weapon Baltimore used to hang 40 points on the scoreboard seemed unstoppable. Little did they know, it would also become the turning point.

When the Stadium Emptied — and the Impossible Began

With 7:50 left in regulation and the Ravens leading 40–25, nearly 20,000 fans exited Highmark Stadium, convinced the Bills were headed for an opening-night loss. Around that time, Dan Parsons came out to the buses and handed each driver a red envelope—a gratuity. Even we doubted a comeback. We congratulated Dan on what appeared to be a Ravens victory, though it wasn't officially earned. Moments after he walked away, everything changed. Josh Allen transformed from Clark Kent into Superman.

He led the Bills on a scoring drive, cutting the deficit to 40–32 with 3:56 remaining. The Bills' defense, fueled by Bills Mafia, rose up next—forcing a Derrick Henry fumble at the Ravens' 38-yard line with 3:09 left. Once again, Allen engineered a drive that ended in a touchdown. The two-point conversion failed, but the score was now 40–38. With 1:58 remaining, the Bills went into the kitchen and cooked up a miracle.

The defense forced a three-and-out. With 1:26 on the clock, Josh Allen calmly marched Buffalo into field-goal range. With Tyler Bass injured, Matt Prater stepped in and drilled the game-winner. **Final score: Bills 41, Ravens 40.** When we realized the Bills had pulled it off, one of the drivers joked that the Ravens might want their tip back. I replied, "If they ask for it, I'm running—yelling, *'I already spent mine!'*"

Grace in Defeat

One might ask—were the Ravens crabby on the ride to the airport? Not at all. They carried themselves with the poise of a first-class organization—competitive, respectful, and professional. Still, they were understandably devastated. They had played like champions and looked destined to win for most of the night. When Coach Harbaugh boarded the bus, his heartbreak was visible. I nearly shed a tear myself.

A World-Class Security Operation

The Baltimore Ravens operate one of the finest security teams in professional sports—staffed by former law enforcement officers, FBI agents, Secret Service members, and canine units. I would like to extend special recognition to **Ross Luciano**, Vice President of Security for the Ravens. A former Secret Service agent, Ross served on presidential protection details across three administrations and worked alongside notable figures such as current FBI Deputy Director Dan Bongino. Ross was elite in every sense—sharp, alert, engaged, and genuinely personable. Among all NFL security teams I've worked with, he stood out as the most interactive and approachable.

Final Farewell

We arrived at the airport, exchanged farewells, and wished the Ravens a safe flight home. Serving the Baltimore Ravens was truly a pleasure, and I look forward to working with them again in the future. Some games are remembered for the score. Others are remembered for the people. **That night had both.** And as the Ravens disappeared into the night sky, I knew the season was already beginning to show its true character—unpredictable, emotional, and unforgiving. One week you're standing in the shadow of heartbreak, the next you're boarding a plane toward the heat, speed, and swagger of a completely different challenge. The road doesn't pause. It only turns. And the next stop on our journey would bring a familiar AFC East rival to town—the Miami Dolphins.

CHAPTER SIXTY-FIVE

THE MIAMI DOLPHINS

Week 3: Urgency Arrives in Buffalo

In Week 3 of the season, the Miami Dolphins came to Buffalo carrying a 0–2 record and a sense of urgency. This was **Thursday Night Football**—prime time, national stage—and Miami was hungry for its first win. On September 15, I reconnected with **Nate Hammett**, the Dolphins' Senior Manager of Team Operations. Working with Nate is always a pleasure. He's precise, professional, and calm under pressure. Together, we reviewed and finalized every detail of the itinerary. For this visit, the Dolphins required six buses.

A Professional Relationship turns Personal

On Wednesday, September 17, I stopped by the hotel to pick up Nate before heading to the airport to meet the rest of the fleet. Our conversation that day felt different—in a good way. Still professional, but more personal than before. We talked about family life, about things beyond football and logistics. It was refreshing. Those moments build trust. And trust matters when things get complicated.

A Locked-Down Stay and a well-dressed Head Coach

Two things stood out immediately during the Dolphins' visit. First, the Dolphins booked every room in the hotel, eliminating any chance of contact with fans. It was a complete lockdown—focused, controlled, and intentional. Second, Head Coach **Mike McDaniel** arrived in style. He wore a soft, light-brown designer suit with perfectly polished matching shoes. He looked sharp—

effortlessly so. Just as Sugar Ray Leonard could've been an NBA star, Coach McDaniel could qualify as a supermodel.

Arrival and the Calm before the Storm

The Dolphins arrived at Buffalo Niagara International Airport via Atlas Air Flight #8086. We transported the team safely to the hotel and returned the following day to take them to Highmark Stadium. As always, games between the Bills and Dolphins are dogfights—either team can win on any given night. But that day, the first battle wasn't on the field. It was traffic.

Game Day Traffic: When Adaptability Becomes Everything

Adaptability is essential in customer service. On game day, it became non-negotiable. Buses 5 and 6 were scheduled to depart at 3:30 p.m., drop off at the stadium, then return to the hotel in time for a 5:00 p.m. run. Even with a police escort, traffic made that impossible. Buses 1 through 4 were staged at the hotel, ready for departure. My lead driver on Bus 5, James Cornelius, radioed in with the truth: they were going to be late. Traffic had won that round. I relayed the information to Nate. But traffic didn't know something important—Nate and I operate on the same wavelength. We both understood immediately: we were getting the team to the stadium with four buses instead of six. Buses 5 and 6 were instructed to remain at the stadium until all buses were staged there.

Quick Decisions, Quiet Leadership

At 4:30 p.m., instead of three buses departing, only Buses 1 and 2 rolled out. Buses 3 and 4 followed at 5:00 p.m., led by David Cercone. One more adjustment was needed—a judgment call. Jack Putnam, my operator on Bus 3, was the newest member of our team. He hadn't yet driven under escort as a lead driver. David, on the other hand, understands the unspoken language of police escorts—the looks, the gestures, the instincts. The solution was simple: we switched the bus signs. As Bus 3, David led the way. Jack followed as Bus 4. Once the job was done, Jack became Bus 3 and David Bus 4, heading to the airport. Problem solved. No drama. No confusion. No red tape.

Taking the Shoulder

The 4:30 p.m. trip to the stadium was brutal—rush hour colliding with stadium traffic. But we weren't stopping. Using headsets instead of phones, I radioed Kenn Hanley on Bus 2. "We're going down the shoulder." "Copy that," he replied. I angled my bus toward the left shoulder of I-90 westbound and flashed my lights. Our lead escort, Tim, read the message without a word. Once we committed, Tim extended his arm out the window and gave a thumbs-up.

Now, with the concrete barrier on the left, traffic on the right, and an Erie County Sheriff escort leading the way, all safety concerns and delays were eliminated. I can't recall who sat directly behind me, but as soon as we hit the shoulder, I heard him say, "Amazing." We rode the shoulder 98 percent of the way to the stadium.

Thursday Night Football Under the Lights

On September 18, 2025, the Bills and Dolphins clashed under the bright lights of **Thursday Night Football**. Buffalo came out on top, winning 31–21. After a loss, the ride to the airport is usually quieter. But professionalism never fades. We delivered the team, exchanged goodbyes, and watched as the Dolphins took wing and flew home. Another mission completed—quietly, efficiently, and exactly as it should be.

Behind the Wheel: Trust, Timing, And the Unspoken Language

What that night reinforced for me—yet again—is that success at this level is never about perfection. It's about trust. It's about timing. And it's about reading situations before they announce themselves. Trust showed up in the relationship Nate Hammett and I have built over time. When plans changed, there was no panic, no second-guessing—just mutual understanding. That kind of trust can't be rushed. It's earned through consistency, honesty, and showing up prepared long before game day.

Timing mattered in every decision. Knowing when to hold buses, when to move fewer assets, and when to adjust the plan without asking for permission is part of leadership. There isn't always time for debate. Sometimes the right call is the quiet one. And then there's the unspoken language—the subtle nods, the hand signals, the instincts shared between professional drivers and law enforcement escorts. No radios needed. No explanations required. Just awareness, experience, and respect for one another's role.

Leadership Is Often Invisible

From the outside, fans see players, coaches, and bright lights. What they don't see is the choreography behind the scenes—the split-second decisions that keep everything moving on time and out of harm's way. Leadership in this space doesn't come with applause. It shows up in calm voices on headsets. In bus numbers switched without a word. In a convoy that arrives exactly when it must—even if the route wasn't the original one. That night, everyone did their job. And because of that, no one noticed anything amiss at all.

Another Thursday Night, Another Standard Met

By the time the Dolphins boarded their aircraft, the work we performed was already fading into memory—as it should. In this profession, the goal isn't to be remembered in the moment. It's to leave behind confidence. Confidence that the plan will work. Confidence that adjustments will be made. Confidence that no matter the score, the operation will be executed with professionalism and care. That's the standard. And on Thursday Night Football in Buffalo, it was met once again.

Rolling on to the next Assignment

As the Dolphins' plane vanished into darkness, Buffalo slipped back into its familiar rhythm. Another prime-time game completed. Another operation executed exactly as required. There's no celebration—only quiet fulfillment. In this work, victory is simple: everyone arrived where they needed to be, safely, professionally, and on time. With that, the wheels kept turning—toward the next team, the next challenge, and the next story ahead.

CHAPTER SIXTY-SIX

THE NEW ORLEANS SAINTS

A Return to Buffalo

Before September 28, 2025, the last time the New Orleans Saints faced the Buffalo Bills in Buffalo was Thanksgiving night, November 25, 2021—a decisive 31–6 Bills victory. Years later, the Saints returned as the same world-class organization they've always been. If there were a new word in the dictionary for *personable*, they'd probably define it. The closest description we could land on was simple and sincere:

Super kind in every way.

First Contact, Clear Trust

On Wednesday, September 24, 2025, I reached out via text to Grant Mathews, the Saints' Team Operations Manager. It was a routine introduction, the same professional courtesy I extend to every NFL logistics coordinator. Text messages handle logistics—but character reveals itself through tone, voice, and presence. Grant explained that, since he would be traveling with the team, there was no need for a hotel pickup prior to airport arrival.

He also shared that while he was my primary contact, Derek Stamnos would serve as the on-site coordinator. Clear. Concise. Thoughtful. An early indicator of the professionalism to come.

A Moment of Adversity — And Response

The Saints required seven buses for their travel needs. As we departed our yard en route to the airport, the unexpected happened. Bus 7—the equipment bus—suffered a mechanical failure due to a blown belt and pulley. While our emergency shop staff is always on call, availability can vary on weekends. Fortunately, one of our mechanics happened to be nearby and responded immediately, repairing the issue in a remarkable 15 minutes. Still, uncertainty is not something we pass along to NFL teams.

Upon arrival at the airport, I texted Grant and asked him to call when convenient. He did so promptly. I explained the situation clearly and reassured him that all buses would be in position before the aircraft touched down. Grant's response never wavered—calm, relaxed, and trusting. He connected me directly with Derek Stamnos, who arrived shortly after our call ended.

"I'll Leave That Up to You"

Derek Stamnos matched the professionalism expected of every NFL team coordinator—but with a unique ease that set him apart. During the standard arrival briefing, most Directors of Operations specify exact bus placement and formation. Derek did the opposite. He smiled and said he'd heard about our efficiency and concluded:

"I'll leave that up to you."

That single sentence spoke volumes—confidence built on reputation and respect earned through consistency.

A Missed Item — And a Masterclass in Service

Saturday night, following the hotel drop-off, our drivers completed their standard bus checks and reported all vehicles clear. Around 8:45 p.m., I received a text from Grant: a garment bag had been left on Bus 3, hanging near the restroom. I assured him that if no one else had retrieved it, we would find it. I immediately called the operator—Kenn Hanley—who was already in bed, preparing for a 4:00 a.m. game-day start. I explained the situation. Kenn's response was instant and absolute:

"I'm on my way."

He found the garment bag hanging behind the last seat—wedged between the seat and the rear wall of the bus. It was a spot no operator would normally think to check. From that moment forward, it became part of our post-trip inspection process.

Above And Beyond — No Questions Asked

Kenn asked what I wanted him to do with the bag. The answer was simple: **Get it back to the hotel tonight.** I called Grant and informed him we had located the item. He said we could bring it the next morning when staging for the stadium. I replied that the bag was already en route and would be left with the front desk. Grant's gratitude was immediate. We wished each other good night.

On Sunday morning, game day, when we arrived at the hotel to transport the Saints to the stadium, I had a chance to speak with Grant in person. He smiled and said:

> "When your driver pulled up in the most beautiful gray Corvette I had ever seen, I said to myself, 'A world-class motorcoach company is serving the New Orleans Saints.'"

I smiled back and replied, "Sir, you got that right." After Kenn dropped the bag off that night, he followed up to confirm delivery. I asked him one last question: "Did you deliver it in uniform?" "No," he said. "I was in my pajamas." Thankfully, Grant noticed the Corvette—not the pajamas. Kenn Hanley, you embodied the spirit of a true customer service specialist. Thank you for your dedication.

A Message That Says It All

Our agent and sales representative, Tammy Kruszka, received the following evaluation from Grant Mathews:

Tammy—

I just wanted to say that the bus service this weekend was top notch. Tommy Seay and the crew were incredibly professional, helpful, and on point with everything that we asked. This was one of the best, if not the very best bus service we've ever had on the road. I told Tommy that we need him to teach all other bus drivers on the road how to run an operation!

Thank you!

Grant Mathews
Team Operations Manager
New Orleans Saints

Turning the Page

The New Orleans Saints reminded us that excellence isn't loud—it's calm, respectful, and deeply human. Trust was extended. Challenges were met. Service rose to the moment when it mattered most. These are the stories that don't always make the scoreboard—but they define the game behind the game. And with that chapter complete, another team, another philosophy, and another lesson in professionalism was already on the horizon—waiting to pull into Buffalo and write the next story.

CHAPTER SIXTY-SEVEN

THE NEW ENGLAND PATRIOTS

Rolling into Buffalo on Confidence

The New England Patriots arrived in Buffalo riding a wave of momentum, fresh off a commanding 42–13 dismantling of the Carolina Panthers the week before. At 2–2, they were finding their footing, while the Bills were chasing a perfect 5–0 start. With the Patriots having added familiar and formidable talent to their roster, this AFC East showdown carried weight well beyond the standings.

By Wednesday, October 1, 2025, I reconnected with Sarah Jackson via text. The tone was upbeat and relaxed—very different from our first year working together, when every detail was checked, rechecked, and polished to perfection. This time, Sarah was calm and confident.

Wonder Woman in Patriots Gear

While Sarah may have been more relaxed as a logistics coordinator, she quietly revealed another side of herself during the team's arrival. She wasn't just coordinating—she was doing. I watched as she helped the equipment staff, hoisting bulky bags and pushing massive trunks toward the equipment truck. She was the only team contact I've ever worked with who seamlessly moved between coordination and physical execution. Adorable, generous, professional, and relentlessly hardworking, Sarah Jackson is a tremendous asset to the New England Patriots. They are fortunate to have her on their staff.

The Meaning Behind the Hats

That year, the drivers were presented with black Patriots hats featuring a vibrant, multicolored logo—something none of us had seen before. For a moment, it puzzled us. Sarah quickly explained that the hats were part of the NFL's **Crucial Catch** initiative, symbolizing the league's commitment to cancer awareness and early detection across all forms of the disease. Once we understood the meaning, those hats went on immediately—and were worn with pride.

Game Time on the Bus

Sarah also has a sharp, effortless sense of humor. During games, while the action unfolds on all five monitors, we're essentially tailgating on the bus alongside our Sheriff escorts. As the game settles in, some drivers change into something more comfortable. That day, driver James Cornelius slipped on a red, white, and blue jersey with his last name proudly stretched across the back.

Perfect Timing

Late in the game, Sarah boarded the bus carrying envelopes with gratuities for the drivers. She took one look at James' jersey, paused, and said—with perfect timing, "Oh… I'm sorry. I think I'm on the wrong bus." Instantly, the bus erupted—drivers shouting, "No, no, no! It's the right bus! Come back with those envelopes!" Sarah couldn't hold it. And neither could we. Laughter filled the bus, turning a routine moment into one none of us will forget.

Leadership Through Connection

Moments like that reveal what makes Sarah Jackson so effective. Her humor isn't loud or distracting—it's perfectly timed, disarming, and human. In an environment built on precision, schedules, and pressure, she knows when a laugh is exactly what's needed. That balance—between seriousness and levity—creates trust. It puts people at ease and reminds everyone involved that while the work is demanding, it can still be joyful. Sarah understands that leadership isn't just about control and coordination. Sometimes it's about connection. And she delivers that effortlessly.

Eight Buses and a Champion's Arrival

The Patriots required eight buses for their stay. On Saturday, October 4, at 2:15 p.m., I picked up Sarah at the hotel and headed to the airport to join the rest of the fleet. At 4:15 p.m., the Patriots' aircraft touched down at Buffalo Niagara International Airport, its vertical stabilizer proudly displaying all five

Super Bowl championships. As the team descended the steps and boarded the buses, Coach Mike Vrabel emerged from the aircraft in a sharp, slim-fit blue designer suit.

I welcomed him to Buffalo, and he returned the greeting with ease and warmth. Coach Vrabel took a seat directly behind me—much like Brian Daboll often does—and from that moment on, it was clear why he is so widely respected. Classy, approachable, and genuinely personable, Mike Vrabel stood out immediately as one of the friendliest head coaches I had ever encountered. The ride to the hotel was smooth and uneventful—just the way professionals on both sides prefer it.

A Leader Forged in The Game

Mike Vrabel's football résumé speaks for itself. Born August 14, 1975, he built a remarkable career spanning nearly three decades. A two-time All-American at The Ohio State University, Vrabel was selected by the Pittsburgh Steelers in the third round of the 1997 NFL Draft before finding his true football home in New England. During eight seasons with the Patriots, he earned three Super Bowl rings, a Pro Bowl selection, and first-team All-Pro honors in 2007.

After finishing his playing career with the Kansas City Chiefs in 2010, Vrabel transitioned seamlessly into coaching. As head coach of the Tennessee Titans from 2018 to 2023, he led the team to an AFC Championship Game, consecutive division titles, and earned NFL Coach of the Year honors in 2021. In 2025, Vrabel returned to New England—this time as head coach—bringing his leadership full circle to the franchise where his legacy was built.

Sunday Night Pressure in Buffalo

Sunday Night Football in Buffalo has a way of amplifying everything. The October 5, 2025 matchup between the Bills and Patriots was no exception. It was a tense, uneasy night for Bills fans as turnovers and penalties repeatedly put the home team in difficult positions. The Patriots capitalized, handing the Bills their first loss of the season, 23–20. It was a divisional defeat that could echo later in the playoff race.

A Wave, A Memory, and a Book in the Making

After the game, as the Patriots boarded the buses, I had a brief moment with Coach Vrabel. I congratulated him on the win and mentioned that I had driven for the Tennessee Titans during their visit to Buffalo on September 19, 2022. He smiled politely—clearly uninterested in revisiting that 41–7 loss—but I remembered that day vividly for another reason. It was the only game that season where I wasn't the lead driver. Assigned to Bus 3, I stood by my coach as Vrabel exited the hotel.

He looked directly at me and waved—smiling as if we were old friends. I remember glancing around, convinced he must be waving at someone else. There was no one there. So, I waved back and called out, "Coach!" From that moment on, I decided Mike Vrabel had to be the most gregarious coach in the NFL. Years later, I told him that in my book, I honored him with **"The Most Gregarious Award."** He laughed and took it in stride.

A Tight Ship Until Takeoff

At the airport following the game, every Patriot expressed appreciation for our service. Coach Vrabel shook my hand and thanked us, adding that he was impressed by our professionalism. "Sir, thank you. It was an honor to serve you and the Patriots. Safe travels," I replied. As he headed through the security checkpoint, he turned back briefly and said, "Good luck with that book."

I remained at the foot of the steps as Mr. Grady—whom I believe was the Assistant Director or Director of Security—conducted a final sweep of the bus. When he descended, he was laughing. "You run a very tight ship," he said. "Very professional." Shaking his hand, I replied, "Sir, the honor is all mine." As always, we stayed until the aircraft was airborne. Only then did we leave the airport.

Turning the Page

Every team brings its own rhythm, its own personalities, and its own lessons. The New England Patriots reminded me that excellence is often quiet, professionalism speaks without shouting, and leadership—when done right—leaves a lasting impression long after the buses pull away. And with that chapter closed, it was time to prepare for the next arrival… Because in the NFL, the next story is always just one flight away.

CHAPTER SIXTY-EIGHT

THE KANSAS CITY CHIEFS

A Rivalry with Everything on the Line

The stakes could not have been higher as the Buffalo Bills prepared for their Week 9 showdown against the Kansas City Chiefs on November 2, 2025. Both teams entered the battle with winning records and a complete understanding of what this game meant—not just for pride, not just for momentum, but for playoff positioning as winter football crept closer.

The Bills were fresh off their bye week, having pushed their record to 5–2 with a decisive victory over the Carolina Panthers. The Chiefs, meanwhile, were riding the wave of their Week 8 win over the Washington Commanders, improving to 5–3 and building steam at precisely the wrong time for Buffalo. Hovering above them all stood the 6–2 New England Patriots—a reminder that the AFC race was tightening like a vise.

The Bills already knew the sting of losing to New England in Week 5. A loss to Kansas City—their recent postseason tormentors—could come back to haunt them once again. To make matters even more compelling, this game marked the third time in less than two years that Kansas City would set foot on Buffalo soil. Their last two appearances—January 21, 2024, and November 17, 2024—were battles etched into Bills history for very different reasons. Now, in 2025, the rivalry continued with renewed urgency.

Planning & Logistics

On Wednesday, October 29, 2025, I reached out to Andrew Schnoebelen, the Chiefs' Manager of Team Operations. Working with Andrew is always a pleasure—he sets the tone with professionalism and genuine kindness, wrapped in a personality that makes the job feel effortless. His return text carried that same warm energy. You could feel the mutual respect before we even rolled a bus out of the garage.

As always, Andrew provided the structure and clarity that make these large-scale operations run smoothly. Every detail was sharp. Every expectation was clear. He treats drivers like valued partners, and that sincerity goes a long way in this business. When he steps onto Bus 1 for the pre-arrival briefing, you immediately know the team is in good hands—on and off the field.

Arrival Day

At approximately 3:35 p.m., United Airlines Flight #3814 touched down in Buffalo. Moments later, the Kansas City Chiefs began exiting the aircraft and making their way toward the motorcade. As had happened during their previous two visits, three familiar figures approached my bus: Coach Andy Reid, Patrick Mahomes, and Travis Kelce. What stood out as they walked toward me was something beyond the sharpness of their attire. Each one carried a quiet, commanding presence that didn't need to be announced. Coach Reid, wearing his signature calm expression, greeted me with the same warmth he always brings.

A Welcome and a Sincere Thanks

I welcomed him to Buffalo, took his bag, and placed it gently into the luggage bay. Coach Reid is rare—soft-spoken, sincere, and always willing to respond in a way that makes you feel like you're part of the Chiefs family, even if only for a moment. This visit was especially gratifying. As Mahomes and Kelce boarded the bus, both expressed their appreciation for our service. Their words were warm, simple, and—most importantly—sincere. You can tell when gratitude is genuine. Throughout their stay, it became clear that the Chiefs were growing increasingly comfortable in our presence.

An Epic Move by Chris Jones

Their star defensive tackle, **Chris Jones**, confirmed that for me on game day. Instead of heading straight for the stadium's security checkpoint, he detoured toward where I stood, reached out, and bumped fists with me before continuing inside, saying, "Good job!" That moment said everything. (For reference, he rode to the game on Bus 2.) The transport from the airport to the hotel was, as expected, safe and on schedule—another seamless start to another professional visit between two organizations with deep mutual respect. But everyone knew the truth: Tomorrow would not feel friendly.

An Unpleasant Surprise

The NFL is a remarkably close-knit community. Good or bad, whatever happens in a city a team visits rarely stays there. News travels fast in this league—through operations offices, coaching staffs, and front offices—long before it ever reaches the public.

When we dropped off the Kansas City Chiefs at their hotel, they were met not by quiet efficiency, but by a line of labor union protesters, shouting at the top of their lungs in opposition to the hotel's non-union status. The scene was loud, uncomfortable, and impossible to ignore. If I felt a sense of embarrassment standing there—which I did—I could only imagine how it felt for the Chiefs as they stepped off the bus and walked straight into the middle of it. It was an unpleasant surprise.

Buffalo, for all its heart and pride, is not a tourist city in the traditional sense. Its hospitality business is largely seasonal, built around sports, conventions, and select times of year. Many hotels already operate on thin margins, and the reality—fair or not—is that some union demands would make it financially impossible for certain properties to survive at all.

None of that changed what the Chiefs experienced in that moment. It didn't take long for word to start circulating around the league. In the NFL, these things always do. Before long, it was widely understood that Kansas City might be considering different accommodations in the future—a reminder that in this business, every detail matters, and every experience leaves a mark.

Game Day: November 2, 2025

The Bills and the Chiefs walked onto the field like two ancient forces preparing for collision—lightning against lightning, thunder against thunder. The November air held its breath as two AFC giants met beneath the gray sky, each fully aware of the stakes. What unfolded was a battle worthy of their history. When the final whistle blew, the Bills claimed a hard-fought 28–21 victory. The stadium erupted. The fans rejoiced. And Buffalo had earned a statement win over the reigning AFC powerhouse. And yet, in defeat, the Chiefs never lost their composure nor their sportsmanship. That is one of the reasons their organization is so deeply respected around the league—and by drivers like me.

Departure

After the game, the Chiefs returned to the buses to head back to the airport. **Patrick Mahomes** approached wearing something far different from his usual tailor-made postgame suits—gray below-the-knee shorts and a black hoodie pulled up over his head. Because the hood covered his face, I didn't recognize him at first. I simply greeted him, took his bag, and loaded it into the luggage bay. In a soft, genuine voice, he said:

"Thank you. I appreciate you."

It was only then that I realized I was speaking with the Super Bowl MVP himself—Patrick Mahomes, franchise quarterback and face of the Chiefs dynasty.

Turning the Page

Moments like that stay with you. At the airport, we wished them blessings and a safe flight home. They boarded, and Kansas City soon faded into the night sky. Another visit complete. Another chapter added to the Bills–Chiefs legacy. And another reminder of why it's an honor to serve these athletes, coaches, and staff—no matter which side of the scoreboard they're on.

CHAPTER SIXTY-NINE

THE TAMPA BAY BUCCANEERS

Dinner Above the Falls

In October 2025, Suzi and I shared dinner at the Watermark Restaurant, perched high atop the Hilton Niagara Fallsview Hotel & Suites, in Ontario, Canada. The food was exceptional, but it was the window table that truly set the scene—a romantic overlook where the falls poured endlessly below, glowing in the night. It was one of those quiet, unhurried evenings where conversation lingers and time feels generous.

A Name in Lights

Midway through dinner, my eye caught the electronic billboard across the street at Fallsview Casino. Bright and unmistakable, the message flashed:

Patti LaBelle – The 80/65 Tour, coming to the OLG Stage at Fallsview Casino.

I hadn't seen Patti perform live since the release of *Chameleon* in 1976. Nearly five decades later, the thought of seeing her again stirred something deep—memory, music, and a lifetime in between.

A Decision Made Too Quickly

The concert was scheduled for November 16, 2025. Without hesitation, I purchased two orchestra pit tickets—$280 well spent, I thought—before doing what experience usually teaches me to do first: Check the Buffalo Bills' schedule.

The moment I clicked "accept," reality hit hard. The Tampa Bay Buccaneers were coming to Buffalo that same day.

Duty Before Desire

The sale was final. No refunds. No luck with resale, despite my efforts. Standing at that crossroads, the choice was clear. As much as Patti LaBelle means to me, my professional responsibility came first. The NFL assignment took priority—even over one of my favorite artists. Rather than let the tickets go unused, I passed them along to a deserving couple, hoping the music would bless them the way it once blessed me.

The Cost of Commitment

Some choices carry disappointment. Others carry purpose. This one carried both. In my line of work, commitment isn't something you schedule around—it's something you honor. And sometimes, honoring it means letting go of a moment you've waited nearly fifty years to relive. The falls keep flowing. The music keeps playing. And the work—always the work—goes on.

Redemption in the Air: When Wounded Teams Collide

Week 11 arrived with both the Buffalo Bills and the Tampa Bay Buccaneers hungry for redemption. Each team was coming off a painful loss—New England had edged out Tampa Bay, while Miami had stunned Buffalo—and the air in Western New York carried that unmistakable tension that only wounded teams bring with them.

Planning & Logistics

On Wednesday, November 12, 2025, I reached out to **Zach Orth**, the Buccaneers' Senior Team Operations Coordinator. This marked our second time working together, and—true to form—Zach brought the same warmth, professionalism, and upbeat energy that made his first visit to Buffalo so memorable. He has a vibrant spirit, a bright smile, and a way of relaxing an entire operation just by stepping into the room.

We reviewed the itinerary and confirmed the details. The Tampa Bay Buccaneers required six buses for their movements. In a slight twist from standard practice, Zach chose to meet us at the airport rather than be picked up at the hotel. Once on-site, he briefed the drivers and handed each of us a commemorative hat honoring the Tampa Bay Buccaneers' 50th Anniversary. It was a classy touch—pure Zach.

Airport Arrival

At approximately 3:40 p.m., Delta Charter #8868 touched down at Buffalo International Airport. The players and staff descended the stairs in steady formation, heading straight toward the awaiting motorcade. Co-owner **Bryan Glazer** settled into the front seat directly across from me. Behind me sat Head Coach **Todd Bowles**—calm, composed, and fully locked into game mode. Their star quarterback, Baker Mayfield, also boarded my bus. The entire Buccaneers organization carried itself with exceptional respect—from ownership to players to support staff.

Security Personnel

One familiar face was missing—**Andres Trescastro**, the longtime Director of Security Operations who had since retired. His absence was noticeable, especially to those of us who had worked closely with him during their last visit to Buffalo. In his place was Ryan Spradlin, who took over the role in October 2024. With more than 25 years as a Special Agent in Charge with the U.S. Department of Homeland Security, Ryan brought a seasoned, steady presence. When I asked him whether he still sees Andres now and then, he grinned and replied:

"More than I like to."

We both laughed—classic Andres. Another member of his staff I wish to acknowledge is a pleasant African-American female, whom I only know as Melanie.

The Baker Mayfield Moment

Of all the NFL luggage I've handled through the years, Baker Mayfield's stands alone. For a simple overnight stay, that little suitcase felt like it was carrying a thousand Lombardi Trophies. When I lifted it into the baggage bay, I instinctively glanced at the ground beneath it—half expecting to see blood spatters. One thing's for sure: Baker doesn't pack light. As I like to say: *If you're worried about forgetting something… just bring everything.*

Being a Buckeye fan, my perspective of Baker has come a long way since 2017, when #5 Oklahoma stunned #2 Ohio State in Columbus and Baker planted the Oklahoma flag right in the middle of the Buckeyes' logo. That moment caused an uproar, prompting an apology he admitted was forced and insincere.

How Forgiveness is Earned

At the time, I wasn't sure I'd ever forgive it. But meeting Baker in person changed everything. Yes, he carries a fiery competitive spirit on the field—but off the field, he was gentle, respectful, and surprisingly soft-spoken. Seeing him up close gave me a more balanced view of his character. From that point forward, forgiveness wasn't just possible. It was guaranteed.

The Game & Departure

Before this visit, the last meeting between the Bills and Buccaneers had been on October 26, 2023, when Buffalo claimed a 24–18 victory. History spectacularly repeated itself on November 16, 2025.

It was explosive.
It was high-energy.
It was unforgettable.

Buffalo won again—44–32. Win or lose, the airport trips are always the same: smooth, orderly, reflective. After the handshakes, farewells, and final checks, the Tampa Bay Buccaneers boarded their aircraft and lifted into the evening sky. Another chapter. Another memory. Another reminder of why I love what I do.

CHAPTER SEVENTY

THE CINCINNATI BENGALS

A Cold Night, Big Stakes, and a Familiar Rivalry

In Week 14, the Cincinnati Bengals arrived in Buffalo with something to prove. Joe Burrow was back—healthy again—and the narrative was already written by many: another chapter in the growing rivalry between Burrow and Josh Allen, one that, coming in, favored Cincinnati. Snow dusted the city. The air was sharp. And everything about the moment hinted at drama. Buffalo had seen this movie before. Nobody expected a quiet ending.

Planning the Arrival

On Wednesday, December 3, 2025, I reached out to the Bengals' Director of Team Operations, **Jeffery Brickner**, to coordinate their itinerary. Jeff and I had crossed paths once before—January 2023, the Divisional Round, a 27–10 Bengals win. That visit was strictly business. Minimal conversation. Minimal interaction. This time felt different. Jeff was relaxed, friendly, and easygoing—his bright smile making frequent appearances. It was the kind of connection that sets the tone before a team even boards the plane.

Touchdown in Buffalo

At 4:00 p.m. on Saturday, December 6, 2025, the Bengals touched down in Buffalo aboard Delta Charter #8860. The transfer from the airport to the hotel went smoothly—no surprises, just professional execution. What was different, though, was who sat across from me. Instead of Head Coach Zac Taylor, the seat was occupied by Cincinnati Bengals owner **Mike Brown**, with Jeff Brickner seated just behind me. The Bengals arrived with a 4–8 record, coming off a statement win against the Baltimore Ravens. Even after an injury-marred stretch for Burrow, they were very much alive in the playoff hunt. And they carried themselves that way.

A Conversation with an NFL Pillar

Game day—Sunday, December 7, 2025—began like many others, but quickly stood apart. Mike Brown was the first to board the bus. I checked to make sure he was comfortable, particularly given the cold Buffalo conditions. A brief remark about the weather sparked an unexpected and genuinely warm conversation. When I mentioned that my son and his family live in Mason, Ohio—and that my grandson, Jayden, is a wide receiver at Lakota East playing under Coach Jon Kitna, soon headed to Army at West Point—Mr. Brown's face lit up. He immediately recalled Kitna as one of his former quarterbacks, and the conversation flowed effortlessly.

What stood out most was how Mike Brown carried himself. Soft-spoken. Sincere. Unhurried. He took the time to listen—not because he had to, but because that's who he is. Modestly dressed and understated, he could walk down any street without drawing a second glance—yet he remains a quiet icon and pillar of the NFL community. In all my years of service, he is the only NFL owner who ever initiated a conversation with me. And that spoke volumes. A genuine pleasure.

A Game for the Archives

The Bengals–Bills matchup delivered on every expectation. It was electric from start to finish—hard hits, precision throws, momentum swings. Both teams played their hearts out, and the snow only added to the atmosphere. When the clock hit zero, the Buffalo Bills emerged with a thrilling 39–34 victory. A classic. No debate. One small surprise stood out: Joe Burrow rode on Bus 5 of 6 both days. Usually, franchise quarterbacks are placed on one of the first three buses. Not **Joe Burrow**.

"I'll Do My Best."

After the game, as we staged outside the stadium waiting to transport the Bengals back to the airport, fellow operator Jack Putnam—who drove Bus 5—shared a gem. Earlier that day, when the Bengals arrived at the stadium, Joe Burrow was the last man off the bus. Jack, hoping to soften the blow of a potential Bills loss, called out politely:

"Mr. Burrow, please don't beat us up too bad today."

Burrow stopped cold. He turned, locked eyes with Jack, and let a slow smirk spread across his face—something straight out of *How the Grinch Stole Christmas* with Jim Carrey. With a wink, he replied:

"I'll do my best."

Platinum-level response. I asked Jeff Brickner whether Burrow was as quiet as he appears. He smiled and said, "Yes—but when he speaks, his voice is very loud without the volume." Burrow proved that point in his postgame interview, leaving the sports world dissecting every word and questioning whether he was signaling a desire to part ways with the Bengals.

Professional to the End

At the airport, I took a moment to thank the Bengals' owner, Mr. Mike Brown—telling him how much of an honor it had been to speak with him and serve his organization. His reply was brief—but revealing: "Very professional. Good job." Jeff Brickner echoed the sentiment. Handshakes were exchanged. Farewells were offered. And the Bengals headed home. Another team transported. Another story earned. And another reminder that sometimes, the most memorable moments aren't in the box score…but in the quiet conversations along the way.

CHAPTER SEVENTY-ONE

THE PHILADELPHIA EAGLES

A Heavyweight Weekend in Buffalo

After a successful two-game road trip, the Buffalo Bills returned home at 11–4 to face the 10–5 reigning Super Bowl champions, the Philadelphia Eagles. With their 40–22 Super Bowl LIX victory over the Kansas City Chiefs now in the rearview mirror, the Eagles arrived in Buffalo focused and hungry—determined to take the next step in defending their championship.

Before the season began, the chatter was already loud—many outlets were forecasting an Eagles–Bills collision in Super Bowl LX. The last time Philadelphia played in Buffalo was October 27, 2019, a 31–13 Eagles win. Back then, I was on staff with Niagara Scenic Tours but not assigned to that charter—another era, another provider. This time, the responsibility was ours.

Setting The Table: First Calls, First Impressions

On Tuesday, December 23, 2025, I connected with the Eagles' Director of Team Travels and Football Logistics, Daniel Ryan. The text was brief, professional, and positive. By Saturday afternoon, the plan was set—but with a twist. Instead of picking Dan up at the hotel, I was told my point of contact would be Football Operations Associate **Clara Montenegro**.

From the first handshake, Clara set the tone. New to the role but far from new to excellence, she carried herself with polish, confidence, and grace—the kind you don't learn on the job. Later, I learned Clara was filling in for a colleague. She didn't just fill in—she upheld the Philadelphia Eagles' standard. They are fortunate to have her.

Shared Roads and Familiar Roots

When Clara mentioned she attended the University of Miami, the door opened. I claimed my Buckeye loyalty—by way of Tommy Jr.—and shared stories from my Coconut Grove Hotel days. The moment I mentioned Monty's restaurant, her face lit up. One shared memory after another—and just like that, rapport turned into trust. At the airport, Clara briefed the drivers, handed out Eagles beanies—much appreciated in the cold—and distributed gratuities during the briefing. That detail was significant. In fact, she was the first and only coordinator who ever gave a gratuity at that moment.

Arrival: The Champions Touch Down

At 3:10 p.m., American Airlines Flight #9745 touched down at Buffalo Niagara International Airport. Among the first off the plane was Head Coach **Nick Sirianni**, dressed in Eagles gear, warm smile intact. I greeted him, took his bag, and welcomed him to Buffalo. On the ride to the hotel, he sat across from me in the second row—comfortable, present, unassuming. Loading took a little longer than usual due to a sealed rear aircraft exit, but it offered a moment I won't forget. As **Jalen Hurts** passed by en route to Bus 3, I greeted him with a crisp salute. He nodded, smiled, and kept moving—quiet confidence in motion. I also welcomed **Saquon Barkley, A.J. Brown, and DeVonta Smith** as they passed to board their buses.

Big Dom, Bigger Heart

Then there's **Domenico DiSandro**—Senior Advisor to the GM, Chief Security Officer, and Gameday Operations leader. "Big Dom" in frame and in spirit. No ego. No demands. Just genuine warmth paired with elite professionalism. Former Penn State lineman, dressed in a collarless white pullover beneath a tan casual suit—fashionably relaxed, unmistakably in charge. Dom is the real deal. The complete package. The ultimate pace-setter. I truly enjoyed working with him.

Game Day Rituals and a Filet Temptation

Sunday morning, game day, at 11:55 a.m., Buses 1–4 staged at the hotel ready for service. That's when I met **Daniel Ryan** in person. Ryan is a gentleman and a scholar with a generous heart—accessible, efficient, and easy to work with. He greeted us with a firm handshake, a sincere smile, and bearing gifts. He gave each driver an envelope—this time, **double the gratuity**. He even invited us to the team's food spread. Mountains of it. I try to keep our drivers disciplined—no waste at the tailgate—but a filet mignon at breakfast tests the strongest resolve.

When A Coach Becomes a Homeboy

Head Coach **Nick Sirianni** boarded first, forty-five minutes before departure. I checked the climate, which he approved. As I turned to step off the bus, he asked, "Are you from Buffalo?" "Born and raised," I said, "but now living on an island that separates Buffalo and Niagara Falls." Then he finished my sentence: **Grand Island**. Surprised, I asked, "Oh, you're familiar with it?" "I grew up in **Jamestown**," he said. At that moment, "Coach" became "Homeboy."

Jamestown is one of those Western New York cities you don't just pass through—you feel it as you arrive. Tucked into the hills near Chautauqua Lake, it carries the quiet strength of a working town built by skilled hands and honest labor. It's also the birthplace of Lucille Ball—but beyond the spotlight, its soul is built on resilience, craftsmanship, and showing up every day to do the job right.

Adding to its legacy, Jamestown can proudly say it produced a Super Bowl–championship head coach in Nick Sirianni—a reminder that excellence often rises from quiet places. I told Coach Nick how proud I was of what he'd accomplished and how honored I was to serve his team. He received it with gratitude. We talked until the next staffer boarded, and that was my cue to step away.

A Locked Door, A Close Call, and a Whole Lot of Laughter

After unloading at the stadium, I was ready to park the bus when someone started knocking like they were auditioning for a fire-escape commercial. I checked both mirrors—nothing. Then I noticed the restroom indicator glowing like a distress beacon.

I opened the door to find Assistant Special Teams Coach **Joe Pannunzio**, looking like a man who had just negotiated a peace treaty with plumbing. "Jesus, thank you for saving me," he said. "Uh, not exactly Messiah, sir," I replied, "but I do have the anointing to open bus bathroom doors." I nearly bit through my lip trying not to laugh. That gentle, soft-spoken man probably believed he was about to miss the game—trapped, forgotten, and eventually written about in a team memo.

There are no locks on the restroom doors. Coach Pannunzio—one of the nicest men you'll ever meet—just didn't know how to work the latch. At the airport, I told Big Dom. He laughed and said, "That's nothing. He locked himself in the elevator last night at the hotel." That was it. I completely lost it. So did Dom. At that point, Joe wasn't just coaching special teams—he was assembling an all-star season of close calls.

The Quiet Win after the Loss

The Bills fell 13–12—a hard loss, earned the hard way. As the team boarded for departure, Big Dom was last, pulling his bag from the tunnel. I met him, took the bag, and heard words that mattered:

"You all are the most professional drivers we've had all season."

That's pride, served cold and honest. I told him about the book and my plan to honor the Eagles properly. He asked questions. Then he said, "I have to buy a copy." "No, sir," I said. "I'm sending you, Coach Nick, Dan Ryan, and Clara Montenegro personalized copies." After seeing the cover, he laughed. "Brother, you look like one of the Four Tops."

Music, Laughter, and a Proper Goodbye

About three minutes from the airport, with traffic light, a phone started playing **"Sugar Pie Honey Bunch"** by the Four Tops. No doubt who cued it up—Big Dom. They told me to sing. I did. It was the first party I'd ever seen on a coach's bus—and somehow, I wasn't just driving it. I was part of it.

At the terminal, Coach Sirianni didn't head straight for security. He came to the luggage bay, shook my hand, thanked me personally, and wished me well. It was the warmest farewell I've ever received from a head coach. No book mentioned. No pitch needed.

Coach Pannunzio thanked me again for the restroom rescue. Clara Montenegro, Daniel Ryan, Big Dom, and I exchanged final goodbyes. Then they cleared security, boarded their flight, and disappeared into the night sky. Some teams pass through a city. Others leave a memory. **The Philadelphia Eagles left one I will never forget.**

CHAPTER SEVENTY-TWO

THE NEW YORK JETS

Where the Road Begins to Turn

As I look at this New York Jets chapter and everything it represents, I realize it naturally wants to sit at the end of my NFL years. It doesn't feel like just another story—it feels like a closing scene. The last regular-season game at Highmark Stadium. The final trips through the airport. The quiet reflection about time and wear on the tires. All of it carries the weight of an ending. That's why this chapter belongs as the final chapter of my NFL section. It feels like the season finale of a long, meaningful run.

I also don't want to rush past what comes next. Instead of forcing this chapter to also explain the new stadium era, I think it deserves a pause—a short bridge between what was and what's coming. One last look at the old stadium as it fades into memory. One thoughtful look at the new one rising. And one honest question in my heart:

Will I be there when the first buses roll in?

That transition deserves its own quiet moment. And in a bigger way, I can see now that this chapter isn't just closing out my NFL stories—it's turning the whole book in a new direction. From here on, the road leads less toward assignments and schedules and more toward meaning, gratitude, faith, family, and legacy. The work was always important. But what it all meant is even more so. This feels like the place where the story stops counting miles...and starts counting blessings.

A Familiar Assignment with a New Face

On Sunday, January 4, 2026, the New York Jets made their second consecutive late-season visit to Buffalo to face the Bills. The game marked not only the conclusion of the Bills' 2025 regular season, but also the final regular-season game ever to be played at Highmark Stadium—unless, of course, the Bills earned a home playoff game and extended its life just a little longer. I was genuinely looking forward to this assignment.

The previous year, I had the pleasure of working with Assistant Director of Football Operations **Mari Jo Kohler**. And among the many professionals in the Jets organization, **Director of Team Operations Aaron Degerness** is another member of the Jets staff I've come to know and genuinely admire. Both were consummate professionals—confident, relaxed, and easy to work with. The kind of people who, within moments of meeting them, make you feel comfortable and respected. But when my work order arrived, I noticed something unexpected. Mari Jo was no longer my point of contact. Instead, the Jets' Manager of Team Operations was listed as **Matteo Lovece**—a name unfamiliar to me.

First Contact

On Wednesday, December 31, 2025, I introduced myself to Matteo via text. As I always do, I told him how honored I was to serve the Jets and then sent back the details of the assignment to confirm that I fully understood their instructions. That simple exchange usually sets the tone. Matteo confirmed everything promptly. Our communication was brief, professional, and efficient. The tone was positive. I was already looking forward to meeting him.

A Handshake in the Lobby

On Saturday, January 3, I picked Mr. Lovece up at the hotel. Instead of meeting at the bus, we met in the lobby. He immediately recognized me as his driver—probably because of the New York Jets cap on my head and the way I was dressed in my uniform, proudly displaying three buttons on the lapels of my blue blazer:

NFL. AFC. New York Jets.

Whatever team I'm serving, I wear the league, the conference, and the team's button. It's my way of showing respect for the shield and for the assignment. We shook hands. I introduced myself with a smile. Matteo returned it with one just as warm and sincere—and even complimented my appearance and greeting. That's all it took. The bond was immediate. We boarded the bus and headed to the airport to join the rest of the fleet.

A Conversation that Traveled the World

While rides to the airport with team coordinators are always pleasant, this one had something extra. Matteo and I talked like two people who had known each other far longer than twenty minutes. I asked about Mari Jo and was glad to hear she had been offered an opportunity she couldn't refuse. *(Mari Jo, I wish you nothing but success and good health in your new role.)*

Matteo had come from the Miami Dolphins, working under the same supervisory structure as **Nate Hammett**. And I can say without hesitation—he is a worthy successor. Matteo Lovece is at the top of his game: personable, sociable, respectful, and genuinely kind. One of the best operations coordinators I've had the pleasure of working with.

A Western New York Connection

Like Chuck Petersen (Vikings), Mitch Reynolds (Chiefs/NFL), and Nick Sirianni (Eagles), Matteo also has a Western New York connection. He attended **Syracuse University**—just a couple of hours from Buffalo. When I told him I had recently led a motorcade transporting the University at Buffalo marching band to Skytop, it tightened that bond even more. Funny how small the world becomes in this line of work.

The Arrival Plan

The Jets reserved six buses for their visit. As always, they mailed their bus number signs and hats ahead of time. Most team coordinators have very specific staging instructions around the aircraft. Matteo didn't. "I've heard about your professionalism," he said. "I'll leave that up to you." We angled the buses toward the plane so the numbers were clearly visible as the players descended the steps—and positioned them to avoid backing up or going under the wing during departure. Clean. Safe. Efficient.

Touchdown In Buffalo

On Saturday, January 3, 2026, at approximately 4:00 p.m., the Jets arrived in Buffalo on United Airlines Flight #3810. That's when I had the pleasure of meeting **Robert Mastroddi**, Senior Vice President of Security. With his bright smile and easy manner, Robert is one of those people whose sincerity you feel immediately. The team boarded the buses, and the ride to the hotel was smooth and uneventful. Like Andres Trescastro before him, **Aaron Degerness** chose to ride standing in the stairwell.

Driving Coach Aaron Glenn

Having Coach **Aaron Glenn** seated in the front seat to my right was a privilege. He is one of the nicest men you could ever meet. Soft-spoken. Professional. Respectful. Although his emotions sometimes show on the sidelines, in person he is calm, dignified, and gracious. A former 12th overall pick in the 1994 NFL Draft, Glenn played 15 seasons in the league, earned three Pro Bowl selections, and finished with 41 career interceptions. Given time, I truly believe he will prove to be an outstanding head coach.

A Buckeye I Missed

Every member of the Jets conducted themselves with class, showing nothing but respect and kindness throughout their stay in Buffalo. Still, true to my Buckeye roots, **Garrett Wilson** remains my favorite Jet. Sadly, he wasn't able to make the trip this time—he had been placed on injured reserve after hyperextending his knee in London earlier in the season. Garrett, if you ever read this, know that I'm wishing you a full, speedy recovery and hoping to see you back where you belong very soon.

Game Day

The Jets arrived in Buffalo in full rebuild mode, carrying a 3–13 record and a season that had tested their resolve. On Sunday, January 4, we staged at the hotel, ready to transport the team to Highmark Stadium—just another game day, but never just another responsibility. Matteo graciously invited us to help ourselves to breakfast. Mindful of the food already waiting for us at our tailgate—and careful not to appear ungrateful—we accepted with quiet restraint, taking only a little. It was a small moment, but one that reflected the unspoken code we always try to live by:

> **Appreciation without excess.**
> **Professionalism in every detail.**

And Gratitude

Though they gave it their best, the Jets couldn't get anything going, even against the Bills' second unit. By the time the clock wound down, the scoreboard told the story: **35–8**. Midway through the third quarter, Matteo came to our bus and walked right into our tailgate, bringing a generous portion of gratuities for the drivers. We invited him to join us. He sampled my grilled gourmet lasagna and Suzi's Slush Cake and said:

"Finger-licking good!"

Words that Matter

After the game, once the team had gone through security at the airport, Matteo Lovece and Aaron Degerness told us that our service was the best part of their visit. I passed those words along to my fellow drivers. We were all proud. We shook hands, watched them disappear through the checkpoint, and stayed until the plane lifted into the night sky. Only then did we head home ourselves.

Looking Toward the Next Chapter

As the Bills' 2025 home schedule comes to a close, I can't realistically see myself working every assignment in 2026. After more than forty years behind the wheel, I don't have much tread left on my tires. That said, I would love nothing more than to work at least one game in the new stadium. To be the first motorcoach operator to lead an NFL motorcade into the Bills' new home would be the crown jewel of my career. And if Niagara Scenic Tours asks me to stay on a little longer? I'll accommodate them in any way I can.

The Long Drive Home

There's a different kind of quiet that settles in after the last bus is parked and the last assignment is complete. It isn't the tired kind. It's the reflective kind—the kind that rides with you all the way home. That night, as I drove through familiar Buffalo streets, I found myself thinking about how many times I've made that same trip after midnight. How many teams. How many seasons. How many stories that began with flashing lights at the airport and ended with a plane lifting into the dark.

I thought about the young man who once stood at the front doors of the Buffalo Hilton in the early 1980s, full of ambition, not knowing that life would one day place him behind the wheel of motorcoaches carrying the biggest names in sports. I thought about the Hyatt, the transit years, the blizzards, the breakdowns, the long nights, the early mornings, and all the people God placed in my path along the way.

A Life Measured in Arrivals and Departures

For more than four decades, my life has been measured in arrivals and departures. In luggage loaded and unloaded. In hotel lobbies and airport tarmacs. In handshakes, head nods, and quiet moments of trust between professionals who depend on one another to get the job done. I've had a front-row seat to moments most people never see. And I never once forgot the responsibility that came with it.

Gratitude Above All

More than anything, I am grateful. Grateful to God for protection over millions of miles. Grateful to Suzi, who has shared this life with me and sacrificed more than most will ever know. Grateful to Niagara Scenic Tours for trusting me with their clients, their equipment, and their reputation. Grateful to the men and women I've had the honor of working beside—drivers, dispatchers, law enforcement escorts, hotel staff, operations people, and team personnel across every league. And grateful to every team that ever placed their trust in my hands.

Still Here, Still Ready

I don't know exactly how many more times I'll pull into the Hamburg yard before dawn. I don't know how many more seasons I'll work. But I do know this:

When the call comes, and if I'm able,
I'll still put on the jacket.
I'll still pin on the shield.
I'll still show up early.

And I'll still do the job the same way I always have—quietly, professionally, and with pride. Because some things aren't just what you do; they're who you are.

CHAPTER SEVENTY-THREE

THE NATIONAL HOCKEY LEAGUE

THE TORONTO MAPLE LEAFS

A New Door Opens

When Grand Tours Motorcoach Company permanently closed its doors, Niagara Scenic Tours suddenly found itself in a position—quite literally—to step into the world of professional sports transportation across Western New York. With that shift came opportunity. At present, Niagara Scenic Tours handles only a select number of NHL charters, while a competitor manages the majority. The reason is simple: name recognition.

One lead driver, formerly employed by Grand Tours, once held the title of lead operator for both the NFL and NHL. But experience has taught me that when name recognition is chosen over higher quality, one often lives beneath their privilege. Progress requires courage. Testing new partnerships matters. And that's exactly what the **Toronto Maple Leafs** chose to do.

First Ice, First Impressions

October 23, 2025, marked a personal milestone—**my first professional hockey assignment**. The Toronto Maple Leafs were in town, and from the opening handshake to the final airport drop-off, the experience was nothing short of first-class. The evening before their arrival, October 22, I sent a courtesy text to the Leafs' Director of Team Operations, **Brad Lynn**, introducing myself as his lead driver for their Buffalo visit. Before I could even set my phone down, it rang. Because I always save my contacts in advance, I recognized his name immediately and answered with a smile. Our conversation was brief, upbeat, and efficient—confirming arrival times, airport procedures, and hotel logistics. In that short exchange, the tone was set. This was going to be smooth.

Arrival In Buffalo

Wednesday, October 23, 3:30 pm. Air Canada Charter #7045 touched down at Buffalo Niagara International Airport. Unlike NFL arrivals—where buses roll directly onto the tarmac—the Maple Leafs deplaned through the terminal before boarding. That's where I met Brad Lynn in person, along with Steven Walker, the team's Director of Security.

The Leafs required two buses for their visit, and I was joined by my trusted colleague and fellow NFL operator, Niles Hardy—one of the finest drivers in our fleet. What stood out immediately was how differently the Maple Leafs traveled compared to NFL teams.

A Different Kind of Setup

In the NHL, things were reversed. Players and security rode with me on the lead bus, while coaches, staff, and ownership followed on Bus Two. In the NFL, it's usually the opposite. That arrangement gave me the privilege of personally driving some of hockey's brightest stars, including:

Forwards: Sammy Blais, Easton Cowan, Max Domi, Calle Järnkrok, Dakota Joshua, Matthew Knies, Scott Laughton, Steven Lorentz, Matias Maccelli, Auston Matthews, Bobby McMann, William Nylander, Nicholas Robertson, Nicolas Roy, and John Tavares.

Defensemen: Simon Benoit, Brandon Carlo, Oliver Ekman-Larsson, Jake McCabe, Dakota Mermis, Philippe Myers, Morgan Rielly, and Chris Tanev.

Goalies: Cayden Primeau and Anthony Stolarz.

Quiet professionals. Focused. Respectful. Every detail mattered to them—and it showed.

Professionalism Recognized

On game day, October 24, 2025, our scheduled spot time was 3:15 p.m. Niles and I arrived early, positioning our buses at the hotel by 3:00 p.m. Two shuttles were planned to KeyBank Center at 4:00 and 4:30 p.m. While waiting, we spoke with Steven Walker, who took the time to compliment our appearance, performance, and attention to detail. "Very professional," he said. Coming from someone who has overseen countless charters across North America, those words carried weight.

Quiet Class

The Maple Leafs arrived dressed more like corporate executives than athletes—understated, polished, and composed. Classy doesn't even begin to describe them. Though Brad Lynn rode on the second bus and our interaction during the trip was brief, his final gesture spoke volumes. At the airport, following the last drop-off, he shook my hand and passed along a generous gratuity—in **American currency**. He elevated himself to a level occupied solely by **Max Thomas of the Miami Marlins**. No one in pro sports was more generous than they were. If given the choice, I'd drive for the Toronto Maple Leafs again in a heartbeat… even over an NFL team. *(LOL)*

The Final Detail Says Everything

One final observation tells the story best. After most NFL charters, my bus typically collects two or three small bags of trash, while other buses fill the dumpster. After transporting the Toronto Maple Leafs? A handful of empty water bottles. That was it. They left the bus as immaculate as they boarded it. If I had to describe the Toronto Maple Leafs in just three words, they would be:

Generous.
Classy.
Clean.

Moving Forward

The Buffalo Sabres won **5–3**. That night, as the Leafs left Buffalo, it was clear that professional excellence looks the same—on ice or grass, skates or cleats. Respect, discipline, and humility travel well. As this new NHL chapter closed, another story was already forming—another team, another city, another chance to show that excellence behind the wheel speaks louder than reputation. **The next bus was already warming up.**

CHAPTER SEVENTY-FOUR

THE CHICAGO BLACKHAWKS

A Back-To-Back Stop In Buffalo

On Thursday, November 20, 2025, the Chicago Blackhawks battled the Seattle Kraken and came up just short in a 3–2 loss. Less than twenty-four hours later, they were scheduled to face the Buffalo Sabres at KeyBank Center. For me, it marked my **second NHL assignment**—a moment I approached with quiet pride and focus. My goal was simple and unwavering: Make the Blackhawks feel comfortable, respected, and well cared for…**without wishing them a victory.**

First Contact: Professionalism Sets the Tone

On Wednesday, November 19, I reached out to the Blackhawks' Vice President of Team Operations, **Tony Ommen**, via text. The exchange was warm, efficient, and professional—exactly what you hope for when first connecting with a team at this level. Mr. Ommen thanked me for reaching out and shared that he was looking forward to meeting us.

The Blackhawks reserved two buses for their stay. **Jack Putnam**—one of my trusted NFL regulars—was assigned to operate Bus 2. Initially, the team had scheduled an 8:30 a.m. practice skate on game day. But hockey travel has a way of rewriting plans. At **2:26 a.m.**, Mr. Ommen texted to cancel the skate after the team arrived in Buffalo at 1:30 a.m. Rest took priority—and rightly so.

Game Day Arrival and New Faces

At 3:00 p.m., we positioned our buses at the team hotel for transport to KeyBank Center. It was there that I met **Brian Higgins**, the Blackhawks' Director of Team Security. From the moment we spoke, it was clear—Brian and

Tony are the kind of professionals every organization hopes to have representing them. Calm. Prepared. Respectful. They set a tone that made our job seamless. I also had the pleasure of meeting **Head Coach Jeff Blashill**. Impeccably dressed and carrying himself with an executive presence, Coach Blashill was composed, reserved, and thoroughly professional. Serving him and his staff was an honor.

A Buffalo Connection: Michael Peca

Jack follows hockey far more closely than I do, and it showed after the game. When Assistant Coach **Michael Peca** boarded my bus, Jack recognized him instantly. In Buffalo, Peca's name still carries weight—and for good reason. Michael Peca played center for the Sabres during one of the franchise's most memorable eras. A relentless defensive forward and natural leader, he served as team captain during the Sabres' **1999 Stanley Cup Final** run. He captured the **Selke Trophy** in 1997 as the NHL's best defensive forward and spent five full seasons in Buffalo. He left behind a legacy built on **grit, discipline, and respect**.

The Details that Define a Team

One detail worth noting was how the Blackhawks assigned their buses. Unlike the Maple Leafs—who did the opposite—the Blackhawks placed their **coaching staff on Bus 1** and the **players on Bus 2**. Every team operates differently, and those subtle variations are part of what makes servicing professional sports so interesting. Another small but telling detail: If the Blackhawks **win**, the driver is asked to find a radio station airing the post-game coverage. If they **lose**, the request is politely disregarded. It's a simple instruction—but it says a lot about understanding the emotional rhythm of a team.

A Respectful Farewell

We truly enjoyed serving the Chicago Blackhawks and would welcome the opportunity to do so again. When we arrived at the airport, goodbyes were exchanged, along with sincere expressions of gratitude for the service provided. They walked through the security checkpoint, boarded their flight, lifted into the night sky, and disappeared above the clouds—returning home, their Buffalo stop now part of the long NHL road behind them.

CHAPTER SEVENTY-FIVE

SURE, LET'S TALK GRATUITIES

When Gratitude Falls Short

Gratuities are rarely a concern for most companies, which is precisely why this issue must be viewed through the eyes of the customer service agents rather than their employers. Although clients may express appreciation for the service they receive, that appreciation isn't always reflected in their gratuities.

No organizations have shown us greater respect in this area than the **Miami Marlins, Toronto Maple Leafs, Miami Dolphins, New England Patriots, New York Jets, Philadelphia Eagles, and the San Francisco 49ers**. None of these teams gave the drivers less than **$150 each**, with the high watermark reaching **$700**—clear, unmistakable signals of respect. Still, not every sports franchise, high school, college, minor league, or professional team values the motorcoach operators who serve them. Ironically, some of the wealthiest franchises have been among the least generous.

When Gratitude Undermines Leadership

In 2022, one NFL team left a **$50 gratuity** on the seat of my bus after we dropped them off at the airport. Their itinerary required **six buses**. Not one of the other drivers received a single dollar. Few things fracture a team faster than a leader accepting a gratuity without regard for the people standing beside them. Integrity and honesty are priceless—and once compromised, they are rarely restored.

I turned the tip over to my fellow drivers to be shared. Split five ways, it amounted to **$10 each over two days**—$5 per day. Split six ways, it dropped to roughly **$4.17 per day**. That level of "gratitude" is not just inadequate—it's embarrassing, especially when weighed against the city and brand that team represents.

A Pattern that Continued

The pattern continued in 2024. Several teams didn't tip at all, despite rating the service as excellent in their evaluations. Others offered a **$300 gratuity**, divided among six drivers over two days of service. That comes to **$25 per day per driver**—a little better, but hardly reflective of a league where billions of dollars circulate annually. Ironically, these same organizations scrutinize every detail—travel efficiency, recovery windows, performance metrics, fuel usage—yet somehow overlook the human beings entrusted with delivering their teams safely through it all. Customer service professionals understand that gratuities are not required—but they are appreciated. And appreciation is not measured by obligation. It's measured by **awareness**.

Where the Responsibility Truly Lies

Let's be clear: players and coaches do not determine gratuities, nor are they typically aware of how their organizations handle them. That responsibility rests with the front office, where decisions are made far from the highways, airports, weather delays, hospitals, hotels, restaurants, event venues, and countless other places where service professionals quietly carry real responsibility every day.

A gratuity isn't a reward for luxury—it's an acknowledgment of responsibility. Motorcoach operators don't simply drive; we manage risk. And in the same way, customer service agents across every field don't simply "do a job"—they carry trust, safety, timing, and outcomes in their hands. Every mile, every shift, every late night, every snow-covered roadway or overcrowded lobby involves judgment calls where lives, well-being, and dignity—not schedules—come first. When nothing goes wrong, that isn't luck. That's professionalism.

Grace, Not Entitlement

Truth be told, no one in the customer service industry is entitled to tips. When a customer adds a gratuity to the bill, it is not because they are required to do so, but because they choose to extend an act of appreciation and grace. Now that America has moved toward making tips tax-exempt, some service workers have begun to act as though gratuities are guaranteed, becoming more aggressive in making that expectation known as customers settle their bills.

Warning! Reverse course or consider another line of work, because that kind of attitude and behavior is not only unacceptable under responsible ownership and management, but if a customer feels harassed, chances are they will not return. Establishments that promote or condone such practices may eventually find themselves forced to close their doors—without ever realizing the true cause.

A Necessary Clarification

When I came to Niagara Scenic Tours, I was already retired and financially stable, and it remains that way today. I don't need to work. I choose to work. I came back because I love serving people, I love being useful, and I still believe in doing things the right way. Gratuities don't determine whether my lights stay on or my refrigerator stays full. But that is not true for most of the men and women who work beside me—or for countless service professionals across this country.

For many drivers, servers, hotel staff, guides, aides, attendants, and customer service agents in every field—from transportation to hospitality, from healthcare to tourism, from food service to events—gratuities aren't extra money. They are part of how bills get paid. They are groceries. They are gas. They are prescriptions. They are the quiet difference between getting by and falling behind.

That's why this conversation isn't about me. It never was. It's about the people who show up every day, early and late, in all weather and all conditions, carrying real responsibility for real people—and who deserve to have that responsibility recognized with something more than a polite thank-you.

When Gratuities Are Necessities

Again, for many customer service agents, gratuities aren't extra money—they're grocery money, gas money, and utility money. If these same organizations applied similar standards after dining at a restaurant with a group of that size, they'd likely be asked not to return. Yet in many industries, this imbalance has become quietly normalized. Over the years, I've worked alongside and served people in transportation, hospitality, tourism, and public service. Nearly all have been courteous—but only a few have shown genuine appreciation, the kind that reflects a real understanding of the responsibility being carried.

Overlooked Behind the Scenes

Schools receive government funding, yet when transporting high school and college athletic teams, the motorcoach driver is often required to remain with the bus to accept the team's food delivery. In most cases, the driver is not offered so much as a sandwich or a slice of pizza. And when a gratuity is involved, it is understandably given to the delivery driver. The moment passes without complaint. But it is a small reminder of how easily the people behind the scenes can be overlooked.

Awareness, Not Entitlement

It's not about entitlement. And it's certainly not about expecting special treatment. It's about **awareness**. Drivers are on duty—often for long stretches—ensuring the safety of students, athletes, and staff alike. We don't leave the bus. We don't step away. We remain present because that's the responsibility entrusted to us. A simple gesture—a word of acknowledgment, a bottle of water, or a modest meal—would go a long way in recognizing the role we play in getting these teams where they need to be, safely and on time. Organizations separate themselves not by what they say—but by what they do. And they are remembered long after the engine cools and the bus doors close.

The Ones who Never ask for Applause

There are professionals in this industry who never ask to be seen. They don't seek recognition, praise, or headlines. Their satisfaction comes from execution—getting it right, every time, without incident. Motorcoach operators live in that space. So do the escorts who clear the roads, the coordinators who work through the night, and the quiet leaders who ensure everything moves as it should. When appreciation is absent, these professionals don't complain. They adjust. They adapt. And they continue to deliver excellence. Because that is who they are.

When Respect Becomes Culture

Organizations that understand gratitude don't treat it as a transaction. They build it into their **culture**. Respect shows up in preparation, communication, and acknowledgment. It's present in how people are spoken to, how challenges are addressed, and how responsibility is shared. When that culture exists, everyone performs better—drivers, staff, and teams alike. It creates a sense of shared mission, where no role is considered insignificant and no contribution is overlooked.

What Excellence Looks Like Up Close

Excellence is rarely loud. More often, it's quiet and consistent. It shows up in drivers who memorize routes before dawn, in escorts who anticipate traffic patterns, in coordinators who think three steps ahead, and in leaders who trust the professionals they've chosen. When those efforts go unnoticed, the work still gets done. But when they are acknowledged, it elevates the entire operation. Gratitude doesn't slow things down. **It strengthens them.**

Carrying the Work Forward

As seasons change and teams come and go, the road remains. So does the responsibility. Those who travel it professionally understand that every trip is a trust placed in human hands. That trust deserves awareness. And when awareness is present, gratitude follows naturally—not as an obligation, but as a reflection of integrity.

A Server Worthy of a Gratuity

On Wednesday, November 1, 2023, my wife and I dined at the Cheesecake Factory inside Walden Galleria Mall in Cheektowaga, New York. Our server, **Samantha H.**, was in training under **Amber C.**, and she was exceptional. Samantha took our order without interruption, then repeated it back flawlessly—clear proof she was truly listening. Her professionalism was well beyond that of a trainee. Our bill totaled **$97.11**. In appreciation of her outstanding service, we left a **$100 tip**. With visible emotion, she accepted our encouragement to extend the same level of care and service to every guest—regardless of whether they gave a gratuity.

A Quiet Turn in the Road

As I pulled into my driveway that night after dropping the Jets off at the airport, I realized something else was ending too—not just a season, not just an era of football, but a long chapter of my own life measured in schedules, staging times, and airport lights. The road had been good to me. Better than I ever deserved. But this story was never only about the teams I served or the miles I drove. It was about the people who stood beside me along the way. The ones who cleared the roads. The ones who opened the doors. The ones who cooked the food, carried the bags, planned the routes, fixed the problems, and made sure everyone got home safely.

Before I set this book down for good, there are some people who deserve to be seen. They are the reason the road always worked. They are the reason I was never really alone out there. And they are the reason the next pages matter just as much as the last game ever did.

CHAPTER SEVENTY-SIX

EITHER WAY, THE SUN COMES UP

Lately, I've found myself thinking about mornings. Not the rushed ones. Not the alarm-clock ones. But the quiet ones—when the world hasn't made up its mind yet, and the sunlight is just starting to stretch across the sky. After more than forty years of showing up early, checking the weather, walking the bus, and putting on the jacket, it feels strange to be standing at a place where the road ahead could bend two different ways. One path says, *keep going*. The other says, *you've done enough*. Truth is, neither one scares me.

Some mornings, Suzi and I sit quietly with our cup of tea, and I catch myself thinking about how many sunrises I've watched from behind a windshield. Airport lots. Hotel driveways. Snow-covered streets. Highways that don't care who you are, only whether you're ready. I think about my parents—about how work was never something you did just for money. It was something you did because it was part of who you were. You showed up. You stayed faithful. You did your job right. And when your day was done, you went home with a clear conscience.

If I keep working, I'll do it the same way I always have—grateful, steady, and proud to still be useful. If I retire, I'll do that with the same gratitude—thankful for the miles, the people, the stories, and the mercy that carried me this far. Either way, the sun comes up. It always has. And I've learned that peace doesn't come from choosing the perfect path. It comes from knowing that whichever path you walk, you're walking it with a pure heart.

CHAPTER SEVENTY-SEVEN

THE UNSUNG HEROES

A Moment Behind the Scenes

On September 28, 2025, while serving the New Orleans Saints, my NFL escorts and I shared a quiet moment together—one of those brief pauses that carry far more meaning than they appear to at first glance. It wasn't staged. It wasn't ceremonial. It was simply a moment of gratitude among professionals who understand what it means to protect, serve, and ensure everyone gets home safely.

Without our dedicated law enforcement partners, life in any community—and especially in high-visibility, high-risk environments like professional sports travel—would be infinitely more difficult. I would like to recognize a group of true unsung heroes from the Erie County Sheriff's Department: our lead escort officer, Warren Luick, along with Donald (Donny), Sal, Emily, Brad, Ricky, Tom, Tim, and Sheriff Howard.

The Quiet Authority that Keeps Everything Moving

These officers are the finest escorts a motorcoach driver could ever ask for. Their work is calm, deliberate, and unwavering—marked by vigilance that never seeks attention, yet never relaxes. When a motorcade moves smoothly through traffic…When an arrival is flawless…When tension never has the chance to escalate…it's because law enforcement is present, prepared, and in command long before anyone else notices. Their presence isn't just about lights, sirens, or clear routes. It's about **judgment**. It's about **reading situations before they unfold**. It's about **protecting players, staff, drivers, fans, and the surrounding community**—all the while remaining professional, composed, and respectful.

Fellowship and a Good Game

As a small token of appreciation, we always make sure our law enforcement partners are well cared for at our tailgate gatherings. After the NFL teams head into the stadium and the pressure eases, the buses become a place of fellowship. We set up two six-foot tables across the tops of the motorcoach seats, lay out the food, and turn on the monitors to catch the game.

I plug my laptop into the bus system so everyone can watch together. In those moments, uniforms fade into shared laughter, conversation, and the simple joy of friendship. It's not about extravagance. It's about acknowledgment. For the last tailgate of the 2025 season, I featured my homemade gourmet grilled Lasagna.

Why Law Enforcement Matters

Law enforcement officers are often most visible in moments of crisis. But their greatest successes are the ones that never make the news—the incidents prevented, the lives protected, the order quietly maintained. They stand between chaos and calm. Often unnoticed. Always essential. That afternoon reminded me that excellence doesn't need applause. Sometimes, it just needs to be **recognized by those who truly understand the weight of responsibility being carried**. It was a special time—one of camaraderie, respect, and fellowship. And it's a memory I will treasure for the rest of my days on this side of heaven.

CHAPTER SEVENTY-EIGHT

AN OFFICER WORTHY OF PRAISE

Springtime in Full Bloom

Each spring, Rochester, New York, comes alive in color and spirit during its beloved Lilac Festival. For ten vibrant days, Highland Park transforms into a gathering place for thousands—locals and visitors alike—drawn by live music, local art, comforting food, and the unmistakable fragrance of lilacs in full bloom. The 2025 festival, held from May 9 through May 18, once again wrapped itself around Mother's Day weekend, continuing a tradition as familiar as the flowers themselves. With the largest collection of lilacs anywhere in the world, the festival is more than an event—it's a celebration of renewal.

A Scenic Excursion with Senior Guests

On May 22, 2022, I was assigned to operate a Scenic Excursion charter carrying a group of our valued senior clients to the festival. The day promised beauty and discovery, including a visit to one of Rochester's true hidden gems—the **Lamberton Conservatory**. Nestled inside Highland Park at 180 Reservoir Avenue, the conservatory is a historic glass house that first opened its doors in 1911.

Named for Alexander B. Lamberton, a former president of the Rochester Parks Commission, the structure reflects the influence of famed landscape architect Frederick Law Olmsted, co-designer of Central Park. Inside, time seems to slow. Tropical rooms echo with the sound of cascading water, desert chambers showcase resilient cacti, and seasonal floral displays change with quiet elegance. For many—especially during Rochester's long winters—it's a sanctuary of warmth and wonder.

A Problem at the Park Gates

But during the Lilac Festival, beauty comes with logistical challenges. Several park roads were closed to vehicle traffic, making motorcoach access to the conservatory nearly impossible. The only available parking area was more than a hundred yards away—far too long a walk for our elderly passengers. I safely pulled the bus aside and approached a traffic officer, explaining our situation and hoping for a bit of flexibility. He understood our concern but couldn't allow us through the closure. Still, he offered an alternate route that might bring us closer. It was a start—but not a solution.

"You Look Like You Could Use Some Help."

As I walked back toward the bus, a calm voice called out behind me. "You look like you could use some help." I turned and met **Officer Moses Robinson** of the Rochester Police Department. Relief washed over me. "Sir," I said honestly, "that's an understatement. I'm not from the area, and these road closures have me stuck." "I overheard your conversation," he replied. "I can get you there—but fair warning, the streets are tight." I smiled. "Officer, as long as the passageway isn't smaller than the eye of a needle, I can make it through."

Guided with Confidence and Care

With calm authority and genuine kindness, Officer Robinson took the lead. He guided our motorcoach through narrow neighborhood streets, cars parked tight on both sides. Inches mattered. Inside the bus, the air grew quiet as passengers held their breath. Then—clearance. At the final barrier, the very street where the conservatory stood, Officer Robinson stepped out of his patrol car, moved the wooden barricade himself, and personally escorted our bus straight to the front entrance. It wasn't just professional. It was compassionate.

Beyond the Call of Duty

Officer Robinson didn't simply help us reach our destination. He ensured that a group of senior citizens could experience a day of beauty, dignity, and joy—without unnecessary hardship. In that moment, he embodied the very best of public service.

A Salute Well Deserved

To Crime Prevention Officer **Moses Robinson** of the Rochester, New York Police Department: You went far beyond the call of duty that day. You demonstrated what it truly means to protect and to serve—with integrity, kindness, and humanity. You are a shining example of the values that strengthen our communities and uplift our country. Thank you for your remarkable service. You are, indeed, **a police officer worthy of praise—an unsung hero.**

CHAPTER SEVENTY-NINE

ILIO DIPAOLO'S RESTAURANT

A Place Where Tradition Meets the Table

Ilio DiPaolo's, at 3785 South Park Avenue in Blasdell, New York, isn't just a restaurant. It's a Western New York institution. From the moment you walk through the doors, you're greeted with the kind of warmth that turns first-time guests into regulars—and regulars into family. The portions are generous, the service is genuine, and the pace is unhurried, the way a great meal should be.

The walls tell stories—photographs of Ilio DiPaolo's Hall of Fame wrestling career and decades of famous faces—but the real story isn't just on the walls. It's in the room. And that story is carried forward every day by Ilio's son, **Dennis DiPaolo**.

The Story Behind the Name

Ilio DiPaolo was born on November 7, 1926, in Introdacqua, Abruzzo, Italy. He became a world wrestling champion, a Hall of Famer, and a man whose name would one day be synonymous with hospitality in Western New York. In 1952, he met his wife, Ethel, and together they built a family—four children, with Dennis proudly the firstborn.

At forty years old, Ilio opened his first restaurant, a small pizzeria. A fire destroyed it, but not the dream. In 1965—the same year he retired from wrestling—he opened the restaurant that still stands today.

In 1995, tragedy struck when Ilio lost his life after being hit by a car during a torrential rainstorm in Hamburg, New York. After his passing, Dennis stepped forward—not just to run a business, but to carry a name, a reputation, and a legacy.

Dennis DiPaolo: Leadership you can Feel

Dennis is not an owner who hides in an office. He's in the dining room, traditionally walking in his father's footsteps. He stops at tables. He makes sure everything is right—not because he has to, but because that's who he is. His leadership style is simple: be present, care deeply, and never forget that people come before plates. Suzi and I have eaten at Ilio's countless times. She loves the Penne with Broccoli. I'm partial to the Seafood Fra Diavolo.

When I bring Scenic Excursion groups there, the reaction is always the same: everyone loves it. Some places serve food. **Ilio's serves memories.** And when milestones matter—weddings, anniversaries, celebrations—the banquet facility is where many Western New York families choose to mark their most important days.

Excellence Behind the Bar: Nino Anzaldi

If you sit in the bar area, you'll likely meet **Nino Anzaldi**, the 2025 Buffalo News *Best of 716 Bartender* award recipient—and one of the finest customer service professionals I've ever encountered. Suzi and I don't sit in the bar area for the drinks. We sit there for the **service**. Nino is disciplined, attentive, and fully present. He never needs to be asked twice. He understands timing, rhythm, and anticipation. Before you realize you need something, it's already there. Before meeting Nino, I didn't even know what the 716 Award was. I do know this: it went to the right man. Professionals like Nino are part of the reason Ilio DiPaolo's doesn't just survive—it **endures**.

A Legacy that Lives in People

Ilio DiPaolo's isn't special because of its history alone. It's special because people like **Dennis DiPaolo** and **Nino Anzaldi** show up every day and protect a standard. That's how legacies last. Quietly. Faithfully. One guest at a time.

CHAPTER EIGHTY

LONGHORN STEAKHOUSE

AN UNSUNG PROFESSIONAL: Dean Walck

Where Everybody Knows Your Name

Dining at LONGHORN Steakhouse on Military Road when **Dean Walck** is working behind the bar feels a little like stepping into *Cheers*: *"Sometimes you wanna go where everybody knows your name…"* It doesn't take long before Dean appears with warm bread, fresh water, and a genuine welcome that immediately sets the tone. His presence is calm, his manner is professional, and his attention is complete. He listens—really listens. He repeats orders back. The food arrives the way it should. And if something isn't right, he fixes it without deflection and without delay. You never have to track Dean down. He already knows.

Service Without Being Asked

What separates Dean from most isn't what he does—it's **when** he does it. The check arrives without interruption. Refills happen before you notice they're needed. The rhythm of the meal is never broken. Nothing feels rushed. Nothing feels forgotten. That kind of service isn't taught in a manual. It comes from discipline, awareness, and pride in doing things right.

A Mind Built for Precision

Behind Dean's calm smile is a mind wired for details. You can feel it in the way he works. Everything is orderly. Everything has a place. Everything is done with intention. He studies the same way he serves: carefully, methodically, and with purpose. His future points toward science and teaching, but the discipline he'll take with him is already on display every night behind the bar.

Quiet Excellence

There's no performance in Dean's work. No flash. No noise. Just consistency. Just pride. Just the quiet confidence of someone who knows that doing things right—every time—is its own reward.

Unsung, but Unforgettable

People like Dean rarely get recognized. They don't ask for it. They don't need it. But places are better because they're there. And guests remember how they were treated long after they forget what they ordered. That's what real professionalism looks like. That's **quiet excellence**.

CHAPTER EIGHTY-ONE

HONORING SCENIC EXCURSIONS AND MY CLIENTS

AN UNSUNG PROFESSIONAL: Maria Burridge

The People Behind the Trips

Over the years, I've driven for professional teams, celebrities, and organizations most people only see on television. But some of the most meaningful miles I've ever driven have been for everyday people—seniors, church groups, community organizations, and friends traveling together simply to enjoy life. That's the world of **Scenic Excursions**. They don't sell tickets. They **create days people remember**. And for nearly a decade, a large part of my professional life has been tied to serving their clients. At the heart of that culture is **Maria Burridge**.

Leadership You Can Trust

Maria is the kind of leader you don't have to worry about. Things are organized. Details are handled. People are respected. And most importantly—**the customer always comes first**. I've had the joy and honor of working with her—and driving for her clients—for almost ten years. In all that time, I've watched her build something special: not just a tour operation, but a **reputation**. Her leadership style is calm, precise, and deeply human. She doesn't just manage trips. She **protects experiences**. She understands that for many of her clients, these outings aren't just vacations—they're highlights of the year. That mindset shows in everything Scenic Excursions does.

A Master of Customer Service

Maria is, in every sense, a master customer service specialist. She leads with professionalism, clarity, and genuine care for people. The standard she sets doesn't just shape the company—it shapes how everyone around her works. And I can say this with complete honesty: **when Maria puts her name on something, it's going to be done right**.

The Clients Who Made It All Worth It

Some of the greatest compliments of my career didn't come from awards or evaluations. They came from **clients who asked for me by name**. To those of you who trusted me to be your driver—thank you. You made me feel like more than just the person behind the wheel. You made me feel like part of the group. The gratuity gifts you gave were neither expected nor required. What mattered wasn't the amount—it was the **kindness behind them**. Each of you left a mark on my heart.

A Roll Call of Gratitude

Though I cannot tell every story, I can certainly remember every kindness. With sincere appreciation, I would like to recognize my valued Scenic Excursions clients:

- AKRON NEWSTEAD SENIORS
  Barbara Gaik

- ALDEN SENIORS
  Helen Brown

- ALLEGANY 60 PLUS
  Judy and Frank Pastore

- AUTUMNWOOD SENIOR CENTER
  Versailles Williams

- BLESSED SACRAMENT
  Dick Nola

- BUFFALO UNDERGROUND: THIS is WNY
  Melanie Chimeto

- CHEEKTOWAGA SENIORS
  Karen Oliver
  Jerri Powers

- CLARENCE SENIORS
  Carolyn Giovino

- COLLINS CENTER SENIORS
  Iren Pfeifer
  Bridgette Farner

- EAST AURORA SENIORS
  Donna Bodekor
  Maria Pitt

- GENESEE COUNTY OFFICE
  Karen Hall

- GLORIA J. PARKS COMMUNITY CENTER
  Solar Ingram
  Phyllis Carver

- HOLY SPIRIT CHURCH
  Joyce Atwell

- LANCASTER SENIOR CITIZENS CENTER
  Rose Marie Janik

- MADE IN AMERICA STORE
  Mark Andol and Family

- MARILLA COMMUNITY CENTER
  Helen Bourgeois

- NORTH COLLINS SENIORS
  Karen Denne
  George Jablonski
  Josephine Bellezza

- ORCHARD PARK SENIORS
  Maria Gally

- RELAY FOR LIFE FUNDRAISERS
  Geri and Dave Courteau

- RICHMOND SENIORS – BUFFALO CITY HALL
  Annette Reid

- SANBORNITES / SANBORN FIRE DEPARTMENT
  Sue Letourneau

- SCHILLER PARK SENIORS
  Annie Pender

- SENECA VOCATIONAL ALUMNI
  Secretary Jim Klapp
  President Ed Mirowski

- ST. JOHN XXIII
  Barbara Oneill

- ST. MARGARET'S SENIORS
  Dick Nola

- ST. MARY OF THE LAKE
  Joe Pietrocarlo

- ST. MARTHA PARISH
  Les Wrobel

- ST. TIMOTHY'S CHURCH
  Donna Cutrona

- THE RAMBLIN' LOU SCHRIVER – WXRL RADIO
  Linda Lou and Joanie Marshal

CHAPTER EIGHTY-TWO

RIDGEVIEW TOURS

AN UNSUNG PROFESSIONAL: Sharon Grover

Some Roads Feel Like Home

There are trips you take because they're on the schedule—and then there are trips you take because they feel like going back to family. For me, **Middlefield, Ohio** has become one of those places. I drive Scenic Excursions charters there at least three times a year, and every time we pull in, I know exactly what's waiting: warmth, laughter, and the kind of hospitality that doesn't need to be advertised. At the heart of that experience is **Sharon Grover**.

Leadership With Heart (and a Great Laugh)

Sharon is the founder and guiding spirit of **Ridgeview Tours**, and she is exactly the kind of person you hope is leading a group of travelers. She is professional, organized, and precise—but just as importantly, she is joyful. Sharon loves to laugh, and her humor has a way of putting everyone at ease before the bus is even fully parked.

Her leadership is calm and steady. Nothing feels rushed. Nothing feels forced. And somehow, everything always seems to work exactly the way it should. Her husband, **Steve**, is right there with her—quietly supportive, helpful, and fully invested. Together, they don't just run tours. They **host people**.

When Two Companies Work Like One

Through a special partnership, Scenic Excursions and Ridgeview Tours work together to offer Amish Country trips to Middlefield. During these tours, Sharon—and sometimes Steve—serve as the guide, making sure everything flows smoothly from start to finish. Though we're two separate companies, on those trips we operate as one team. Every tour includes an Amish wedding feast, and every visit feels thoughtfully planned, authentic, and unhurried—the way experiences like this should be.

Built On Trust and Familiar Miles

Over the years, a real friendship has grown between Sharon, her family, and me. There's a comfort that comes from working with people who value relationships as much as results. Middlefield isn't just a destination anymore. It's a place where we're greeted by name.

"Traffic Jam" and a Thousand Little Kindnesses

When my bus arrives to begin the tour, Sharon and Steve always greet the driver with one of my favorite traditions in all my years of driving: a jar of their homemade **"Traffic Jam"** jelly. It's a small thing. But it tells you everything. As long as nature provides, every passenger also receives a plant, along with a small-to medium-sized Amish-grown pumpkin—gracious gifts from the Grovers. And because shopping is part of the experience, guests are given large, sturdy bags to carry their purchases. Nobody has to do any of that. They do it anyway. That's what hospitality looks like when it's real.

More than a Tour—A Shared Journey

On October 14, 2025, I drove another charter to Middlefield. Before starting the three-hour ride back home, Sharon and I paused to take a photo together. It was one of those moments that captures more than it shows. Ridgeview Tours isn't about places. It's about **people**. About laughter on the bus. About stories shared. About travelers who start the day as guests and end it feeling like family.

Quiet Excellence

Sharon Grover is an unsung professional in the truest sense of the word. She doesn't seek attention. She doesn't chase recognition. She simply shows up, takes care of people, and makes sure every journey is better than it would have been without her. And that is exactly the kind of excellence this book is about.

CHAPTER EIGHTY-THREE

THE ERIE NIAGARA SUNRISE EXCHANGE CLUB

AN UNSUNG PROFESSIONAL: Phyllis Gentner

Where Community Still Shows Up Early

Some of the best work in a community happens before most people finish their first cup of coffee. The **Erie Niagara Sunrise Exchange Club** is proof of that. They gather early, not for attention or recognition, but to figure out how to help—who needs support, where service is needed, and how they can make their corner of the world a little better. At the heart of that group is **Phyllis Gentner**.

An Invitation that Meant More than She Knew

On Wednesday, November 19, 2025, Phyllis—then president of the club—invited me to attend their breakfast meeting and share some of the stories from this book. It was an honor I didn't take lightly. That morning, the room was filled with familiar warmth and open faces. In attendance were:

> Ruth Bland, Linda Colkitt, Debbie Gajewski, Sue Gilbert, Joanne Guercio, Ken and Carol Hamm, Donna Hutton, Sherran Lockwood, Jerry Maragliano, Linda Matuszewski, Sandy Olear, Chris Stanz, Tami Stengel, and Barbara Tucker. My wife, Suzi, was there as well—along with Gary Gentner, Phyllis' husband.

More Than Neighbors

Gary and Phyllis aren't just associates. They're our neighbors—directly across the street. Over time, we've become something more like extended family. We watch out for each other. If someone needs a ladder, a tool, a lawn mower, or even a cup of sugar, it's understood: you just walk across the street. That's the kind of neighborhood—and the kind of people they are.

A Morning of Stories and Laughter

After the meeting, I shook hands with everyone. More than one person told me how much they enjoyed the morning, adding, "We've never had anyone speak to our club that kept our undivided attention as much as you did—while laughing along the way." That meant more to me than they probably realized. Later, in their community newsletter dated November 19, 2025, they wrote:

> "Tom's background stories, from growing up as one of 11 children to his jobs from 'the bottom' to today's accomplishments, were one humorous story after another… Tom's comedic way of speaking left us wishing there was more time to hear his stories."

Phyllis Gentner: A Servant's Heart

Phyllis Gentner embodies professionalism with a warmth that immediately puts people at ease. Her bright smile carries wisdom, creativity, and a deep kindness that makes people feel seen and valued. But what stands out most is the way she **ministers to others**—with a mother's care. She listens. She encourages. She reassures. She serves quietly and faithfully, without ever needing the spotlight. In June 2024, Phyllis received multiple honors, including her elevation to President of the Erie Niagara Sunrise Exchange Club and recognition as the distinguished Member of the Year.

As for Gary—if our wives didn't keep us busy with house projects, he and I would probably spend entire days sitting around solving the world's problems one conversation at a time.

Why This Work Matters

Organizations like the Erie Niagara Sunrise Exchange Club rarely make headlines. But communities are held together because of them. Because of people like **Phyllis Gentner**—who show up, care deeply, and keep doing the work that needs to be done, long after the applause has faded.

With Gratitude

With heartfelt appreciation, I dedicate this tribute to **Phyllis and Gary Gentner** and to every member of the Erie Niagara Sunrise Exchange Club. Thank you for your service. Thank you for your compassion. And thank you for all the hard work you do—often before the rest of the world even wakes up.

CHAPTER EIGHTY-FOUR

BUFFALO UNDERGROUND: THIS IS WNY

AN UNSUNG PROFESSIONAL: Melanie Chimento

Sometimes One Day Changes Everything

Over a lifetime, you meet thousands of people. Most pass through your days like scenery outside a bus window—present for a moment, then gone. And then, once in a great while, someone enters your story **briefly**… and leaves something behind that never leaves you. That's what happened when I met **Melanie Chimento**.

A Trip that started Like Any Other

When I had the opportunity to drive for **Buffalo Underground: THIS is WNY** on a trip to **Covered Wagon Tours in Wellsboro, Pennsylvania**, I had no idea it would become one of the most meaningful single-day assignments of my career. From the very beginning, the people in Melanie's group treated me not as "the driver," but as part of the journey. They were warm, genuine, and full of stories. The miles passed easily, carried by conversation and laughter. Before heading out on the wagon tour, we all sat down together for a meal—BBQ chicken, pulled pork, potatoes, and corn. The food was good. The fellowship was better.

A Question I Didn't Expect

During that day, as we talked about many things—including the book project I had been working on and the stories it would one day hold—Melanie asked me something simple and unexpected:

"Do you know what the front cover of your book is going to look like?"

I answered honestly. "No. Not yet." It wasn't modesty. It was truth. I hadn't seen the story clearly enough to imagine its face. At some point in our conversation, I showed her the photograph of me standing at the front entrance of the Buffalo Hilton, in uniform, wearing my top hat. To me, it was just a snapshot. A moment. Another day at work. Melanie looked at it and said, without hesitation:

"That's your front cover!"

Just like that. In one sentence, she gave shape to something I had spent a lifetime living—but had never quite seen. In that image was **service**. In that image was **consistency**. In that image was **dignity, pride, and quiet professionalism**. There could be no substitute.

The Kind of Insight that Can't be Taught

Some people have a gift for seeing what others miss. Melanie is one of them. She is a master customer service specialist in her own right—not because of titles, but because of **perception**. Because she listens. Because she notices. Because she understands people and stories. We only met once. I only drove her group one time. And yet, she clarified something that took me **a lifetime** to fully understand.

A Leadership that Doesn't Need Time to Prove Itself

Some people leave an impact through years of presence. Others do it in a single, perfectly-timed moment. That kind of leadership doesn't need volume. It doesn't need repetition. It doesn't need a spotlight. It simply **sees**. And when it speaks, something permanent changes.

What I Carried Home

What made that day so special was how naturally it unfolded. A trip. A meal. A conversation. A moment of insight. What began as just another charter became a **defining chapter** in my journey—not because of the distance traveled, but because of the understanding gained.

The Lesson that Stays

This book is for everyone who believes:

- That excellence doesn't need a spotlight
- That leadership can be quiet
- And that the way you serve others is the truest measure of success

I am grateful to **Melanie Chimento**, to **Buffalo Underground: THIS is WNY**, and to the wonderful people who shared that table in Wellsboro for reminding me that sometimes, the most meaningful legacy isn't built behind the wheel…but in the way people see you.

Some Journeys

Some journeys last a lifetime. Others take only a day—and reveal a truth that stays with you forever.

CHAPTER EIGHTY-FIVE

STILL HERE, AND STILL GRATEFUL

There's a strange kind of silence that comes when the engine finally cools. Not the empty kind. Not the lonely kind. The reflective kind. It's the kind of quiet that settles in after the last bag is unloaded, the last bus is parked, and the paperwork is done. The kind that rides with you all the way home. The kind that makes you turn the radio down and just think. I've made that drive more times than I can count.

Through snowstorms and summer nights. Through wins and losses. Through seasons that seemed to fly by and years that felt like they took a lifetime. I've driven past stadium lights, hotel marquees, quiet neighborhoods, and empty highways—carrying everyone else's stories while slowly writing my own. I didn't set out to build a career. I set out to do a job.

I was a kid once, standing at the front doors of the Buffalo Hilton, trying to look professional in a uniform that felt bigger than I was. I had no idea that life would one day place me behind the wheel of motorcoaches carrying presidents, athletes, celebrities, and teams whose logos are known all over the world. I didn't know I'd drive through blizzards, black ice, construction zones, and moments that required more prayer than planning. I only knew how to show up. And somehow, that turned into a life. The Hyatt years. The transit years. The long nights. The early mornings. The breakdowns that taught patience. The smooth runs that taught gratitude. And the people—so many people—who walked into my story and left fingerprints on my heart.

I think about my parents, Ezelle and Claudia, and the foundation they laid without ever knowing how far it would carry me. I think about Suzi—who has lived this life with me, not beside it. Who has waited up, worried, prayed, sacrificed, and supported more than any book could ever fully explain. I think about my children, my grandchildren, and the quiet hope that somehow, in all of this, I showed them what faithfulness looks like. Both Suzi and I came from homes where marriage was built to last. Our parents each spent more than sixty years together, and their example shaped how we understood commitment, perseverance, and loyalty. Long before we realized it, they were teaching us how to build a life that would stand the test of time.

I think about the drivers. The dispatchers. The mechanics. The escorts. The hotel staff. The coordinators. The unsung professionals who never make headlines but make everything work. We don't do this job for applause; we do it because we care, and know that the job must be done right.

For more than forty years, my life has been measured in arrivals and departures. In luggage loaded and unloaded. In handshakes and head nods. In trust. Every trip was a responsibility. Every mile carried weight. When nothing went wrong, nobody noticed. And that was exactly how we wanted it. People sometimes ask me how many miles I've driven. I don't know. I stopped counting a long time ago. What I do know is this: every mile mattered. Not because of where it went—but because of who was on board. I don't know how many more times I'll make an airport pick up. I don't know how many more seasons I'll work. But I do know this: if the call comes—and if I'm able—I'll still show up early. And I'll still do the job the same way I always have. Quietly. Professionally. With pride. Because some things aren't just what you do. They're who you are.

And if tomorrow never brings another assignment, that's okay too. Because this road has been good to me. God has been good to me. Life has been good to me. Better than I ever deserved. The engine will cool. The bus will rest. And I will too. But for now, I'm "Still Here, And Still Grateful."

Appendix

Selected Concerts and Major Artists Appearing in Buffalo (1975–1977)

The following listings document a portion of the extraordinary live-music era that passed through Buffalo during my years at the Holiday Inn Midtown. I personally served at least eighty-five percent of the artists listed. Most of these performers and their touring crews stayed at one of our Holiday Inn properties, but they often chose to stay at our location due to its proximity to the concert venues. These records reflect the remarkable cultural moment that surrounded my early career in hospitality and service.

Kleinhans Music Hall

1975

- JAN 18 Barry Manilow, Robert Klein
- JAN 22 Gentle Giant, Alvin Lee
- FEB 16 Van Morrison
- MAR 01 Billy Joel, Tom Rush
- MAR 04 Average White Band, Les McCann
- MAR 11 Tom Rush
- MAR 17 Humble Pie, Joe Vitale
- APR 03 Golden Earring
- APR 08 Maria Muldaur
- APR 10 Santana
- APR 18 Supertramp, Chris de Burgh
- APR 25 LaBelle
- MAY 15 Jesse Colin Young, Leo Kottke
- MAY 20 James Taylor
- OCT 12 Rick Wakeman
- OCT 24 The Lettermen
- OCT 26 LaBelle
- DEC 14 Ohio Players

- DEC 17 Bruce Springsteen

1976

- JAN 16 Benny Goodman Sextet
- FEB 21 Supertramp
- MAR 05 Blackfoot, Roxy Music
- MAR 21 B.B. King
- APR 10 Laura Nyro
- APR 26 Ray Charles
- JUN 10 Vinton, Frankie Yankovic
- OCT 29 LaBelle, Tower of Power
- NOV 18 The Irish Rovers

1977

- FEB 09 Bruce Springsteen
- MAR 08 Bob Seger & The Silver Bullet Band, Starz
- MAR 09 Barry Manilow
- APR 12 Weather Report
- APR 21 Jean-Luc Ponty
- JUN 10 Grover Washington Jr.
- JUL 23 Lou Rawls
- JUL 29 KC and the Sunshine Band
- AUG 25 Helen Reddy
- SEP 09 Benson, Melba Moore
- OCT 02 Randy Newman, John Prine
- OCT 11 Ronnie Laws
- OCT 12 Harry Chapin
- OCT 30 Lonnie Liston Smith & The Cosmic Echoes
- NOV 14 Neil Sedaka
- NOV 19 Tammy Wynette

Buffalo Memorial Auditorium

1975

- APR 22 Seals & Crofts
- JUN 15 The Gap Band, The Rolling Stones
- JUL 31 Uriah Heep, Point Blank, Blue Öyster Cult
- SEP 26 Jethro Tull, Richie Havens
- OCT 18 The Jacksons, Tavares, KC and the Sunshine Band
- OCT 29 The Doobie Brothers, Poco, Outlaws
- NOV 14 The Temptations, Natalie Cole, Leon Haywood
- DEC 08 The Allman Brothers Band
- DEC 10 The Who
-

1976

- MAR 19 David Bowie
- MAR 31 Tony Orlando and Dawn
- APR 07 Peter Frampton, The J. Geils Band
- JUN 25 Elvis Presley
- JUL 23 Aerosmith, Rick Derringer, Henry Gross
- SEP 02 The Beach Boys, Jeff Beck
- SEP 24 The Isley Brothers
- OCT 08 Frank Sinatra
- OCT 15 Neil Diamond
- OCT 22 Frank Zappa
- OCT 29 The Alpha Band, The J. Geils Band, Lynyrd Skynyrd
- NOV 08 John Denver
- NOV 12 Chicago
- DEC 15 KISS, Uriah Heep

1977

- FEB 28 Genesis
- MAR 29 Cheap Trick, Boston, Jethro Tull
- MAY 09 Grateful Dead
- JUN 10 Crosby, Stills & Nash
- JUL 2–3 Fleetwood Mac, Kenny Loggins
- JUL 06 Aerosmith, Nazareth
- OCT 15 The Commodores, The Emotions
- OCT 17 Rod Stewart
- OCT 21 The Oak Ridge Boys
- NOV 01 Chicago, The Doobie Brothers
- NOV 18 Utopia, Starcastle

Shea's Performing Arts Center

1976

- MAR 13 Michael Martin Murphey
- JUN 27 Carmen McRae
- OCT 22 Frank Zappa
- NOV 16 Richie Havens
- NOV 18 Styx
- NOV 19 Phoebe Snow

1977

- MAR 12 Muddy Waters, James Cotton
- MAR 19 B.B. King, Bobby "Blue" Bland
- MAY 01 Little Feat
- MAY 10 Utopia
- JUN 08 Foreigner, Uriah Heep, The Dictators
- JUL 08 Herbie Hancock

- SEP 15 Johnny Winter
- OCT 07 Gato Barbieri
- OCT 21 Frankie Valli & The Four Seasons
- OCT 28 Phoebe Snow
- OCT 29 The Crusaders
- OCT 31 Styx
- DEC 09 Lake, Nektar, City Boy

Melody Fair (North Tonawanda)

Notable performers appearing during this era included: Nat King Cole, Harry Belafonte, Johnny Cash, Duke Ellington, Ray Charles, Little Richard, Sammy Davis Jr., Gladys Knight, The Bee Gees, and many others.

www.ingramcontent.com/pod-product-compliance
Ingram Content Group UK Ltd.
Pitfield, Milton Keynes, MK11 3LW, UK
UKHW041858190726
13854UKWH00002B/973

9 798995 089315